Lecture Notes in Computer Science 12614

More information about this subseries at http://www.springer.com/series/7409

Felix Wolf · Wanling Gao (Eds.)

Benchmarking, Measuring, and Optimizing

Third BenchCouncil International Symposium, Bench 2020
Virtual Event, November 15–16, 2020
Revised Selected Papers

Springer

Editors
Felix Wolf (ID)
Department of Computer Science
Technical University of Darmstadt
Darmstadt, Germany

Wanling Gao (ID)
Institute of Computing Technology
Chinese Academy of Sciences
Beijing, China

ISSN 0302-9743 ISSN 1611-3349 (electronic)
Lecture Notes in Computer Science
ISBN 978-3-030-71057-6 ISBN 978-3-030-71058-3 (eBook)
https://doi.org/10.1007/978-3-030-71058-3

LNCS Sublibrary: SL3 – Information Systems and Applications, incl. Internet/Web, and HCI

This Springer imprint is published by the registered company Springer Nature Switzerland AG
The registered company address is: Gewerbestrasse 11, 6330 Cham, Switzerland

Preface

This volume contains the papers presented at Bench 2020: the Third BenchCouncil International Symposium, held virtually in November, 2020. The Bench conference has three defining characteristics. First, it provides a high-quality, single-track forum for presenting results and discussing ideas that further the knowledge and understanding of the benchmark community. Second, it is a multi-disciplinary conference. This edition of the conference attracted researchers and practitioners from different communities, including architecture, systems, algorithms, and applications. Third, the program features both invited and contributed talks.

The Bench symposium solicits papers that address pressing problems in benchmarking, measuring, and optimizing systems. The call for papers for the Bench 2020 conference attracted a large number of high-quality submissions. During a rigorous review process, in which each paper was reviewed by at least four experts, the program committee selected 13 papers for the Bench 2020 conference. The papers in this volume include revisions requested by program committee members.

Bench 2020 had three keynote lectures. Torsten Hoefler, professor of scalable parallel computing at ETH Zurich, explained how to design performance experiments and report their results, both fundamental for scientific progress in our field. David J. Lilja, professor of electrical and computer engineering at the University of Minnesota, presented a stochastic computing model and showed how we can learn from mistakes, errors, and noise. Kristel Michielsen, an expert in quantum computing at Jülich Supercomputing Centre and professor of quantum information processing at RWTH Aachen University, introduced methods to evaluate the capabilities of quantum computers and presented benchmarking results for state-of-the-art quantum hardware and software.

Moreover, our program included one invited talk by Arne J. Berre from SINTEF Digital, Tomás Pariente Lobo from Atos, and Todor Ivanov from Lead Consult, who introduced DataBench, a software toolbox supporting big data and AI benchmarking. In addition, conference general chair Jianfeng Zhan presented AIBench, the BenchCouncil AI benchmarks for datacenters, HPC, IoT, and the edge, including their performance rankings.

During the conference, the International Open Benchmark Council (BenchCouncil) sponsored four different types of awards to recognize important contributions to the area of benchmarking, measuring, and optimizing. The BenchCouncil Achievement Award recognizes a senior member who has made long-standing contributions to the field. David J. Lilja was named the 2020 recipient of the achievement award. The BenchCouncil Rising Star Award recognizes a young researcher who demonstrates outstanding research and practice related to the theme of the conference. Torsten Hoefler was named the 2020 recipient of the rising star award. The BenchCouncil Best Paper Award is to recognize a paper presented at our conference with high potential impact. The BenchCouncil Award for Excellence for Reproducible Research rewards reliable and reproducible research using benchmarks from a variety of organizations. In 2020, we had two best papers, both earning equally high scores, and three papers receiving the award for excellence for reproducible research. Douglas Pereira Pasqualin, Matthias Diener, André Rauber Du Bois and Maurício Lima Pilla from Universidade Federal de Pelotas and University of Illinois at Urbana-Champaign received the Bench 2020 best paper award and the award for excellence for reproducible research for their paper *Characterizing the Sharing Behavior of Applications using Software Transactional Memory*. Bangduo Chen, Mingzhen Li, Hailong Yang, Zhongzhi Luan, Lin Gan, Guangwen Yang, and Depei Qian from Beihang University and Tsinghua University received the best paper award and the award for excellence for reproducible research for their paper *swRodinia: A Benchmark Suite for Exploiting Architecture Properties of Sunway Processor*. In addition, Lin Li, Eric Rigall, Junyu Dong, and Geng Chen from Ocean University of China and Inception Institute of Artificial Intelligence received the excellence for reproducible research award for their paper *MAS3K: An Open Dataset for Marine Animal Segmentation*.

We are very grateful to all the authors for contributing such excellent papers to the Bench 2020 conference. We appreciate the indispensable support of the Bench 2020 Program Committee and thank its members for the time and effort they invested in maintaining the high standards of the Bench symposium.

December 2020   Felix Wolf
                                                       Wanling Gao

Organization

General Chair

Jianfeng Zhan — BenchCouncil & Chinese Academy of Sciences, China

Program Chairs

Felix Wolf — Technical University of Darmstadt, Germany
Wanling Gao — Chinese Academy of Sciences, China

Program Committee

Matthew Bachstein — University of Tennessee, Knoxville, USA
Woongki Baek — UNIST, Korea
David Bermbach — TU Berlin, Germany
Arne Berre — SINTEF, Norway
Ben Blamey — Uppsala University, Sweden
K. Selçuk Candan — Arizona State University, USA
Florina Ciorba — University of Basel, Switzerland
Zhihui Du — Tsinghua University, China
Vladimir Getov — University of Westminster, UK
Ryan E. Grant — Sandia National Laboratories, USA
Cheol-Ho Hong — Chung-Ang University, Korea
Yunyou Huang — Guangxi Normal University, China
Sascha Hunold — TU Vienna, Austria
Khaled Ibrahim — Lawrence Berkeley National Laboratory, USA
Todor Ivanov — Goethe University Frankfurt, Germany
Zhen Jia — Amazon, USA
Nikhil Jain — Lawrence Livermore National Laboratory, USA
Juby Jose — Intel, USA
Gwangsun Kim — POSTECH, Korea
Huan Liu — Arizona State University, USA
Gang Lu — Huawei, China
Xiaoyi Lu — The Ohio State University, USA
Piotr Luszczek — University of Tennessee, Knoxville, USA
Lucas Mello Schnorr — UFRGS, Brazil
Benson Muite — University of Tartu, Estonia
Bin Ren — College of William and Mary, USA
Rui Ren — Cyberspace Security Research Institute Co., Ltd., China
Hyogi Sim — Oak Ridge National Laboratory, USA
Shuaiwen Leon Song — The University of Sydney, Australia
Salman Zubair Toor — Uppsala University, Sweden

Blesson Varghese	Queen's University Belfast, UK
Feiyi Wang	Oak Ridge National Laboratory, USA
Lei Wang	Chinese Academy of Sciences, China
Bo Wu	Colorado School of Mines, USA
Biwei Xie	Chinese Academy of Sciences, China
Jungang Xu	University of Chinese Academy of Sciences, China
Chen Zheng	Chinese Academy of Sciences, China
Xie-Xuan Zhou	Max Planck Institute of Biochemistry, Germany

Award Committee

Lizy Kurian John	The University of Texas at Austin, USA
Dhabaleswar K. (DK) Panda	The Ohio State University, USA
Geoffrey Fox	Indiana University, USA
Jianfeng Zhan	Chinese Academy of Sciences and University of Chinese Academy of Sciences, China
Tony Hey	Rutherford Appleton Laboratory STFC, UK

BenchCouncil Rising Star Award Lecture

Scientific Benchmarking of Parallel Computing Systems

Torsten Hoefler

ETH Zurich

Abstract. Measuring and reporting performance of parallel computers constitutes the basis for scientific advancement of high-performance computing (HPC). Most scientific reports show performance improvements of new techniques and are thus obliged to ensure reproducibility or at least interpretability. Our investigation of a stratified sample of 120 papers across three top conferences in the field shows that the state of the practice is not sufficient. For example, it is often unclear if reported improvements are in the noise or observed by chance. In addition to distilling best practices from existing work, we propose statistically sound analysis and reporting techniques and simple guidelines for experimental design in parallel computing. We aim to improve the standards of reporting research results and initiate a discussion in the HPC field. A wide adoption of this minimal set of rules will lead to better reproducibility and interpretability of performance results and improve the scientific culture around HPC.

Scientific Benchmarking of Parallel Computing Systems

Torsten Hoefler

Abstract

BenchCouncil Achievement
Award Lecture

It's a Random World: Learning from Mistakes, Errors, and Noise

David J. Lilja

University of Minnesota, Minneapolis, USA

Abstract: The world is a random place. As computer performance analysts, we learn how to statistically quantify randomness and errors to prevent mistakes, usually. For example, computer designers must use yesterday's benchmark programs to design systems today that will be evaluated with tomorrow's benchmarks. The results of this "benchmark drift" can be ugly, as we learn from measurements on a real microprocessor that showed significantly less performance improvement than simulations predicted. Additionally, the continued scaling of devices introduces greater variability, defects, and noise into circuits, making it increasingly challenging to build systems that rigidly transform conventional binary inputs into binary outputs. Yet these changes also provide opportunities through some unexpected connections. We have been investigating a stochastic computing model that treats randomness as a valuable computational resource by transforming probability values into probability values. Through these examples, I hope to demonstrate how we can learn from mistakes, errors, and noise.

Keynote

Benchmarking Quantum Computers

Kristel Michielsen

Institute for Advanced Simulation, Jülich Supercomputing Centre

Abstract: Significant advances in the system- and application-oriented development of quantum computers open up new approaches to hard optimization problems, efficient machine learning and simulations of complex quantum systems. In order to evaluate quantum computing as a new compute technology, profound test models and benchmarks are needed to compare quantum computing and quantum annealing devices with trustworthy simulations on digital supercomputers. These simulations provide essential insight into their operation, enable benchmarking and contribute to their design.

We present results of benchmarking quantum computing hardware and software. We show benchmarking outcomes for the IBM Quantum Experience and CAS-Alibaba gate-based quantum computers, the D-Wave quantum annealers D-Wave 2000Q and Advantage, and for the quantum approximate optimization algorithm (QAOA) and quantum annealing. For this purpose, also simulations of both types of quantum computers are performed by first modeling them as zero-temperature quantum systems of interacting spin-1/2 particles and then emulating their dynamics by solving the time-dependent Schrödinger equation.

Invited Talks

AIBench and Its Performance Rankings

Jianfeng Zhan

Chair of BenchCouncil Steering Committee

Abstract: Modern real-world application scenarios like Internet services not only consist of a diversity of AI and non-AI modules with very long and complex execution paths, but also have huge code size, which raises serious benchmarking or evaluating challenges. Using AI components or micro benchmarks alone can lead to error-prone conclusions. Together with seventeen industry partners, we extract nine typical application scenarios, and identify the primary components. As the proxy to real-world applications, the AIBench scenario benchmarks let the software and hardware designers obtain the overall system performance and find out the key components within the critical path. Following the same methodology, we propose Edge AIBench for benchmarking end-to-end performance across IoT, edge and Datacenter.

Earlier-stage evaluations of a new AI architecture/system need affordable AI training benchmarks, while using a few AI component benchmarks alone in the other stages may lead to misleading conclusions. We present a balanced AI benchmarking methodology for meeting the conflicting requirements of different stages. We identify and implement seventeen representative AI tasks with state-of-the-art models to guarantee the diversity and representativeness of the benchmarks. Meanwhile, we keep the benchmark subset to a minimum for affordability, and release AI chip rankings. Furthermore, on the basis of the AIBench training subset, we present the HPC AI500 benchmarks and their rankings for evaluating HPC AI systems for both affordability and representativeness. For AI Inference, as its cost is trivial, we provide comprehensive AI inference benchmarks. Meanwhile, we propose AIoTBench for considering diverse lightweight AI frameworks and models.

DataBench Toolbox Supporting Big Data and AI Benchmarking

Arne J. Berre[1], Tomás Pariente Lobo[2], and Todor Ivanov[3]

[1] SINTEF Digital
[2] Associate Head of AI, Data & Robotics Unit, Atos
[3] Senior Consultant at Lead Consult

Abstract: The DataBench Toolbox offers support for big data and AI benchmarking based on existing efforts in the benchmarking community. The DataBench framework is based on classification of benchmarks using a generic pipeline structure for Big Data and AI pipelines related to the Big Data Value Association (BDVA) Reference Model and the ISO SC42 AI Framework. Based on existing efforts in big data benchmarking and enabling inclusion of new benchmarks that could arise in the future, the DataBench Toolbox provides an environment to search, select and deploy big data benchmarking tools, giving the possibility to identify technical metrics and also relate to and derive business KPIs for an organization, in order to support Evidence-Based Big Data and AI Benchmarking to improve Business Performance. The Handbook and the DataBench Toolbox are essential components of the DataBench project results. The DataBench Toolbox is a software tool which will provide access to benchmarking services, KPIs and various types of knowledge; the DataBench Handbook plays a complementary role to the Toolbox by providing a comprehensive view of the benchmarks referenced in the Toolbox, and of how technical and business benchmarking can be linked. The DataBench Handbook and Toolbox are aimed at industrial users and technology developers who need to make informed decisions on Big Data and AI Technologies investments by optimizing technical and business performance.

Contents

Benchmarking on GPU

Application and Dataset

Best Paper Session

Characterizing the Sharing Behavior of Applications Using Software Transactional Memory

Douglas Pereira Pasqualin[1]([✉]) [iD], Matthias Diener[2] [iD],
André Rauber Du Bois[1] [iD], and Maurício Lima Pilla[1,3] [iD]

[1] Computer Science Graduate Program (PPGC), Universidade Federal de Pelotas,
Pelotas, RS, Brazil
{dp.pasqualin,dubois,pilla}@inf.ufpel.edu.br
[2] University of Illinois at Urbana-Champaign, Urbana, IL 61801, USA
mdiener@illinois.edu
[3] Google LLC, Sunnyvale, CA 94089, USA

Abstract. Software Transactional Memory (STM) is an alternative abstraction for process synchronization in parallel programming. It is often easier to use than locks, avoiding issues such as deadlocks. In order to improve STM performance, many studies have been made on transactional schedulers. However, in current architectures with complex memories hierarchies, it is also important to map threads in such a way that threads that share data are executed close to each other in the memory hierarchy, such that they can access data protected by STM faster. For a successful thread mapping of an STM application, it is important to perform an in-depth analysis of its sharing behavior to determine its suitability for different mapping policies and the expected performance gains. This paper characterizes the sharing behavior of the STAMP benchmark suite by using information extracted from the STM runtime, providing information to guide thread mapping based on their sharing behavior. Our main findings are that most of the STAMP applications are suitable for a static thread mapping approach to improve the performance since (1) the applications do not present dynamic behavior and (2) the sharing pattern does not change between executions. Furthermore, we show that sharing information gathered from the STM runtime can be used to analyze and reduce false sharing in TM applications.

Keywords: Software transactional memory · STAMP · Sharing behavior · Communication matrix · Thread mapping · Characterization

1 Introduction

Transactional memory (TM) is an alternative abstraction for process synchronization in parallel programming. The most commonly used abstraction, locks,

This study was financed in part by the Coordenação de Aperfeiçoamento de Pessoal de Nível Superior - Brasil (CAPES) - Finance Code 001 and PROCAD/LEAPaD.

F. Wolf and W. Gao (Eds.): Bench 2020, LNCS 12614, pp. 3–21, 2021.
https://doi.org/10.1007/978-3-030-71058-3_1

is error-prone and often leads to problems such as deadlocks. On the other hand, TM provides an easy to use abstraction which only requires enclosing critical sections of an application in atomic blocks. Each block is executed as a transaction, and the TM runtime guarantees a consistent execution of these transactions. Although TM can be implemented both in hardware or software, this work is focused on software TM (STM), not hardware TM (HTM). Advantages of STM over HTM include a higher flexibility, allowing the implementation of many kinds of algorithms; easier integration with other language features such as garbage collection; and fewer resource limitations, such as cache size [21,24].

Most studies to improve STM performance focus on reducing the number of conflicts (transactional aborts), relying on the use of transactional schedulers [13]. In multicore systems, there are additional challenges due to the complex memory hierarchies with different access latencies. In these architectures, it is important to exploit memory affinity, i.e., place threads and the data they access close to each other. The majority of the studies in this area focus on general applications [5,15,23,28,41,42], and only few target STM applications [8,9].

In modern parallel architectures, the performance of STM transactions depends to a large degree on the speed of which threads can access shared data [36]. STM provides interesting mapping opportunities since the STM runtime has precise information about memory areas that are shared between threads, their respective memory addresses, and the intensity with which they are accessed by each thread [35]. However, for a successful mapping, it is necessary to perform an in-depth analysis of STM applications, for instance, if the memory access pattern changes in each execution; the number of addresses accessed inside transactions, etc. This analysis is important to guide decisions regarding mapping, such as determining if an application is suitable for a thread mapping based on communication behavior and defining the type of mapping policy (static or dynamic).

In this paper, we characterize the applications from STAMP [32], a frequently used TM benchmark suite [6,10,14,34,38,45], by gathering sharing information through a modified TinySTM [18] runtime, providing information to guide thread placement based on their sharing behavior. The modified runtime gathers information about the suitability for thread mapping of each application, its communication pattern, and its dynamic behavior, among others. We also show how the runtime can be used to detect false sharing of cache lines of STM operations.

Using the proposed characterization, we show that the majority of STAMP applications are suitable for a sharing-aware mapping, as they do not have dynamic communication patterns. In that case, for those applications that are suitable for thread mapping, a *static* mapping mechanism is sufficient to improve the performance of applications. Compared to other tools to determine the communication behavior, our modified runtime has a much lower overhead and is more accurate, due to only tracking STM operations and not all memory accesses of an application. Compared to the default OS scheduler, we achieved speedups from thread mapping of up to 58.3% (online mechanism) and 56% (static mechanism), with averages of 7.4% with online and 13.5% with static. Reducing false sharing resulted in gains of up to 10.9%.

2   Background

This section presents a brief overview of software transactional memory, sharing behavior, thread mapping, and the STAMP applications.

2.1   Software Transactional Memory

Software transactional memory (STM) is an abstraction to synchronize accesses to shared resources. One of its main objectives is to simplify parallel programming, replacing the use of explicit locks with atomic blocks. Thus, developers only need to mark the block of code, the critical section, that should be executed as a transaction. The STM system is responsible for ensuring a consistent execution without race conditions or deadlocks. A transaction that executes without conflicts with other transactions *commits*, i.e., all its operations are made visible to other transactions. If any conflicts are detected, a transaction *aborts*, discarding all its operations and restarting it until a commit is possible.

There are many design choices available for implementing an STM system. Examples are transaction granularity (word or object), version management, and conflict detection and resolution. Another important component is the contention manager (CM). Its objective is to choose what to do when two transactions conflict, including aborting the oldest transaction immediately, waiting a period before restarting, and aborting the enemy transaction, among others [22]. TinySTM [18] is one of the most used STM libraries and is considered a state-of-art STM implementation [10, 14, 38]. TinySTM uses word granularity and has configurable version management and CMs.

2.2   Sharing Behavior and Thread Mapping

Modern systems have multiple cores and sometimes multi-sockets, where each socket is connected to a memory module. In such architectures, it is important to consider how cores are connected, where the memory of the program is allocated, and how it is accessed [19]. Thus, placement of threads and data is important for application performance, by achieving better data locality and load balance [30]. One technique for improving memory locality is to map threads and data of an application to the system by considering their sharing (or communication) behavior [11], expressed as memory accesses to the same data by different threads. To determine a better placement of threads and data, an affinity measure is required. A common measure is a communication matrix [4, 31], in which each cell represents the amount of communication between pairs of threads [10]. A communication matrix can be represented graphically, where darker cells indicate more communication between pairs of threads [15].

2.3   STAMP Applications

Stanford Transactional Applications for Multi-Processing (STAMP) [32] is a benchmark suite frequently used for testing TM systems [6, 10, 14, 34, 38, 45]. It is composed of eight applications and represents many realistic application domains such as Bioinformatics, security, data mining, machine learning, and others. Its applications cover many aspects of transactional cases such as level of contention, transaction length, variation length of read and write sets, among others.

3   Methodology of the Characterization

This section discusses the methodology of the characterization.

3.1   Detecting Sharing in STM Applications

The characteristics of memory access behavior presented in this paper are based on the communication matrices of applications. To extract the matrices we have adapted a mechanism proposed in our previous work [36]. This mechanism is triggered on each transactional data access operation (read or write). When at least two different threads accessed the same memory address, a communication event between them is stored in a communication matrix. Examples of communication matrices are shown in Fig. 2. Axes show threads IDs. The mechanism was implemented in the TinySTM library [18], version 1.0.5. TinySTM was configured to use the default configuration: *lazy* version management, *eager* conflict detection and contention manager *suicide*. STAMP was compiled with gcc 8.3.0. If not specified otherwise, all applications were executed ten times using 64 threads and the default input parameters shown in Table 1. Most parameters are larger than the largest ones suggested in the original paper [32] to achieve more substantial execution times on modern machines.

3.2   Machine

Applications were executed on an eight-socket Intel Xeon E5-4650 system, running Linux kernel 4.19.0-9. Each socket has 12 2-HT cores, totaling 96 cores. Each socket corresponds to a NUMA node (for a total of 8 NUMA nodes), and 12 × 32 KB L1d, 12 × 32 KB L1i, 12 × 256 KB L2 and 30 MB L3 caches.

Table 1. Default parameters for the STAMP programs used in the experiments.

Application	Arguments
bayes	-v32 -r8192 -n10 -p40 -i2 -e8 -s1 -t num_threads
genome	-g49152 -s256 -n33554432 -t num_threads
intruder	-a10 -l128 -n262144 -s1 -t num_threads
kmeans	-m40 -n40 -t0.00001 -i random-n65536-d32-c16.txt -p num_threads
labyrinth	-i random-x1024-y1024-z9-n1024.txt -t num_threads
ssca2	-s21 -i1.0 -u1.0 -l3 -p3 -t num_threads
vacation	-n4 -q90 -u100 -r1310720 -t16777216 -c num_threads
yada	-a15 -i ttimeu1000000.2 -t num_threads

3.3 Mean Squared Error (MSE)

Since the analysis of the communication behavior of the applications is based on communication matrices, we used *Mean squared error* (MSE) [44] metric to compare the difference between them, which has been used in prior work for this purpose [15]. The equation to calculate the MSE is shown in Eq. 1.

$$MSE(A, B) = \frac{1}{N^2} \sum_{i=0}^{N-1} \sum_{j=0}^{N-1} (A[i,j] - B[i,j])^2 \qquad (1)$$

where:

A, B = input matrices
N = matrix order, i.e., number of threads
i, j = matrix indexes

If the MSE of two matrices is zero, then the matrices are exactly the same. Higher MSE values indicate higher differences. This metric is useful to compare, for instance, if the memory access behavior of one application changes on each execution.

3.4 Experiments

We performed the following experiments to characterize the sharing behavior of the STAMP applications:

1. We collected information about the total of accessed addresses inside the STM library. The information is useful to understand how much data is accessed by STM operations (Sect. 4.1).
2. We executed the same application ten times to verify if the communication pattern changes between executions. This experiment will show if a communication matrix collected in a previous execution can be used to make a static thread mapping (Sect. 4.2).
3. We executed the same application ten times, changing the input parameters from the default. This experiment will show if it is possible to use a collected communication matrix with different input parameters to make a static thread mapping (Sect. 4.3).
4. We executed the same application ten times, changing the total number of threads from the previous experiments, with the same goal as in the previous item (Sect. 4.4).
5. We collected the communication matrix several times during the execution of an application, to determine if an application needs an online mechanism to detect the sharing behavior and perform the thread mapping multiple times during execution (Sect. 4.5).

4   Characterization of STM Sharing Behavior

This section presents the characterization of the STAMP applications.

4.1   STM Memory Access Information

The first data set is not directly related to sharing behavior but is useful to explain further the behavior of applications. The total number of distinct memory addresses accessed by STM operations was collected as well as the total number of accesses made to these addresses such as read or write operations. With this data, it is possible to calculate other information:

- **Number of distinct cache lines**: This was calculated based on the default cache line of most current microarchitectures, 64 bytes.
- **Number of distinct pages**: This was calculated based on the default page size of many current microarchitectures, 4096 bytes.
- **Percentage of cache lines with false sharing**: We consider that a cache line has false sharing when multiple threads perform STM operations on more than one word on the same line.

Results are shown in Table 2 and indicate that the applications have different characteristics regarding the number of accessed addresses. *kmeans* has the lowest amount of distinct addresses accessed. However, it has a large number of total accesses made to these addresses. On the other hand, *ssca2* has the largest amount of distinct addresses accessed, but not the largest total of accesses, whose belongs to *vacation*. Regarding false sharing, the majority of applications have a large percentage of false sharing. For instance, in *kmeans*, all addresses share common cache lines. On the other hand, *genome* has the least amount of false sharing which indicates that more than half of the accessed addresses has at least 64 bytes or the addresses that conflict in the same cache line are accessed outside the STM library.

Table 2. Analysis of accessed STM memory addresses in STAMP applications.

Application	Distinct addresses	Distinct cache lines	Distinct pages	Total accesses	% of lines with false sharing
bayes	1,082	497	122	15,928,303	89.33
kmeans	682	101	4	833,954,131	100.00
labyrinth	824,126	290,083	18,213	1,994,315	83.05
genome	19,750,104	11,216,870	452,651	2,840,508,725	36.21
intruder	23,292,164	8,131,906	297,629	4,105,619,590	99.00
yada	25,055,077	13,932,226	848,045	610,446,722	81.38
vacation	33,671,744	10,796,118	799,129	7,212,365,036	99.08
ssca2	91,335,091	13,907,852	528,387	270,369,505	99.90

4.2   Stability of Sharing Behavior Across Different Executions

The goal of this experiment is to determine if the communication pattern changes across different executions of the same application, using the same input parameters and the number of threads. To answer this question, we run all applications one time and collected the communication matrix, to be used as a baseline for comparison. After that, we run each application nine more times, collecting the communication matrix in each execution. Then, we calculated the MSE of each resulting matrix, comparing it to the first execution. Results are shown in Fig. 1.

Some applications, for instance *bayes*, *genome* and *labyrinth*, present the same communication behavior in all executions. This observation can be visualized in two different communication matrices of *bayes* (Fig. 2(a) and (b)). Axes show threads IDs. In contrast to *bayes*, *ssca2* presents a not so similar behavior on each execution. However, looking at two *ssca2* matrices (Fig. 2(c)) and (d)) it is possible to note that although the basic communication behavior is the same (all-to-all [3]), the total amount of communication between threads is very different. This can be explained by the non-deterministic behavior of TM applications, mainly due to the fact that the total number of aborts varies in each execution. More aborts imply in more work to be done, consequently more communication between threads. In that case, even having a higher MSE between executions,

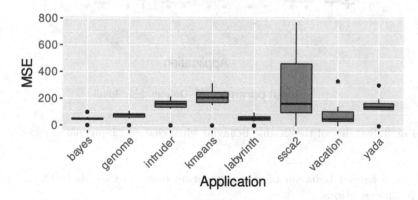

Fig. 1. Stability of the sharing behavior across different executions.

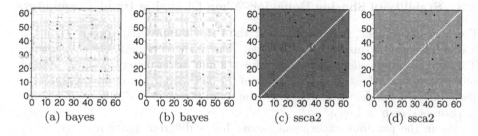

Fig. 2. Matrices with highest and lowest MSEs between different executions.

Table 3. Small input parameters used in the experiments in Sect. 4.3.

Application	Arguments
bayes	-v16 -r4096 -n15 -p40 -i2 -e8 -s1 -t num_threads
genome	-g16384 -s64 -n16777216 -t num_threads
intruder	-a10 -l64 -n131072 -s1 -t num_threads
kmeans	-m15 -n15 -t0.00001 -i random-n65536-d32-c16.txt -p num_threads
labyrinth	-i random-x512-y512-z7-n512.txt -t num_threads
ssca2	-s18 -i1.0 -u1.0 -l3 -p3 -t num_threads
vacation	-n4 -q60 -u90 -r1048576 -t4194304 -c num_threads
yada	-a20 -i ttimeu100000.2 -t num_threads

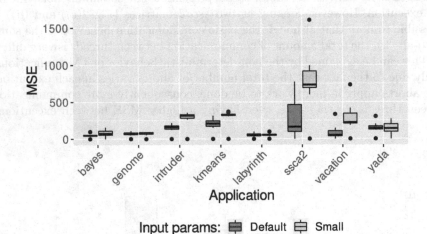

Fig. 3. Stability of the sharing behavior when changing input parameters.

ssca2 has a similar behavior of communication between threads (all-to-all pattern) in all executions.

4.3   Stability of Sharing Behavior When Changing Input Parameters

For this experiment, instead of using the default input parameters shown in Table 1, we used a smaller input data set. The changed parameters are shown in Table 3. Then, we collected ten communication matrices using the same methodology of Sect. 4.2. Lastly, a comparison of the MSE using the default parameters (Sect. 4.2) was made, comparing with the small parameters (Table 3). This comparison is shown in Fig. 3.

As in the previous experiment, *ssca2* has a different pattern on each execution. For instance, Fig. 4(c) and (d) show two different executions of *ssca2*, using the small parameters (Table 3). However, with the new parameters, it is

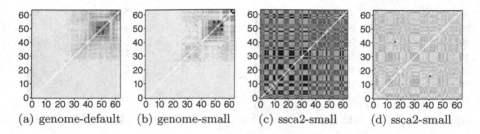

(a) genome-default   (b) genome-small   (c) ssca2-small   (d) ssca2-small

Fig. 4. Matrices with highest and lowest MSEs.

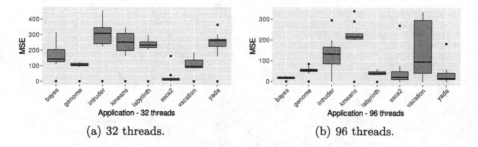

(a) 32 threads.   (b) 96 threads.

Fig. 5. Stability of the sharing behavior when changing the number of threads.

possible to observe that some groups of threads communicate more often than others (Fig. 4(c)). Besides, there is a difference between communication patterns taking into consideration the default and small parameter sets. This can be visualized by comparing Fig. 2(c) and Fig. 4(c). Other applications such as *intruder*, *kmeans*, and *vacation* have a small difference between communication patterns when changing input parameters. While others, such as *genome* have almost the same communication pattern, even when changing the input parameters (Fig. 4(a) and (b)).

4.4 Stability of Sharing Behavior with Different Numbers of Threads

Figure 1 in Sect. 4.2 showed the communication matrices for 64 threads. We used the same methodology to collect them for 32 and 96 threads, and show the results in Fig. 5. The most different behavior occurs with *vacation* and 96 threads. However, looking at the communication pattern of two executions with the highest MSE (Fig. 6(c) and (d)) we saw the same behavior for *ssca2* in Sect. 4.2. With 96 threads, *vacation* has an all-to-all communication pattern, and the main difference between executions is the total amount of communication, which can be explained by the difference of aborts between each execution. On the other hand, applications such as *genome* present a similar behavior even changing the number of threads, for instance, with 32 threads (Fig. 6(a) and (b)).

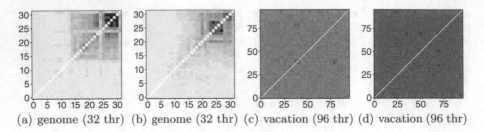

(a) genome (32 thr) (b) genome (32 thr) (c) vacation (96 thr) (d) vacation (96 thr)

Fig. 6. Matrices with the lowest and highest MSEs.

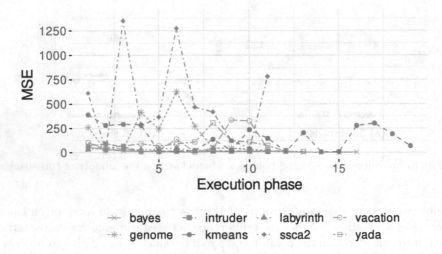

Fig. 7. Comparing the MSE on different execution phases.

4.5   Dynamic Behavior During Execution

The goal of this experiment is to determine if the communication pattern changes during the execution of the application. For this experiment, we store multiple communication matrices in different execution phases of the applications. We analyzed the total of addresses accessed by each application (Table 2) and used it as a parameter to define a *save interval*, i.e., when to collect the communication matrix. After collection, we reset the data structure responsible to store the communication matrix. For instance, for *labyrinth* the mechanism collected eight matrices, whereas for *kmeans* nineteen matrices were collected. We run the applications using the default parameters (Table 1) and 64 threads.

In the previous sections, the MSE was compared with the first collected matrix, i.e., the baseline was the first execution. For this experiment, the baseline was the last collected matrix. For instance, after two matrices collected it is possible to calculate the MSE between them. When a third matrix is collected, we calculated the MSE between the third and the previous execution (second matrix) onward. Figure 7 presents the results.

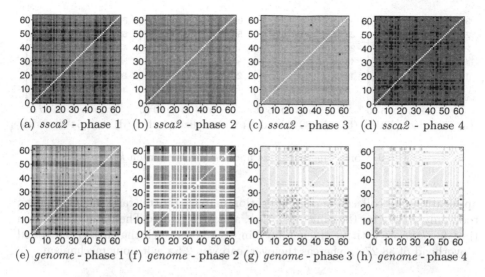

(a) *ssca2* - phase 1   (b) *ssca2* - phase 2   (c) *ssca2* - phase 3   (d) *ssca2* - phase 4

(e) *genome* - phase 1 (f) *genome* - phase 2 (g) *genome* - phase 3 (h) *genome* - phase 4

Fig. 8. Communication matrices in different execution phases.

Analyzing the graph, *ssca2* has the highest difference in communication patterns during the execution, followed by *genome*. However, as in Sects. 4.2 and 4.3 the biggest difference in the communication matrices was in the amount of communication between threads since this application has an all-to-all behavior. This is visualized in Fig. 8(a)–(d). On the other hand, *genome* has a varying communication pattern during its execution. There is an intense communication between threads in the beginning of the application, whereas in the end there is little communication (Fig. 8(e)–(h)). Other applications have a similar communication behavior during their execution.

4.6   Overhead of the Behavior Detection

To compare the overhead generated by tracking and generating the communication matrices, we compare our mechanism with a memory tracing tool called numalize [16]. Unfortunately, numalize crashes in applications with large numbers of memory accesses. This problem was observed in others studies that have used this tool [41]. Hence, we were only able to run *kmeans* using numalize.

Numalize depends on Intel's Pin tool [29] to instrument the application and trace all accessed addresses, not only the ones accessed by the STM system. Therefore, numalize captures a different memory access behavior compared to our mechanism. This is visualized in Fig. 9 which compares the collected matrices of *kmeans* with 32 and 64 threads using both mechanisms. The MSE between the matrices collected by numalize and our mechanism is 824.72 (32 threads) and 524.97 (64 threads).

Another disadvantage of numalize is the overhead added to trace all memory accesses. On *kmeans*, using 64 threads, numalize took 690.90 s to execute the

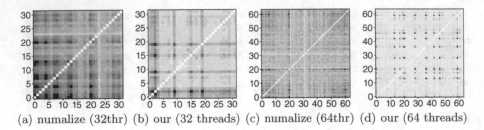

(a) numalize (32thr) (b) our (32 threads) (c) numalize (64thr) (d) our (64 threads)

Fig. 9. Comparing `numalize` and our mechanism on *kmeans*.

application and collect the communication matrix. By contrast, our mechanism took only 46.20 s for the same operation, almost 15× less. The normal execution time for *kmeans* without tracing anything is 18.05 s, such that `numalize` added a overhead of 38.27×, whereas the overhead was 2.5× with our mechanism.

5   Case Studies

In this section, we present two performance experiments based on the characterization shown in the last section.

5.1   Performance Gains from Sharing-Aware Thread Mapping

Since we only observed high MSE values in applications that have an all-to-all pattern, which can be explained by the different number of aborts in each execution, our hypothesis is that a *static* thread mapping mechanism (where threads are mapped to cores at the beginning of execution, and never migrated) is sufficient for the `STAMP` applications, and an *online* mechanism (where mapping is performed periodically during execution) is not necessary. In order to show how the characterizations made in this paper can be used, and to verify this hypothesis, we performed an experiment to compare these two types of thread mapping mechanisms. The default OS scheduler, which we refer to as *Linux*, was used as a baseline.

For the *static* approach, we used the same mechanism proposed in [36], which was used to collect the matrices in this paper. Moreover, we tested the static mapping with communication matrix collected by `numalize` for *kmeans*. We used the `TopoMatch` [26] mapping algorithm to calculate the best thread placement based on the communication matrix. Finally, applications were re-executed, binding threads to cores using the function `pthread_setaffinity_np`. For the *online* approach, we performed these steps while the application was running [35]. To reduce the overhead, we performed a sampling of STM operations (limited to 10%) and triggered the mapping algorithm with an interval of 50,000 operations by the master thread. The applications were run with 32, 64, and 96 threads on the machine shown in Sect. 3. Results are presented in Fig. 10.

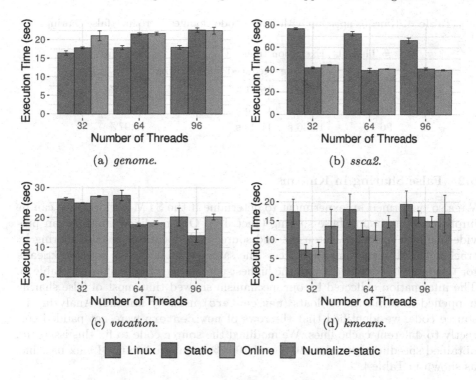

(a) *genome.*

(b) *ssca2.*

(c) *vacation.*

(d) *kmeans.*

■ Linux ■ Static ■ Online ■ Numalize-static

Fig. 10. Comparing the performance of various thread mappings.

The results indicate that the *online* mechanism performed similarly to the *static* one. As discussed in [36], *genome* is not suitable for a communication aware mechanism. Nevertheless, we are interested in comparing the difference between *static* and *online* mechanisms only. The major difference was in *vacation* with 96 threads, where the *online* thread mapping mechanism was not triggered often enough. The result was similar to *Linux* in this case.

The highest performance gains were achieved with kmeans in 32 threads: 58.3% using the online mechanism and 56% with static compared to the default OS scheduler. Overall, taking into consideration all applications and thread configurations, the static mechanism improved performance by 13.5% and the online mechanism by 7.4%. With kmeans, the *static* mapping based on numalize performed worse than our mechanism with 32 and 64 threads. With 96 threads, the performance was similar, however numalize has a higher overhead to collect the matrix.

These experiments have shown that the conclusions made through the characterization done in Sect. 4 were accurate. A *static* mapping mechanism is sufficient for the STAMP applications. However, according to the results, it is possible to develop an *online* mechanism with a low overhead, sampling the accessed memory addresses, and using TopoMatch to calculate the mapping. Hence, an *online* mechanism can be interesting, since it is not be necessary to perform a prior execution only to collect the communication matrix.

Table 4. Kmeans speedup with source code changes to reduce false sharing.

# Threads	Execution time		Speedup
	Baseline	Reduced false sharing	
32	17.36 s	16.01 s	7.81%
64	18.05 s	17.15 s	4.97%
96	19.36 s	17.24 s	10.97%

5.2 False Sharing in Kmeans

We also performed an experiment to determine if the STM performance can be improved by reducing false sharing (Sect. 4.1). Our modified runtime can provide memory addresses, intensity, and source code locations of false sharing by tracking STM operations that access the same cache lines. We selected kmeans for this experiment since it had the highest percentage of false sharing (Table 2). The information collected by our mechanism showed that most of false sharing happened in a matrix of floats (new_centers) used by kmeans. Analyzing its source code, we identified that the rows of new_centers were not padded correctly to different cache lines. We modified the source code to fix this issue and obtained speedups between 4.97% and 10.97% compared to the Linux baseline, as shown in Table 4.

6   Related Work

In [3], the Splash-2 and Parsec benchmark suites were characterized regarding their memory access behavior. They also showed other characteristics such as temporal and spatial characterization of the communication. All information was gathered through the use of a simulator. Using the collected information, they proposed changes to the communication systems to be used in future chip multiprocessors (CMP). Different communication characteristics of Splash-2 and Parsec were also studied in [33]. Rane and Browne [39] proposed to instrument the source code of applications using the LLVM compiler, to extract memory trace of applications. Then, they compute metrics using the collected data, such as cycles per access; NUMA hit ratios; access strides; etc. With this information, they manually changed a subset of programs of the Rodinia benchmark suite and were able to improve the performance. The numalize tool to extract information about communication behavior was proposed in [16]. Also, they have analyzed different benchmark suites and proposed metrics that describes spatial, temporal, and volume properties of memory accesses to shared areas.

Hughes et al. [25] proposed a set of transactional characteristics to classify the similarity of transactional workloads. The main idea is to select a subset of programs that present distinct transactional characteristics, to be used in benchmarks or tests. In [7], a generic mechanism was proposed to intercept any function of STM libraries. The mechanism is implemented as an external tool, allowing developers to extract and calculate information accessed inside the STM library. Baldassin et al. [2] characterized the memory allocation of STAMP.

Mapping algorithms are used to map tasks to cores according to a metric, for instance, a communication matrix. Scotch [37] is a graph-partitioning framework that can be used for mapping. TreeMatch [27] focuses on mapping in hardware hierarchies that can be represented as a tree. TopoMatch [26] integrates Scotch and TreeMatch in the same library to deal with any topology, not only trees. EagerMap [12] uses a greedy heuristic to match application communication patterns to hardware hierarchies. It can also consider the task load of the processes. ChoiceMap [41] generates a mapping that considers mutual priorities of tasks.

Castro et al. [8] use the abort ratio of transactional applications to decide the thread mapping strategy dynamically. Zhou et al. [46] created a mechanism to dynamically define the best number of threads allowed to run transactions concurrently. Based on the number of threads, the thread mapping strategy is changed. In [9], the main idea was to map threads with transactions that conflict often to sibling cores that share caches since they are accessing the same shared data. Góes et al. [20] focused on STM applications that have a worklist pattern and proposed a mechanism for improving memory affinity that relies on the use of static page allocation (bind or cyclic) and data prefetching by using helper threads. In our previous work [35,36], a thread mapping for STM is proposed based on the memory access behavior of the applications.

In hardware TM (HTM), false sharing is one of the main causes of conflicts [1,43], since the granularity of conflict detection is normally the cache line [21]. However, in STM there is a concern in avoiding false sharing too, for instance, using different kinds of memory allocators [2] or increasing the size of the lock array table [17], which maps memory locations to their related versioned locks.

7 Conclusion

This paper presented a characterization of the STAMP applications regarding their sharing behavior. We show that by only taking memory accesses from STM operations into consideration, it is possible to create an accurate and low overhead mechanism to determine sharing behavior. We found that the STAMP applications do not present a dynamic sharing behavior during and between executions. Hence, a *static* thread mapping approach is sufficient to improve the performance of the applications that are suitable for a thread mapping based on their sharing behavior. We were also able to analyze and reduce false sharing in STM memory areas, and achieved substantial performance gains from performing thread mapping based on the detected sharing behavior, as well as the reduction of false sharing. As future work, we intend to characterize the accesses to memory pages and memory allocations of STAMP applications and other TM applications in order to use them for data mapping in NUMA architectures.

All software and instructions necessary to reproduce the experiments in this paper are available at https://github.com/douglaspasqualin/Bench-20-STM.

References

1. Amslinger, R., Piatka, C., Haas, F., Weis, S., Ungerer, T., Altmeyer, S.: Hardware multiversioning for fail-operational multithreaded applications. In: 2020 32nd International Symposium on Computer Architecture and High Performance Computing (SBAC-PAD), pp. 20–27. IEEE CS, September 2020. https://doi.org/10.1109/SBAC-PAD49847.2020.00014
2. Baldassin, A., Borin, E., Araujo, G.: Performance implications of dynamic memory allocators on transactional memory systems. In: Proceedings of the 20th ACM SIGPLAN Symposium on Principles and Practice of Parallel Programming, PPoPP 2015, pp. 87–96. Association for Computing Machinery, New York (2015). https://doi.org/10.1145/2688500.2688504
3. Barrow-Williams, N., Fensch, C., Moore, S.: A communication characterisation of Splash-2 and Parsec. In: 2009 IEEE International Symposium on Workload Characterization (IISWC), pp. 86–97 (2009). https://doi.org/10.1109/IISWC.2009.5306792
4. Bordage, C., Jeannot, E.: Process affinity, metrics and impact on performance: an empirical study. In: Proceedings of the 18th IEEE/ACM International Symposium on Cluster, Cloud and Grid Computing, pp. CCGrid 2018, pp. 523–532. IEEE Press (2018). https://doi.org/10.1109/CCGRID.2018.00079
5. Bylina, B., Bylina, J.: OpenMP thread affinity for matrix factorization on multicore systems. In: 2017 Federated Conference on Computer Science and Information Systems (FedCSIS), pp. 489–492 (2017). https://doi.org/10.15439/2017F231
6. de Carvalho, J.P.L., Honorio, B.C., Baldassin, A., Araujo, G.: Improving transactional code generation via variable annotation and barrier elision. In: 2020 IEEE International Parallel and Distributed Processing Symposium (IPDPS). pp. 1008–1017 (2020). https://doi.org/10.1109/IPDPS47924.2020.00107
7. Castro, M., Georgiev, K., Marangozova-Martin, V., Méhaut, J., Fernandes, L.G., Santana, M.: Analysis and tracing of applications based on software transactional memory on multicore architectures. In: 2011 19th International Euromicro Conference on Parallel, Distributed and Network-Based Processing, pp. 199–206 (2011). https://doi.org/10.1109/PDP.2011.27
8. Castro, M., Góes, L.F.W., Méhaut, J.F.: Adaptive thread mapping strategies for transactional memory applications. J. Parallel Distrib. Comput. **74**(9), 2845–2859 (2014). https://doi.org/10.1016/j.jpdc.2014.05.008
9. Chan, K., Lam, K.T., Wang, C.L.: Cache affinity optimization techniques for scaling software transactional memory systems on multi-CMP architectures. In: 14th Internationl Symposium on Parallel and Distributed Computing, pp. 56–65. IEEE CS, June 2015. https://doi.org/10.1109/ISPDC.2015.14
10. Chen, D.D., Gibbons, P.B., Mowry, T.C.: Tardis, TM.: Incremental repair for transactional memory. In: Proceedings of the Eleventh International Workshop on Programming Models and Applications for Multicores and Manycores, PMAM 2020. Association for Computing Machinery, New York (2020). https://doi.org/10.1145/3380536.3380538
11. Cruz, E.H.M., Diener, M., Navaux, P.O.A.: Thread and Data Mapping for Multicore Systems. SCS. Springer, Cham (2018). https://doi.org/10.1007/978-3-319-91074-1
12. Cruz, E.H.M., Diener, M., Pilla, L.L., Navaux, P.O.A.: EagerMap: a task mapping algorithm to improve communication and load balancing in clusters of multicore systems. ACM Trans. Parallel Comput. 5(4) (Mar 2019). https://doi.org/10.1145/3309711

13. Di Sanzo, P.: Analysis, classification and comparison of scheduling techniques for software transactional memories. IEEE Trans. Parallel Distrib. Syst. **28**(12), 3356–3373 (2017). https://doi.org/10.1109/tpds.2017.2740285
14. Di Sanzo, P., Pellegrini, A., Sannicandro, M., Ciciani, B., Quaglia, F.: Adaptive model-based scheduling in software transactional memory. IEEE Trans. Comput. **69**(5), 621–632 (2020). https://doi.org/10.1109/tc.2019.2954139
15. Diener, M., Cruz, E.H.M., Alves, M.A.Z., Navaux, P.O.A.: Communication in shared memory: Concepts, definitions, and efficient detection. In: 24th Euromicro International Conference on Parallel, Distributed, and Network-Based Processing, pp. 151–158, February 2016. https://doi.org/10.1109/PDP.2016.16
16. Diener, M., Cruz, E.H., Pilla, L.L., Dupros, F., Navaux, P.O.: Characterizing communication and page usage of parallel applications for thread and data mapping. Performance Evaluation **88–89**, 18–36 (2015). https://doi.org/10.1016/j.peva.2015.03.001
17. Felber, P., Fetzer, C., Riegel, T.: Dynamic performance tuning of word-based software transactional memory. In: Proceedings of the 13th ACM SIGPLAN Symposium on Principles and Practice of Parallel Programming, PPoPP 2008, pp. 237–246. ACM, New York (2008). https://doi.org/10.1145/1345206.1345241
18. Felber, P., Fetzer, C., Riegel, T., Marlier, P.: Time-based software transactional memory. IEEE Trans. Parallel Distrib. Syst. **21**, 1793–1807 (2010). https://doi.org/10.1109/TPDS.2010.49
19. Gaud, F., et al.: Challenges of memory management on modern NUMA systems. Commun. ACM **58**(12), 59–66 (2015). https://doi.org/10.1145/2814328
20. Góes, L.F.W., Ribeiro, C.P., Castro, M., Méhaut, J.-F., Cole, M., Cintra, M.: Automatic skeleton-driven memory affinity for transactional worklist applications. Int. J. Parallel Programm. **42**(2), 365–382 (2013). https://doi.org/10.1007/s10766-013-0253-x
21. Grahn, H.: Transactional memory. J. Parallel Distrib. Comput. **70**(10), 993–1008 (2010). https://doi.org/10.1016/j.jpdc.2010.06.006
22. Guerraoui, R., Herlihy, M., Pochon, B.: Towards a theory of transactional contention managers. In: Proceedings of the Twenty-fifth Annual ACM Symposium on Principles of Distributed Computing, PODC 2006, pp. 316–317. ACM, New York (2006). https://doi.org/10.1145/1146381.1146429
23. Gustedt, J., Jeannot, E., Mansouri, F.: Automatic, abstracted and portable topology-aware thread placement. In: 2017 IEEE International Conference on Cluster Computing (CLUSTER), pp. 389–399 (2017). https://doi.org/10.1109/CLUSTER.2017.71
24. Harris, T., Larus, J., Rajwar, R.: Transactional Memory, vol. 2. Morgan and Claypool Publishers, San Rafae (2010). https://doi.org/10.2200/S00272ED1V01Y201006CAC011
25. Hughes, C., Poe, J., Qouneh, A., Li, T.: On the (dis)similarity of transactional memory workloads. In: 2009 IEEE International Symposium on Workload Characterization (IISWC), pp. 108–117 (2009). https://doi.org/10.1109/IISWC.2009.5306790
26. Jeannot, E.: TopoMatch: Process mapping algorithms and tools for general topologies (2020). https://gitlab.inria.fr/ejeannot/topomatch. Accessed 20 July 2020
27. Jeannot, E., Mercier, G., Tessier, F.: Process placement in multicore clusters: algorithmic issues and practical techniques. IEEE Trans. Parallel Distrib. Syst. **25**(4), 993–1002 (2014). https://doi.org/10.1109/TPDS.2013.104

28. Khaleghzadeh, H., Deldari, H., Reddy, R., Lastovetsky, A.: Hierarchical multicore thread mapping via estimation of remote communication. J. Supercomput. **74**(3), 1321–1340 (2017). https://doi.org/10.1007/s11227-017-2176-6

29. Luk, C.K., et al.: Pin: Building customized program analysis tools with dynamic instrumentation. In: Proceedings of the 2005 ACM SIGPLAN Conference on Programming Language Design and Implementation, pp. 190–200. ACM, New York (2005). https://doi.org/10.1145/1065010.1065034

30. Majo, Z., Gross, T.R.: Memory system performance in a NUMA multicore multiprocessor. In: Proceedings of the 4th Annual International Conference on Systems and Storage, SYSTOR 2011, pp. 12:1–12:10. ACM, New York (2011). https://doi.org/10.1145/1987816.1987832

31. Mazaheri, A., Wolf, F., Jannesari, A.: Unveiling thread communication bottlenecks using hardware-independent metrics. In: Proceedings of the 47th International Conference on Parallel Processing. ICPP 2018. ACM, New York (2018). https://doi.org/10.1145/3225058.3225142

32. Minh, C.C., Chung, J., Kozyrakis, C., Olukotun, K.: STAMP: stanford transactional applications for multi-processing. In: IEEE International Symposium on Workload Characterization. pp. 35–46. IEEE CS, September 2008. https://doi.org/10.1109/IISWC.2008.4636089

33. Mohammed, M.S., Abandah, G.A.: Communication characteristics of parallel shared-memory multicore applications. In: 2015 IEEE Jordan Conference on Applied Electrical Engineering and Computing Technologies (AEECT), pp. 1–6 (2015). https://doi.org/10.1109/AEECT.2015.7360553

34. Mururu, G., Gavrilovska, A., Pande, S.: Quantifying and reducing execution variance in STM via model driven commit optimization. In: 2019 IEEE/ACM International Symposium on Code Generation and Optimization (CGO), pp. 109–121 (2019). https://doi.org/10.1109/CGO.2019.8661179

35. Pasqualin, D.P., Diener, M., Du Bois, A.R., Pilla, M.L.: Online sharing-aware thread mapping in software transactional memory. In: 2020 32nd International Symposium on Computer Architecture and High Performance Computing (SBAC-PAD), pp. 35–42. IEEE CS, September 2020. https://doi.org/10.1109/SBAC-PAD49847.2020.00016

36. Pasqualin, D.P., Diener, M., Du Bois, A.R., Pilla, M.L.: Thread affinity in software transactional memory. In: 2020 19th International Symposium on Parallel and Distributed Computing (ISPDC), pp. 180–187. IEEE CS, July 2020. https://doi.org/10.1109/ISPDC51135.2020.00033

37. Pellegrini, F.: Static mapping by dual recursive bipartitioning of process architecture graphs. In: Proceedings of IEEE Scalable High Performance Computing Conference, pp. 486–493 (1994). https://doi.org/10.1109/SHPCC.1994.296682

38. Poudel, P., Sharma, G.: Adaptive versioning in transactional memories. In: Ghaffari, M., Nesterenko, M., Tixeuil, S., Tucci, S., Yamauchi, Y. (eds.) Stabilization, Safety, and Security of Distributed Systems. pp. 277–295. Springer International Publishing, Cham (2019). https://doi.org/10.1007/978-3-030-34992-9_22

39. Rane, A., Browne, J.: Performance optimization of data structures using memory access characterization. In: 2011 IEEE International Conference on Cluster Computing, pp. 570–574 (2011). https://doi.org/10.1109/CLUSTER.2011.77

40. Sasongko, M.A., Chabbi, M., Akhtar, P., Unat, D.: ComDetective: a lightweight communication detection tool for threads. In: Proceedings of the International Conference for High Performance Computing, Networking, Storage and Analysis. SC 2019 ACM, New York (2019). https://doi.org/10.1145/3295500.3356214

41. Soomro, P.N., Sasongko, M.A., Unat, D.: BindMe: A thread binding library with advanced mapping algorithms. Concurr. Comput. Pract. Exp. **30**(21), e4692 (2018). https://doi.org/10.1002/cpe.4692
42. Stirb, I.: NUMA-BTDM: A thread mapping algorithm for balanced data locality on NUMA systems. In: 2016 17th International Conference on Parallel and Distributed Computing, Applications and Technologies (PDCAT), pp. 317–320 (2016). https://doi.org/10.1109/PDCAT.2016.074
43. Waliullah, M.M., Stenstrom, P.: Removal of conflicts in hardware transactional memory systems. Int. J. Parallel Program. **42**(1), 198–218 (2012). https://doi.org/10.1007/s10766-012-0210-0
44. Wang, Z., Bovik, A.C.: Mean squared error: Love it or leave it? a new look at signal fidelity measures. IEEE Signal Process. Mag. **26**(1), 98–117 (2009). https://doi.org/10.1109/MSP.2008.930649
45. Yu, Z., Zuo, Yu., Zhao, Y.: Convoider: a concurrency bug avoider based on transparent software transactional memory. Int. J. Parallel Program. **48**(1), 32–60 (2019). https://doi.org/10.1007/s10766-019-00642-1
46. Zhou, N., Delaval, G., Robu, B., Rutten, E., Méhaut, J.F.: An autonomic-computing approach on mapping threads to multi-cores for software transactional memory. Concurr. Comput. Pract. Exp. **30**(18), e4506 (2018). https://doi.org/10.1002/cpe.4506

swRodinia: A Benchmark Suite for Exploiting Architecture Properties of Sunway Processor

Bangduo Chen[1], Mingzhen Li[1], Hailong Yang[1,2(✉)], Zhongzhi Luan[1], Lin Gan[3], Guangwen Yang[3], and Depei Qian[1]

[1] School of Computer Science and Engineering, Beihang University, Beijing 100191, China
hailong.yang@buaa.edu.cn
[2] State Key Laboratory of Mathematical Engineering and Advanced Computing, Wuxi 214125, Jiangsu, China
[3] Department of Computer Science and Technology, Tsinghua University, Beijing 100084, China

Abstract. The Sunway processor has been demonstrated with superior performance by various scientific applications, domain specific frameworks and numerical algorithms. However, the optimization techniques that can fully exploit the architecture features are usually buried deep in large code bases, which prevents average programmers to understand such optimization techniques. Thus, the existing complex software fails to provide guidance for more programs embracing the computation power of Sunway processor. In this paper, we build a benchmark suite *swRodinia* by porting and optimizing the well-known *Rodinia* benchmark on Sunway processor. Specifically, we demonstrate several optimization techniques by tailoring the benchmarks to better leverage the architecture features for higher performance. Moreover, based on the optimization experiences, we derive several useful insights from both software and hardware perspectives, that not only guide the better utilization of current Sunway processor, but also reveal the direction of hardware improvements for future Sunway processor. We open source the *swRodinia* benchmark suite and encourage the community to enhance the benchmark with us continuously.

Keywords: Sunway processor · Benchmark suite · Heterogeneous manycore · Parallelization · Performance optimization

1 Introduction

Sunway Taihulight is the first supercomputer to achieve more than 100PFlops peak performance (in double precision) around the world. It is equipped with 40,960 pieces of Sunway SW26010 heterogeneous manycore processors. Each SW26010 processor can achieve 3.06TFlops, and several unique architecture

F. Wolf and W. Gao (Eds.): Bench 2020, LNCS 12614, pp. 22–38, 2021.
https://doi.org/10.1007/978-3-030-71058-3_2

designs contribute to this remarkable peak performance. *1)* It has 260 cores contained in 4 Core Groups (CG), each CG includes 1 Management Processing Elements (MPE) and 64 Computing Processing Elements (CPEs). *2)* Each CPE has a 64 KB local device memory (LDM) with access latency of 4–5 cycles (similar to L1 data cache), but the LDM requires explicit control by programmers. *3)* The register communication allows efficient data communication between CPEs with transferring 256-bit data package at 10–11 cycles. *4)* The direct memory access (DMA) to the main memory has higher bandwidth when accessing continuous memory space than discrete load/store instruction. While these unique architecture features bring extremely high floating-point computing capabilities, they also introduce significant challenges to write efficient parallel programs for Sunway processor.

Currently, there are two parallel programming paradigms supported on Sunway processor, including OpenACC [20] and Athread [1]. OpenACC primarily focuses on productivity, and allows the programmers to port existing programs to Sunway by annotating with parallel pragmas. OpenACC can give programmers a taste of running parallel programs on Sunway easily, but never the eventual programming paradigm for squeezing the performance (as we demonstrate through benchmark evaluation in Sect. 4). At the other hand, Athread exposes the architecture details to the programmers such as LDM memory allocation, register communication, and DMA access, which for sure increases the learning curve and is less friendly to application programmers. Since most programmers on Sunway are to pursue the ultimate goal of higher performance, they are willing to overcome such learning obstacle in return of the ability to leverage the architecture features for performance at extreme through intricate manipulation of program execution. Thus, Athread becomes the de-facto parallel programming paradigm on Sunway.

Many applications from various fields, such as atmospheric dynamics [24], earthquake simulation [9], and graph processing [16], have achieved promising performance on Sunway TaihuLight, which have demonstrated the superior performance and efficiency of Sunway processor. Although effective optimization techniques on Sunway have been proposed in previous studies [9,16,24], these techniques are tightly coupled with the application logics and buried deeply in the large code base of the application (e.g., millions of lines of Fortran code). Therefore, it is prohibitive for average programmers to learn and understand these optimization techniques on Sunway. In the meanwhile, we notice there is no benchmark suite available for Sunway processor so far. To fill the missing piece of benchmark suite and expose the optimization techniques accessible to average programmers on Sunway, we propose to establish a benchmark suite for Sunway with various optimization techniques applied. The importance of the benchmark suite can be understood from two-folds. First, from the software perspective, it clearly illustrates various optimization techniques with representative benchmarks, that can be understood by programmers with manageable code sizes. The benchmark suites can also guide the performance optimizations of applications in similar domains. Second, from the hardware perspective, through the performance analysis (e.g., roofline model) of the benchmark suite, we can identify the deficiency of hardware design, which reveals optimization direction for future generation of Sunway processor.

Specifically, we select six benchmarks from six distinct dwarves in the well-known *Rodina* benchmark suite [3,4], and port them to Sunway processor with various optimization techniques applied to fully exploit the architecture features. For comparison, each benchmark is implemented using both OpenACC and Athread on Sunway. We name the ported and optimized benchmark suite on Sunway as *swRodinia*, which is open source for the community to leverage[1]. We encourage the community to contribute and improve *swRodinia* continuously, which can serve as the reference codes lowering the entry point for average programmers to embrace the computation power of Sunway processor. In addition, we perform performance evaluation with roofline analysis to understand the efficiency of performance optimizations. We also derive useful insights for not only better utilizing the existing architecture features of Sunway for higher performance through various optimization techniques, but also the optimization directions for hardware improvements of future generation of Sunway processors for better programmability and performance. In sum, this paper makes the following contributions:

- We provide a benchmark suite for Sunway processor, *swRodinia*, which contains six representative benchmarks with various optimization techniques applied to fully exploit the architecture features for better performance.
- We evaluate the benchmarks with in-depth analysis to understand the effectiveness of various optimization techniques, as well as identify the limiting factors for further performance optimization.
- We highlight several insights based on our experiences of benchmark optimization and evaluation on Sunway, to provide general guidance for the software optimizations and hardware improvements of Sunway processor.

2   Background

2.1   Architecture of Sunway Processor

Each Sunway SW26010 processor contains 4 Core Groups (CGs), and each CG consists of a Memory Controller (MC), a Management Processing Element (MPE) and 64 Computing Process Elements (CPEs). MPE and CPEs play different roles. MPE is similar to a modern CPU processor, which supports the complete interrupt functions, memory management, and out-of-order execution. Whereas, CPEs are simplified cores that are specially designed for acceleration.

In terms of memory hierarchy, each CG connects 8 GB memory module, which is shared by MPE and all CPEs. Each MPE has a 32 KB L1 cache and a 256 KB L2 cache for both instruction and data. Each CPE has a 16 KB L1 instruction cache and a 64 KB programmable Local Data Memory (LDM). The

---

[1] https://github.com/JackMoriarty/rodinia_3.1_SW.

LDM needs to be explicitly controlled by programmers, which can then serve as a software data cache. CPEs can use both Direct Memory Access (DMA) and normal global load/store (Gload/Gstore) instructions to access data in main memory. However, when the memory addresses to be accessed are continuous, the DMA outperforms Gload/Gstore by order of magnitudes in both bandwidth and latency.

Moreover, the CPEs are organized in 8 × 8 mesh, which supports register communication between CPEs along the same row/column at low latency. Each register communication operation can get/put 256-bit data packets. Each CPE has 6 × 288 bits (256 bits for data and 32 bits for ECC checksum) receive buffer, which is shared by both row and column, as well as 4 × 256 bits send buffer for row and column separately. If a CPE tries to put data when its send buffer is full, its pipeline stalls until the send buffer is available again. If a CPE tries to get a data when its receive buffer is empty, its pipeline stalls until the data in receive buffer is ready. Therefore, it is important for programmers to manage the register communication carefully to avoid deadlock.

2.2 Parallel Programming Paradigms on Sunway Processor

2.2.1 OpenACC

The OpenACC program follows the execution model that the MPE and the CPEs cooperate under the guidance of MPE. The program first starts on the MPE, and executes serially with a **main thread** and the computation-intensive code region is offloaded and run on CPEs as **accelerated threads** under the control of the main thread. In terms of memory hierarchy, the memory managed by OpenACC can be divided into three parts: *1)* MPE thread data space, which is located in main memory, and visible to both MPE and CPE threads. *2)* CPE thread private space, which is located in main memory, and visible to the CPE threads. *3)* CPE thread LDM space, which is located in the LDM of one CPE, and only visible to this CPE. To use the CPE thread LDM space, the programmers need to manage the data transfer between main memory and LDM explicitly.

2.2.2 Athread

The execution model of Athread is similar to OpenACC. However, it requires the programmers to write codes for MPE and CPEs separately. The program first starts and runs on the MPE, and executes serial code with a main thread. When the program needs to run in parallel on CPEs, the MPE thread invokes the startup function of CPEs to launch the parallel acceleration. Then, the MPE can run asynchronously with CPEs before calling the waiting function. Once the CPEs finish their work, MPE can continue to execute subsequent codes. The memory model of Athread can be divided into two parts: *1)* MPE data space, which is located in main memory, and visible to all CPEs. *2)* CPE LDM space, which is located in LDM, and visible to the CPE which owns the LDM. Specifically, the most important APIs in Athread are listed in Table 1.

Table 1. The most important APIs in Athread programming model.

APIs	Function description
Athread_halt()	Shutdown CPEs
Athread_spawn()	Launch the codes in parallel among CPEs
Athread_join()	Block the MPE execution and wait for the completion of CPE executions
Athread_get()	Load data from main memory to LDM
Athread_put()	Write the data in LDM back to main memory

2.3   Rodinia Benchmark

The Rodinia benchmark suite [3,4] developed by University of Virginia is one of the most widely used parallel benchmarks in both academia and industry. It consists of 23 benchmarks covering a wide spectrum of application domains such as graph traversal, dense linear algebra, N-Body and etc. The application domains (a.k.a *dwarfs*) are carefully selected based on the well-known white paper [2] for parallel computation from University of Berkeley (e.g., nine *dwarfs* identified in Rodinia). The Rodinia provides parallel implementations for the benchmarks targeting heterogeneous architectures (e.g., CPU, GPU and FPGA) using the programming models such as OpenMP, CUDA and OpenCL. We think the Rodinia benchmark suite could be the perfect candidate for us to port and optimize on Sunway processor based on the following two reasons. Firstly, the benchmarks reflect important application domains, which are also the domains to be supported on Sunway currently and in near future. Secondly, the parallelization methods are well identified in existing Rodinia implementations (e.g., OpenMP). Based on Rodinia, we can focus on the realization of optimization techniques that fully exploit the architecture features of Sunway processor.

3   Porting and Optimizing Rodinia Benchmarks

In this section, we introduce the benchmarks of *swRodinia*, and we show how we port and optimize them on Sunway processor. For each benchmark, we implement two versions, including the OpenACC version and the Athread version. For the OpenACC version, we only need to replace the optimization primitives from **omp** (OpenMP) to **acc** (OpenACC). Occasionally, we change the OpenMP primitives to OpenACC primitives with the same meaning (e.g., replace **for** with **loop**). For simplicity, we omit the optimizations using OpenACC, and focus on the optimization techniques using Athread as follows.

3.1   Back Propagation

Back Propagation (*Backprop*) is a machine-learning algorithm that trains the weights of connected nodes on a layered neural network. The application is comprised of two parts: *1)* the forward phase, in which the activation is propagated

---

Algorithm 1. The Athread version of the forward phase in *Backprop*

```
 1: Input: l1, conn, n1, n2
 2: Output: l2
 3: malloc LDM for local_l2, local_conn and local_sum
 4: local_sum ← 0
 5: left, right ← boundary according to CPE_ID
 6: size ← right − left
 7: for k ← 0 → n1 + 1 do
 8:     DMA: get data from main memory and put into local_l1, local_conn
 9:     for j ← 0 → size do
10:         local_sum[j+left] += local_conn[k][j] * local_l1[k]
11:     end for
12: end for
13: for j ← left → right do
14:     local_l2[j] = squash(local_sum[j])
15: end for
16: DMA: put the data we modified in local_l2 back to main memory
```

---

from the input layer to the output layer, and *2)* the backward phase, in which the error between the observed and requested values in the output layer is propagated backward to adjust the weights and the biases. In each layer, the processing of all the nodes can be done in parallel. Since the computation patterns of the forward phase and the backward phase are similar, we only analyze the forward phase here.

In Athread implementation (Algorithm 1), we need to offload the two-layer nested loops to CPEs, so we **split** the outermost loop and assign the corresponding computation to the CPEs. In the original code, inner loop index changes the fastest, but it corresponds to the highest dimension of the array *conn*. To improve memory locality, we **exchange the loop order** of the inner loop and the outer loop (line 7 and line 9). Then the exchanged inner loop index corresponds to the lowest dimension of the array *conn*, which makes it convenient to transfer data between main memory and LDM through **DMA**. Besides, due to the size of first dimension of the array *conn* is larger than the LDM size, we divide the array into several data blocks (the **blocking** optimization technique) and load one block at a time to reduce the occupation of LDM (line 8).

3.2 Breadth-First Search

Breadth-First Search (*BFS*) is one of the classical graph algorithms. BFS is a traversing algorithm. It starts traversing from a selected node and explores all of the neighbor nodes at the present depth prior to moving on to the nodes at the next depth level. In this part, we implement and optimize *BFS* on Sunway processor.

For the Athread implementation, we **split** the outermost loop, and assign the workloads to CPEs according to the CPE id. Array *h_graph_edge* and array *h_graph_mask* are too large to be loaded into LDM. So we apply the **blocking** optimization, to load data block by block. Besides, we apply the **double buffer** optimization to overlap the data loading and computation.

As shown in Fig. 1, block loading and double buffering need double space of the loaded data, one for computation buffer, the other one for preloading buffer.

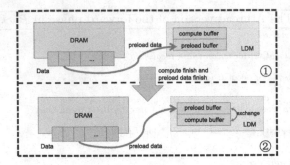

Fig. 1. The process of double buffer in *BFS*.

At the beginning, there is no data in LDM, so CPEs will load data for the next stage. In stage ①, the CPEs can perform computation. And CPEs should call DMA transfer function in advance to preload data for next stage. Because the DMA function is asynchronous, the data transfer and the computation are performed at the same time. In stage ②, the data to use has been preloaded by the previous stage. So we preload data for the next stage, and compute at the same time. And repeat, till all computation is completed.

3.3   Hotspot3D

Hotspot3D computes the heat distribution of a 3D grid iteratively. In each iteration, a new temperature value is computed according to its last value, the surrounding value, and the power value.

Algorithm 2. The Athread version of *Hotspot3D*

1: Input: *pIn, tIn_t, nx, ny, nz*
2: Output: *tOut_t*
3: *left, right* ← boundary of *z* according to CPE_ID
4: **for** *z* ← *left* → *right* **do**
5:     DMA: load partial data of *pIn, tIn_t* into LDM
6:     **for** *y* ← 0 → *ny* **do**
7:         DMA: preload partial data of *pIn, tIn_t* which will be used in next stage into LDM asynchronously
8:         **for** *x* ← 0 → *nx* **do**
9:             Do the computation and put the result into *local_tOut_t*
10:         **end for**
11:         Wait for the completion of DMA preload
12:         Wait for the completion of DMA put of the previous stage
13:         DMA: put result back to main memory asynchronously
14:     **end for**
15: **end for**

For Athread version (Algorithm 2), we also **split** the outermost loop. And all discrete scalars are **packaged** into a *struct*, and its pointer is transferred to CPEs as a parameter of the *Athread_spawn* function. Besides, the sizes of array *pIn*, array *tOut_t*, and array *tIn_t* exceed the size of LDM, so we apply block loading and double buffer optimizations (line 5 and line 7), and we **overlap** the computation and the DMA loading (line 11–13).

We also analyze the memory access pattern of the program, and improve the ratio of **data reuse**. In this benchmark, the data C at an arbitrary position is related to its neighbors along the x, y, z axis directions, including E, W, N, S, T, and B, as shown in Fig. 2a. At the next loop (Fig. 2b), C moves to the position of N and becomes C'. And the computation of data C' relies on the data in position N', C, T', B', and the neighboring data along x axis. We find that the data of N and C are already in the LDM, we can reuse them directly.

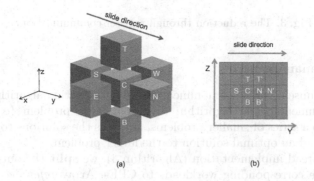

Fig. 2. The implementation of data reuse in *Hotspot3D*.

3.4 Kmeans

Kmeans is a widely used clustering algorithm in data-mining for its simplicity. And it shows a high degree of data parallelism. In the Athread implementation, we also **split** the outermost loop. And we divide the array *membership*, array *partial_new_centers*, and array *partial_new_centers_len* into **blocks**, then we load the blocks and the entire array *clusters* into CPE's LDM through **DMA**. We also need to push them back through DMA after finishing the computation. For variables *delta*, we leverage the register communication to accelerate the reduction operation on it.

The CPEs of a CG on Sunway processor are organized in 8×8 mesh. And the implementation of **reduction using register communication** inside the mesh is shown in Fig. 3. Firstly, each CPE sends its local reduction variable to the first CPE at the same row (i.e., CPE 0, 8, 16, ⋯ 56). Then the CPEs at the first column receive the variable, perform the reduction on the received variables, and derive a partial result of its row individually. Secondly, the CPEs in the first column send the partial reduction result to the first CPE at the same column (i.e., CPE 0). Then CPE 0 performs the reduction and derives the final result. Finally, CPE 0 writes the final result to main memory.

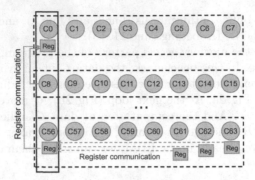

Fig. 3. The reduction through register communication.

3.5   Needleman-Wunsch

Needleman-Wunsch (NW) is a nonlinear global optimization algorithm for DNA sequence alignments. The algorithm divides a large problem (e.g., the full sequence) into a series of smaller problems, and uses the solutions to the smaller problems to find an optimal solution to the larger problem.

In the Athread implementation (Algorithm 3), we **split** the outermost loop and assign the corresponding workloads to CPEs. Array *reference* (read-only) and array *input_itemsets* (read and write) are crucial to the performance. These arrays are already divided into **blocks** in the serial version, so we just need to load them to CPEs block by block (line 6 and line 7). Once the computation corresponding to the *input_itemsets* block is finished, we write it to main memory through **DMA** (line 13). Then, we load the next blocks, perform the computation, and write the block back repeatedly till all blocks are processed.

Algorithm 3. The Athread version of NW

1: Input: *refernece, input_itemsets, blk*
2: Output: *input_itemsets*
3: *left, right* ← block boundary divided according to CPE_ID
4: **for** $x \leftarrow left \rightarrow right$ **do**
5:      Allocate local memory for *input_itemsets_l, reference_l*
6:      DMA: load partial data of array *refernece* into LDM
7:      DMA: load partial data of array *input_itemsets* into LDM
8:      **for** $i \leftarrow 0 \rightarrow BLOCK + 1$ **do**
9:          **for** $j \leftarrow 0 \rightarrow BLOCK + 1$ **do**
10:            *input_itemsets_l*[i][j] =
                   max(*input_itemsets_l*[i-1][j-1]+*reference_l*[i-1][j-1],
                   input_itemsets_l[i][j-1]-*PENALTY*,
                   input_itemsets_l[i-1][j]-*PENALTY*)
11:         **end for**
12:     **end for**
13:     DMA: put the partial result(*input_itemsets_l*) back to main memory
14: **end for**

3.6   Pathfinder

Pathfinder uses dynamic programming to find a path from the bottom row to the top row with the smallest accumulated weights on a 2D grid, where each step moves straight ahead or diagonally ahead. And in each iteration, a node selects a neighboring node in the previous row with the smallest accumulated weight.

Similar to other benchmarks, in the Athread version, we **split** the outermost loop. And after careful analysis, we find each CPE only reads part of array *src* and array *wall*, so we just need to load these partial data into LDM through **DMA**. As for the array *dst*, it is write-only. So we just gather its intermediate data using *local_dst*. Finally, CPEs put the array *local_dst* back to *dst* in the main memory by DMA at the end of execution.

4   Evaluation

4.1   Performance Comparison

In the experiments, we use a CG of Sunway SW26010 processor for performance evaluation. For the OpenACC version and the Athread version of the benchmarks, we set the number of CPEs to 64. We record the average time obtained from 5 runs as the final result. And the baseline is the serial version of benchmarks on MPE. The performance comparison is shown in Fig. 4. The standard deviation for speedup across runs is $-0.01 \sim +0.02$ and $-0.04 \sim +0.03$ for OpenACC and Athread, respectively.

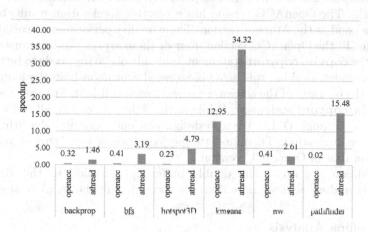

Fig. 4. The performance comparison of OpenACC and Athread across *swRodinia* benchmarks. The x-axis indicates the different benchmarks. The y-axis indicates the speedup normalized to baseline (the serial version on MPE).

As shown in Fig. 4, the average speedup of the OpenACC versions and the Athread versions over the baseline is $2.39\times$ and $10.31\times$ respectively. It is obvious that the performance of Athread versions are much better than that of OpenACC versions, while most of the OpenACC versions of the benchmarks have negative results. This is because OpenACC can not make good use of the architectural features of Sunway processor. We take *Hotspot3D* as an example to explain, and other benchmarks (including *Backprop*, *BFS*, *Pathfinder*, and *NW*) have similar problems.

In the OpenACC version of *Hotspot3D*, we split the outermost loop by splitting the loop index. Array *pIn*, array *tOut*, and array *tIn* need to be loaded into CPEs' LDM, which is crucial to performance. However, array *tOut* and array *tIn* cannot be split according the outermost loop, because they are accessed by pointers (*tOut_t* and *tIn_t*) in the loop. Consequently, these arrays cannot be added to **cache** statement of OpenACC (because it is not supported by OpenACC). Therefore, each data of the arrays can only be accessed through inefficient Gload/Gstore. Even though the array *pIn* can be added to the **cache** statement, the low-level implementation of **cache** is still less efficient. Because the size of software cache is only 256 bytes, and CPEs have to read/write the main memory frequently.

On the contrary, the Athread version of *Hotspot3D* doesn't have such problems. Programmers can analyze the relationship between these three arrays and the index of outermost loop, which is too difficult for the OpenACC compiler. So programmers can divide the arrays and load them into LDM through DMA, which is much better comparing to accessing main memory directly as well as using software cache. And the performance result proves that.

Notably, the speedup of the OpenACC version and the Athread version of Kmeans reaches 12.95× and 34.32× respectively, which outperforms that of other benchmarks. The OpenACC version has a positive acceleration result, but it is still not as good as the Athread version. There are five performance crucial arrays in Kmeans. In the OpenACC version, four of these arrays can be transferred to LDM by the **copyin/copyout** statement, and only one array needs to be put into **cache** statement. Besides, this array is accessed continuously in the loop, which improves the hit ratio of the software cache. However, it is still not as efficient as the **copyin/copyout** statement. While in the Athread version, all of the arrays are accessed through DMA. We also design efficient reduction algorithm using register communication. Therefore, the performance of the Athread version is better than that of OpenACC version.

In addition, we apply the double buffer optimization to the *BFS* and *Hotspot3D*, and we achieve more than 3× speedup over the serial version.

4.2 Roofline Analysis

We analyze the benchmarks using the roofline model to better understand the effectiveness of our benchmarks on Sunway architecture (shown in Fig. 5). Because the performance counters are quite limited on Sunway CPEs, it is very difficult for us to measure the operational intensity. We calculate the operational intensity through algorithmic analysis. But we still need to measure the attainable performance of benchmarks through actual running.

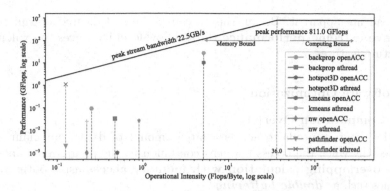

Fig. 5. The roofline model of *swRodinia* benchmark suite on Sunway processor.

The advantage of roofline model is that it builds up relationships among peak floating-point performance, operational intensity and memory bandwidth, which can reveal the intrinsic characteristics of the applications and provide guidance for performance optimization. We only analyze the OpenACC versions and the Athread versions. Since *BFS* does not perform any floating-point operation, we exclude it from the roofline analysis in Fig. 5.

The roofline model of a Sunway CG reveals that in order to fully utilize its performance, 36 Flops calculations should be performed when accessing one-byte data in memory. It can be clearly seen from Fig. 5 that the operational intensity of our benchmark is under the slope of the roofline model, and thus our benchmarks are mostly bounded by the memory bandwidth. Therefore, increasing the operational intensity has become the key to improving the performance of these benchmarks, which we leave for optimization in the future work.

5   Insights

5.1   Programmability vs. Performance

Although both OpenACC and Athread are available parallel programming models for Sunway processor, they usually emphasize on different aspect in terms of programmability and performance. When using **OpenACC**, it requires **trivial code modifications** especially when the codes have already been parallelized (e.g., with OpenMP). Programmers can insert limited pragmas to optimize OpenACC codes to some extent (e.g., using LDM for better data locality), in general it is **difficult to fully exploit the architecture features** (e.g., register communication) due to its high-level abstraction. Whereas using **Athread**, it requires **higher programming efforts** to manage the codes running efficiently. The programmers are responsible for explicitly controlling the parallelization on CPEs, such as handling the DMA transfer between LDM and main memory, as well as initiating register communication between CPEs. Such intricacy usually leads to error-prone Athread programs (e.g., register communication deadlocks), and thus costs a large amount of time to debug. However, the advantages of Athread are apparent. Because users can perform dedicated optimizations to **achieve extreme performance** through low-level interfaces to exploit the architecture features.

5.2   Software Optimization

5.2.1   Computation Overlap

When the program needs to access a large amount of data from main memory, especially when the access happens continuously, the programmers need to consider **overlapping calculation with memory access** using optimization techniques such as *double buffering*.

On Sunway, the DMA transfer invoked by CPEs returns intermediately, and its corresponding flag bit will be set when the DMA transfer is completed, which makes the overlapping possible. In the implementation of *double buffering*, a CPE allocates two data buffers for each DMA transfer, one for calculation, and one for DMA transfer. Once the data buffer for calculation is empty, programmers should first check whether the DMA transfer is finished. If finished, programmers can exchange the pointers or references of the two buffers so that the recently transferred data can be used for calculation, and the original calculation buffer can be used for the next DMA transfer. Otherwise, programmers should keep waiting for the completion of DMA transfer. In ideal cases, the DMA transfer can be completely overlapped by the calculation. In *swRodinia*, benchmark *BFS* and *Hotspot3D* benefit from the *double buffering* optimization.

5.2.2   Data Locality

When accelerating program on CPEs, the latency of LDM access (about 4 cycles) is much lower than DMA transfer (more than hundreds of cycles). Therefore, it is crucial to **leverage data locality**, by loading frequently used data in LDM, reusing the data during calculation, and thus eliminating unnecessary DMA transfers.

For program with fixed memory access patterns, for example in *Hotspot3D*, the adjacent loops share similar data accesses. In such case, we can **keep the data of previous loop in LDM**, and reuse the data in the adjacent loop, which can effectively reduce the DMA transfers and save the limited memory bandwidth.

For program dealing with matrix, the mis-matched data access (e.g., column-major) with the matrix storage (e.g., row-major) could lead to poor data locality even when using LDM on CPEs. For example, the matrix $A^{m \times n}$ is stored in row-major order, however if the matrix is accessed in column-major order (e.g., $A[0:m][j]$), such access pattern would lead to frequent data eviction in LDM and thus more data access to main memory. To address such problem, programmers can apply the optimization technique to **re-order the iterations of nested loops**, so that the matrix is accessed in a row-major order, which improves the program's data locality. In *swRodinia*, benchmark *Back Propagation* benefits from the *loop re-order* optimization.

5.2.3   Parallel Communication Primitive

When a CPE needs to aggregate the value of a certain variable from other CPEs, **register communication can be used to implement the parallel** *reduce* **primitive**.

To implement the *reduce* primitive, one commonly used optimization technique consists of two steps. Firstly, all CPEs perform register communication along the rows, which means each CPE sends the value of reduction variable to the CPE at n-th column at the same row, so each CPE at n-th column receives a partial reduction result. Then, the CPEs at n-th column perform register communication along the column, and each sends the partial result to the CPE at m-th row. Eventually, the CPE at (m-th, n-th) obtains the final reduction result. In *swRodinia*, benchmark *Kmeans* benefits from the parallel *reduce* primitive.

Moreover, to implement the *allreduce* primitive, one commonly used optimization technique is to realize butterfly-structured communication using register communication. Firstly, a butterfly-structured communication is performed at each row, so each CPE obtains the partial reduction result of its row. Secondly, a butterfly-structured communication is performed at each column, so all CPEs obtain the final result of the reduction variable.

5.3   Hardware Improvements

Firstly, several benchmarks in our evaluation exhibit irregular memory accesses. Due to the limited LDM size, the required data cannot always be loaded into LDM, therefore these programs have to access the main memory with high latency. A typical benchmark is the *BFS*, such graph processing programs hardly have regular memory patterns due to the irregular structure of the input graph. In the meanwhile, we observe the LDMs scattered among CPEs if aggregated, could provide a logically shared LDM with large capacity, which is able to alleviate the main memory access of irregular applications. Thus, we suggest to add hardware support that enables **LDM sharing among CPEs** for better performance of irregular applications.

Secondly, the manipulation of register communication is too complicated. When dealing with a large amount of data, the data much be split into a series of data packets with each packet less than 256 bits. The CPEs that receive the packets need to reassemble the packets considering their sequences. Such pre-processing and post-processing of the packets introduce non-negligible overhead. In addition, when the receiver CPE and the sender CPE are not located in the same row or column, the communication between them needs to be forwarded by a third CPE, which not only doubles the latency at least, but also introduces programming burden for complicated processing logic. Thus, we suggest to improve **register communication efficiency** and support **all-to-all communication pattern**. Such hardware improvements can greatly reduce the programming complexity and increase the parallel efficiency of benchmarks such as *Stencil* and *lavaMD*.

6   Related Work

Scientific Application: Many scientific applications across various fields [5,6, 9,10,16,22,24,26] can make full use of up to tens of millions cores of Sunway TaihuLight supercomputer. For example, Atmospheric Dynamics [24] realize the fully implicit simulation of the global atmospheric dynamics; Molecular Dynamics [6] simulates the physical movements of atoms and molecules at Peta-scale; Earthquake Simulation [9] provides a highly scalable nonlinear simulation tool.

Domain Specific Framework: In order to ease the development of deep learning applications on Sunway, many deep learning frameworks tailored for Sunway are proposed. swTVM [18] is a deep learning compiler based on TVM and is optimized for Sunway processor. swTVM can achieve better data locality and generate efficient code. swCaffe [13] and swDNN [8] can accelerate the DNN training/inference on Sunway.

Numerical Algorithm: There are also high-performance algorithms designed for Sunway TaihuLight, including sparse triangular solver (SpTRSV) [15, 19], sparse Cholesky factorization [14], tile-low-rank GEMM [11], sparse matrix-vector multiplication (SpMV) [17,21], gradient boosted decision trees (GBDT) [25], canonical polyadic decomposition (CPD) [7], as well as common midopint (CMP) and common reflection surface (CRS) algorithms [12]. The optimizations from these work are valuable reference for us to optimize the *swRodinia* benchmark suite.

The paper [23] benchmarks Sunway processor with mini-programs written in C and assembly language. However, neither the mini-programs are representative, nor they are publicly available to reveal useful optimization techniques for Sunway programmers.

7   Conclusion

In this paper, we implement *swRodinia*, a benchmark suite tailored on Sunway processor. In *swRodinia*, we demonstrate several effective optimization techniques, such as parallel *reduce* primitive using register communication, memory access overlapping using *double buffering*, and *loop re-ordering* to improve LDM data locality, which can fully exploit the architecture features on Sunway processor for better performance. Moreover, we highlight several useful insights for both software optimizations on current Sunway processor, and directions of hardware improvements for next-generation Sunway processor.

Acknowledgment. This work is supported by National Key R&D Program of China (Grant No. 2020YFB150001), National Natural Science Foundation of China (Grant No. 62072018, 61502019 and 61732002), and the Open Project Program of the State Key Laboratory of Mathematical Engineering and Advanced Computing (Grant No. 2019A12).

References

1. Athread user guide. http://www.nsccwx.cn/guide/. Accessed 16 Aug 2020
2. Asanovic, K., et al.: The landscape of parallel computing research: A view from berkeley (2006)
3. Che, S., et al.: Rodinia: a benchmark suite for heterogeneous computing. In: 2009 IEEE International Symposium on Workload Characterization (IISWC), pp. 44–54 (2009)
4. Che, S., Sheaffer, J.W., Boyer, M., Szafaryn, L.G., Wang, S.L., Kadron, K.: A characterization of the Rodinia benchmark suite with comparison to contemporary CMP workloads. In: IEEE International Symposium on Workload Characterization (IISWC 2010), pp. 1–11 (2010)
5. Duan, X., et al.: Neighbor-list-free molecular dynamics on sunway taihulight supercomputer. In: Proceedings of the 25th ACM SIGPLAN Symposium on Principles and Practice of Parallel Programming, PPoPP 2020, pp. 413–414. Association for Computing Machinery, New York (2020)
6. Duan, X., et al.: Redesigning lammps for peta-scale and hundred-billion-atom simulation on sunway taihulight. In: Proceedings of the International Conference for High Performance Computing, Networking, Storage, and Analysis, SC 2018, IEEE Press (2018)
7. Dun, M., Li, Y., Yang, H., Li, W., Luan, Z., Qian, D.: swCPD: optimizing canonical polyadic decomposition on sunway manycore architecture. In: 2019 IEEE 21st International Conference on High Performance Computing and Communications; IEEE 17th International Conference on Smart City; IEEE 5th International Conference on Data Science and Systems (HPCC/SmartCity/DSS), pp. 1320–1327. IEEE (2019)
8. Fang, J., Fu, H., Zhao, W., Chen, B., Zheng, W., Yang, G.: swDNN: a library for accelerating deep learning applications on sunway taihulight. In: 2017 IEEE International Parallel and Distributed Processing Symposium (IPDPS), pp. 615–624. IEEE (2017)
9. Fu, H., et al.: 18.9-pflops nonlinear earthquake simulation on sunway taihulight: Enabling depiction of 18-hz and 8-meter scenarios. In: Proceedings of the International Conference for High Performance Computing, Networking, Storage and Analysis. SC 2017. Association for Computing Machinery, New York (2017)
10. Gao, P., et al.: Millimeter-scale and billion-atom reactive force field simulation on Sunway Taihulight. IEEE Trans. Parallel Distrib. Syst. **31**(12), 2954–2967 (2020)
11. Han, Q., Yang, H., Luan, Z., Qian, D.: Accelerating tile low-rank gemm on sunway architecture: Poster. In: Proceedings of the 16th ACM International Conference on Computing Frontiers, pp. 295–297 (2019)
12. Hu, Y., Yang, H., Luan, Z., Gan, L., Yang, G., Qian, D.: Massively scaling seismic processing on Sunway Taihulight supercomputer. IEEE Trans. Parallel Distrib. Syst. **31**(5), 1194–1208 (2019)
13. Li, L., et al.: swCaffe: a parallel framework for accelerating deep learning applications on Sunway Taihulight. In: 2018 IEEE International Conference on Cluster Computing (CLUSTER), pp. 413–422 (2018)
14. Li, M., Liu, Y., Yang, H., Luan, Z., Gan, L., Yang, G., Qian, D.: Accelerating sparse Cholesky factorization on sunway manycore architecture. IEEE Trans. Parallel Distrib. Syst. **31**(7), 1636–1650 (2020)

15. Li, M., Liu, Y., Yang, H., Luan, Z., Qian, D.: Multi-role spTRSV on sunway many-core architecture. In: 2018 IEEE 20th International Conference on High Performance Computing and Communications; IEEE 16th International Conference on Smart City; IEEE 4th International Conference on Data Science and Systems (HPCC/SmartCity/DSS), pp. 594–601. IEEE (2018)

16. Lin, H., et al.: Shentu: processing multi-trillion edge graphs on millions of cores in seconds. In: Proceedings of the International Conference for High Performance Computing, Networking, Storage, and Analysis, SC 2018. IEEE Press (2018)

17. Liu, C., Xie, B., Liu, X., Xue, W., Yang, H., Liu, X.: Towards efficient spMV on sunway manycore architectures. In: Proceedings of the 2018 International Conference on Supercomputing, pp. 363–373 (2018)

18. Liu, C., et al.: swTVM: exploring the automated compilation for deep learning on sunway architecture. arXiv preprint arXiv:1904.07404 (2019)

19. Wang, X., Liu, W., Xue, W., Wu, L.: Swsptrsv: a fast sparse triangular solve with sparse level tile layout on sunway architectures. SIGPLAN Not. **53**(1), 338–353 (2018)

20. Wienke, S., Springer, P., Terboven, C., an Mey, D.: OpenACC—first experiences with real-world applications. In: Kaklamanis, C., Papatheodorou, T., Spirakis, P.G. (eds.) Euro-Par 2012. LNCS, vol. 7484, pp. 859–870. Springer, Heidelberg (2012). https://doi.org/10.1007/978-3-642-32820-6_85

21. Xiao, G., Li, K., Chen, Y., He, W., Zomaya, A., Li, T.: CASpMV: a customized and accelerative spMV framework for the Sunway Taihulight. IEEE Trans. Parallel Distrib. Syst. 1 (2019)

22. Xu, K., et al.: Refactoring and optimizing WRF model on Sunway Taihulight. In: Proceedings of the 48th International Conference on Parallel Processing, ICPP 2019. Association for Computing Machinery, New York (2019). https://doi.org/10.1145/3337821.3337923

23. Xu, Z., Lin, J., Matsuoka, S.: Benchmarking SW26010 many-core processor. In: 2017 IEEE International Parallel and Distributed Processing Symposium Workshops (IPDPSW), pp. 743–752. IEEE (2017)

24. Yang, C., et al.: 10m-core scalable fully-implicit solver for nonhydrostatic atmospheric dynamics. In: Proceedings of the International Conference for High Performance Computing, Networking, Storage and Analysis, SC 2016. IEEE Press (2016)

25. Yin, B., Li, Y., Dun, M., You, X., Yang, H., Luan, Z., Qian, D.: *swGBDT*: efficient gradient boosted decision tree on sunway many-core processor. In: Panda, D.K. (ed.) SCFA 2020. LNCS, vol. 12082, pp. 67–86. Springer, Cham (2020). https://doi.org/10.1007/978-3-030-48842-0_5

26. Zhang, T., et al.: Sw_gromacs: accelerate gromacs on Sunway Taihulight. In: Proceedings of the International Conference for High Performance Computing, Networking, Storage and Analysis, SC 2019. Association for Computing Machinery, New York (2019)

Data Management and Storage

Impact of Commodity Networks on Storage Disaggregation with NVMe-oF

Arjun Kashyap[2(✉)], Shashank Gugnani[1], and Xiaoyi Lu[2]

[1] The Ohio State University, Columbus, USA
gugnani.2@osu.edu
[2] University of California Merced, Merced, USA
{akashyap5,xiaoyi.lu}@ucmerced.edu

Abstract. NVMe-based storage is widely used for various data-intensive applications due to their high bandwidth and low access latency. The NVMe-over-Fabrics (NVMe-oF) protocol specification provides efficient remote access to NVMe-SSDs over storage networking fabrics. NVMe-oF provides the opportunity to make storage disaggregation practical by reducing the cost of remote access. Unfortunately, the performance characteristics of different NVMe-oF networking protocols are not well understood. In this paper, we propose a four dimensional (network protocol, I/O pattern, I/O size, and number of cores) evaluation methodology to understand NVMe-oF performance over various commodity networks. We conduct comprehensive microbenchmark analyses using the user-space Intel SPDK library to compare the TCP, IPoIB, RoCE, and RDMA transports. Our analysis reveals interesting, and often counter-intuitive insights and performance tradeoffs among the different transports. We find that Infini-Band with native RDMA is able to deliver the best performance among all tested networking protocols in most experiments. Contrary to expectation, IPoIB could achieve better CPU utilization and lower tail-latency for large I/O operations in some of our experiments. We believe that our analysis helps gain insight into the deployment implications of NVMe-oF in datacenters.

Keywords: NVMe-over-Fabrics · SPDK · Disaggregated storage · Performance characterization

1 Introduction

Storage disaggregation is gaining popularity in cloud datacenters recently [13–15] due to the ability to scale and manage storage and compute results with increased flexibility and better resource utilization. A large body of work [4,5,14–16] has looked at how storage systems can be efficiently designed to take advantage of disaggregated storage. Other works [10,13,26] have looked at improving the network costs of disaggregation. Taking this trend into consideration, it is imperative to gain a better understanding of the impact of commodity networks on storage disaggregation.

Fast NVMe [18] drives are becoming ubiquitous in datacenters. Their low latency and inherent parallelism make them a perfect fit for cloud storage. The recently

This work was supported in part by NSF research grant CCF #1822987.
This work was done by the authors A. Kashyap and X. Lu while at Ohio State University.

© Springer Nature Switzerland AG 2021
F. Wolf and W. Gao (Eds.): Bench 2020, LNCS 12614, pp. 41–56, 2021.
https://doi.org/10.1007/978-3-030-71058-3_3

proposed NVMe over Fabrics (NVMe-oF) standard [19] allows fast remote access to NVMe devices over various network transports. NVMe-oF has overtaken Serial Attached SCSI (SAS) and Serial AT Attachment (SATA) as the state-of-the-art approach to access storage remotely. The standard was designed to leverage the increased parallelism available in modern solid state drives (SSDs) and networks, such as InfiniBand (IB) and Remote Direct Memory Access (RDMA) over Converged Ethernet (RoCE). Studies [2, 3] have shown that NVMe-oF has extremely low overhead at the application level compared to traditional I/O paths. However, the standard allows several network protocols to be used for remote I/O and prior work has not considered the breadth of available protocols.

We believe that there is a lack of studies which evaluate the tradeoffs of different networks and try to gain an in-depth understanding of their performance characteristics on storage disaggregation. This is even more important when considering NVMe-oF because the network overhead constitutes a significant portion of remote access latency. Protocols such as SAS and SATA were designed for spinning disks where data storage was significantly slower than network I/O. Therefore, it was not beneficial to study the impact of network protocols until now. For cloud vendors, there is a lack of sufficient information to make informed decisions on the network protocol to deploy in datacenters. For instance, the tail latency characteristics of networks are not known. Therefore, it is hard to choose which network to use to achieve a given latency service level objective. We seek to solve this information gap through an in-depth performance characterization.

In this paper, we propose a four dimensional (network protocol, I/O pattern, I/O size, and number of cores) evaluation methodology to understand NVMe-oF over various commodity networks. We conduct a set of comprehensive microbenchmark analyses using the userspace Intel SPDK library to compare the TCP, IP-over-IB/IPoIB, RoCE, and RDMA transports. Our analysis reveals interesting insights and performance tradeoffs between the different transports.

To summarize, the contributions of our work are as follows:

- An extensive four dimensional (network protocol, I/O pattern, I/O size, and number of cores) characterization methodology of NVMe-oF protocols
- In-depth NVMe-oF protocol performance characterization and tradeoff analysis using the userspace Intel SPDK library
- The community can leverage the findings in this paper to make informed decisions on the transport type to deploy for NVMe-oF based on latency, bandwidth, and CPU utilization constraints of the system in datacenters

We conduct extensive experiments on a local cluster with NVMe-SSDs and several networks connecting each server. Overall, our findings reveal interesting insights – RoCE is able to achieve bandwidth similar to IPoIB and IB for most of the write workloads despite having only 40 Gbps network card when compared to 100 Gbps card for InfiniBand. This shows that moderate network bandwidth is sufficient to achieve good performance for write operations on current-generation NVMe-SSDs. Overall, we find that InfiniBand with native RDMA can deliver the best performance among all tested networking protocols in most experiments.

Contrary to expectation, IPoIB could achieve better CPU utilization and lower tail-latency for large I/O operations in some of our experiments. IPoIB has similar CPU utilization to TCP with ~45% CPU time in user mode and ~50% in kernel/system mode but its bandwidth are similar to RoCE and IB whose CPU utilization is ~92% in user mode. Apart from TCP, the other three network protocols - RoCE, IPoIB, and IB have similar average latency but varying tail latency depending upon the I/O size. Increasing the number of cores on client and target for NVMe-oF protocol does not change the throughput for TCP, RoCE, and IB transports for random read operation but raises the latency for all transports.

The rest of this paper is organized as follows. Section 2 discusses background on storage disaggregation, NVMe-oF, and SPDK. Section 3 presents the characterization methodology we propose, Sect. 4 presents our in-depth experimental analysis, and Sect. 5 summarizes our analysis with a discussion. Section 6 discusses related work and Sect. 7 presents the conclusion and future work.

2   Background

In this section, we discuss storage disaggregation, the NVMe-oF standard, and the SPDK library.

2.1   Storage Disaggregation and NVMe-oF

Storage disaggregation is a commonly used technique to improve resource utilization in cloud environments. In this approach, storage devices are physically separated from compute servers and are typically accessed over the network using a remote access protocol. This separation allows applications to only provision storage in an ad-hoc manner and scale it up or down depending on utilization. Disaggregation comes at the cost of the network overhead of remote access and indeed a lot of research [10,13,26] has looked into limiting the performance overheads of remote access. Nevertheless, the flexibility and resource savings of disaggregation are worth the overhead.

The NVMe-oF protocol specification [19] allows remote access of NVMe devices over different transports/network protocols. It allows fast access to any remote NVMe device via NVMe block storage protocol over the network as seen in Fig. 1. NVMe-oF currently supports three types of transports:

* NVMe over Fabrics using RDMA (Infiniband, RoCE, and iWARP)
* NVMe over Fabrics using Fibre Channel
* NVMe over Fabrics using Ethernet (TCP)

The specification terms NVMe-oF client/initiator as the node which contains drivers to send NVMe commands over the transport and NVMe-oF target as the node which contains drivers for local NVMe storage device (connected via PCI-e) and different transports.

2.2   Intel SPDK

Intel SPDK [25] is a userspace library that provides NVMe drivers, storage protocols (iSCSI target, NVMe-oF target, and vhost-scsi target), and storage services (blobstore

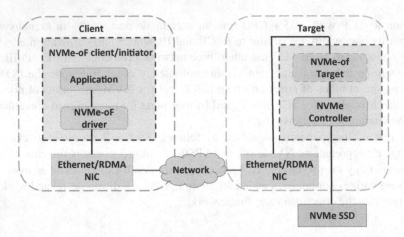

Fig. 1. NVMe-oF architecture

and block device abstraction layer). It uses polling rather than interrupts to complete asynchronous I/O operations via queue pairs. It provides a userspace NVMe-oF application which consists of NVMe-oF target [7] and NVMe-oF client/initiator drivers. The client is responsible for establishing a connection and submitting I/O requests (similar to local NVMe devices) over the network to an NVMe subsystem exposed by an NVMe-oF target. Apart from avoiding costly syscalls and data copy overheads, SPDK is also able to scale and avoid synchronization overheads by pining its connections to CPU cores.

3 Characterization Methodology

Our methodology involves evaluating NVMe-oF across four dimensions - transport type or network protocol, I/O pattern or workload, number of cores involved in I/O, and I/O size as seen in Fig. 2. The network transport under consideration are TCP, RoCE, IPoIB, and IB as these are widely available in today's datacenters. We did not consider iWARP and fibre channel because we did not have access to these networks. Moreover, they are not widely used in datacenters. I/O pattern studied are sequential/random read/write and read-write and I/O sizes are varied from 1KB to 1MB. Number of cores represent the threads (one thread is pinned to one core) performing I/O at NVMe-oF client and NVMe-oF target side. I/O pattern, I/O size, and the number of cores represent most of the workloads different applications generate while reading or writing from/to NVMe-SSDs.

For benchmarking NVMe-oF we choose SDPK's NVMe-oF implementation [25] as it provides both a user-space NVMe-oF target and client and is the current state-of-the-art approach. The SPDK NVMe-oF target uses NVMe driver in polled-mode for I/Os. Being in user-space, it helps us avoid software processing overheads and obtain the actual latency of I/O transactions. The metrics reported are throughput/bandwidth, average and tail (p50, p90, p99, p999, and p9999) latency, client CPU utilization, and SSD parallelism or concurrency. These metrics were chosen as they help in quantifying

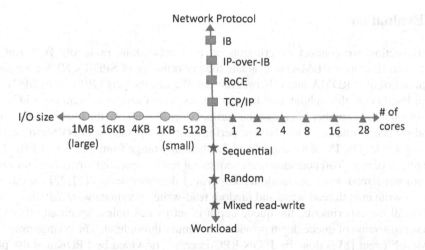

Fig. 2. Four-dimensional characterization approach

the performance and efficiency of various network transports and are typically the most important for cloud vendors and applications. Throughput, bandwidth, and latency are measured using the NVMe perf tool [20] as it has the capability to generate various workloads (sequential/random read/write and read-write), vary queue depth, I/O size, pin threads to CPU cores, and specify different transport types (ethernet and RDMA).

In our experiments, first we find out the maximum bandwidth of each transport type by trying out different combinations of I/O size, workload, and queue depth while performing I/Os. The observation here was that higher queue depth always provided higher bandwidth keeping all other factors same. Hence, all of our experiments are performed at a queue depth of 128. Even at a queue depth of 128, the system is not able to achieve its peak bandwidth when only one core is involved in I/O at both NVMe-oF client and target side. To fully utilize/saturate the network and SSD, we differ the number of cores and noticed bandwidth scaling with number of cores for IPoIB, though not linearly. Once we obtain the maximum throughput of all four transport types, we decide to study the variation in maximum bandwidth according to I/O pattern or workload as workload type has a profound impact on the bandwidth. Keeping other factors, like number of cores and queue depth constant, we evaluated the change in bandwidth for 1 KB and 4 KB I/O sizes. We choose these I/O sizes as it is representative of the typical size of objects in systems, such as key-value stores. Efficiency of the network transports is determined by the latency and CPU utilization at peak bandwidth. Average, p90, p99, p999, and p9999 latencies for each transport were noted when system has maximum throughput. Again, the increase in latency is proportional to the I/O size. The CPU utilization of a transport was broken down into the time spent by an I/O operation in user/system/idle mode. NVMe-SSDs support multiple levels (channel, plane, chip, and die) of parallelism. We calculate the concurrency/parallelism each transport could attain by varying the queue depth. This helps us to learn how well each network transport can exploit the parallelism within an NVMe-SSD. These metrics could allow a user of NVMe-oF protocol to determine a suitable transport type for their application based on its operating environment and latency constraints.

4   Evaluation

In this section, we conduct experiments on four networking protocols TCP, RoCE, IPoIB, and IB (native RDMA) to evaluate the performance of SPDK's NVMe-oF storage protocol over RDMA and Ethernet fabrics. We use the perf [20] tool of SPDK to obtain bandwidth, throughput, and latency results across various dimensions- I/O pattern, I/O size, and number of cores. The number of cores indicate the total threads (each thread pinned to one core) involved in performing I/O operations at NVMe-oF client and target side. The I/O sizes considered for the study range from 512 B to 1 MB. The I/O pattern or workload considered are sequential read, sequential write, random read, random write, read-write and random read-write. Like other studies [21,22] the ratio of reads to write in both read-write and random read-write operations were 70:30.

For all the experiments, the queue depth is set to 128 unless specified otherwise because this value of queue depth provides maximum throughput. The configuration of NVMe-oF target [8] is done by JSON-RPC interface provided by SPDK and the perf tool is run on the client. Each experiment is performed three times and the average value is reported.

4.1   Experimental Setup

Our cluster consists of two Linux servers directly connected, each equipped with a two-socket, 28-core Intel broadwell CPU (E5-2680v4@2.40 GHz), 512 GB DRAM, an Ethernet (1 Gbps) NIC, a ConnectX-3 RoCE (40 Gbps) NIC, and a ConnectX-5 IB-EDR (100 Gbps) NIC. One server has an Intel DC P3700 NVMe-SSD attached via PCIe and acts as the NVMe-oF target while the other server is used as the NVMe-oF client performing I/O reads and writes over the network. We use SPDK v20.04.1 for all of our evaluations. In our experiments, the legend *TCP* refers to TCP over 1 GbE, *RoCE* refers to RoCE over 40 GbE, *IPoIB* refers to IP-over-InfiniBand over a 100Gb IB card, and *IB* refers to native RDMA over a 100 Gb IB card.

4.2   Bandwidth Evaluation

First, we wish to discover the peak throughput for all transports as we vary the number of cores or workload or I/O size. Thus, we vary one of the factors and keep the others fixed. The number of cores/threads are set to 28 as maximum bandwidth is achieved when all 28 cores are performing I/O operations. We study the variation in bandwidth with respect to I/O size in Fig. 3 for random read operation with number of threads/cores set to 28 (full subscription) at both NVMe-oF target and client. The peak bandwidth for this configuration is 3599 MiB/s at 1 MB I/O size for IB transport and 3611 MiB/s for local SSDs. IPoIB has a slightly lower peak bandwidth of 3426 MiB/s. An interesting observation is that RoCE, IPoIB, and IB are able to almost achieve their respective peak bandwidths after I/O size crosses 4 KB. Thus, small I/O sizes are sufficient to achieve near peak bandwidth of an NVMe SSD over the network. TCP transport has the lowest peak bandwidth at 466 MiB/s which is 13% of the peak bandwidth achieved by other transports. This is because of the low bandwidth of the ethernet NIC.

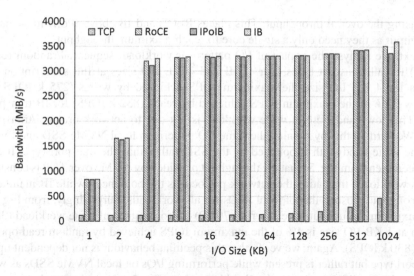

Fig. 3. Bandwidth with varied I/O sizes at full subscription for random read I/O

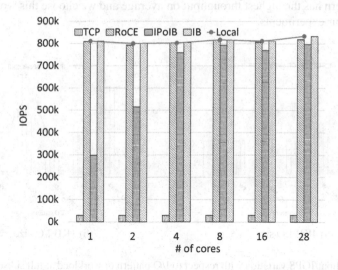

Fig. 4. Throughput with varied cores/threads for 4KB random read I/O

Second, we discuss the effects of number of cores/threads on throughput. For this experiment, we equally vary the number of threads performing I/O at the NVMe-oF client and target between 1–28 and measure the bandwidth for random read I/O at 4KB. We observe from Fig. 4 that the throughput/IOPS does not scale with the increase in the number of cores for TCP transport type and remains fixed at maximum throughput for RoCE and IB. On the other hand, IPoIB' throughput increases until 4 cores and then reaches its peak value. The low throughput of IPoIB for only 1 or 2 cores is due to the execution of kernel code in IPoIB network stack that dominates the total I/O time decreasing the overall throughput. This places RoCE and IB above IPoIB in terms of throughput as they need only a single core to reach maximum throughput.

Next, we analyse the impact of I/O pattern or workload (sequential/random read-/write) for all transport types over 1 KB and 4 KB I/O sizes at full subscription. In Fig. 5a for 4 KB I/O size the maximum IOPS achieved by writes (275 k IOPS) is roughly 33% of the maximum IOPS achieved by reads (832 k IOPS) for IB transport type. This low bandwidth of write workload is not due to network protocol/transport type. We verified this by running the same I/O pattern on local NVMe-SSD and found that the write bandwidth is bounded by the SSD rather than the transport type. It can also been seen from Fig. 5a that the throughput provided by NVMe over TCP is constant across workloads indicating the network protocol is the bottleneck while IB maintains the throughput close to that of local SSDs for all workloads. Surprisingly, from Fig. 5b the maximum throughput of read-write (70:30) and/or sequential write workload (35 k IOPS) at 1 KB I/O size is 4% of the maximum IOPS achieved by random read operations (830 k IOPS). Again, we verify that this peculiar behaviour is not dependent upon transport type but rather is present while performing I/Os on local NVMe SSDs as well due to write amplification at smaller sized I/Os. From Fig. 5 we can observe that random read I/O pattern has the highest throughput on average and we choose this workload for majority of our experiments.

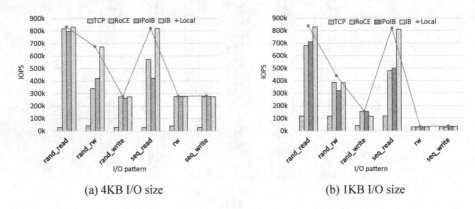

(a) 4KB I/O size   (b) 1KB I/O size

Fig. 5. Throughput/IOPS variation with respect to I/O pattern or workload at full subscription (28 cores/threads). For random read-write (rand_rw) and read-write (rw) workloads the read to write ratio was 70:30

4.3   Latency Evaluation

In latency analysis we study the impact of transport types on latency and the overhead they introduce. We first compare average, p90, p99 and p9999 latency of local NVMe-SSDs and NVMe-oF for all four transport types with 512 B (the minimum block size of a SSD) and 1 MB I/O sizes at full subscription. This shows us the overhead incurred by both small and large I/Os due to the transport type. As expected, from Table 1, the average latency of TCP transport is approximately 20 times that of average latency of

RoCE/IPoIB/IB transport types. Similarly, the p99 and p9999 latency of TCP transport is roughly 30 times that of p99 latency of RoCE/IPoIB/IB transport. In fact, in terms of bandwidth IB is the closest to local NVMe-SSDs for small (Table 2) and large sized I/Os whereas in terms of latency IPoIB adds the least amount of overhead at peak utilization for large I/Os. This could be related to the configuration of various transports in SPDK library. For small I/O requests, IPoIB incurs a higher overhead with its tail latency being $1.5\times$ of IB.

Table 1. Latency at peak bandwidth and full subscription for 1MB random read I/O

	Bandwidth (MiB/s)	Avg Latency (s)	p90 (s)	p99 (s)	p9999 (s)
Local	3626.10	0.96	1.1	1.33	1.40
TCP	466.60	19.44	28.72	29.23	29.27
RoCE	3512.67	0.99	1.16	1.71	1.75
IPoIB	3366.23	1.05	1.12	1.35	1.42
IB	3599.87	0.97	1.15	1.60	1.64

Table 2. Latency at full subscription for 512 bytes random read I/O. RoCE was not reported to due to testbed limitations

	Bandwidth (MiB/s)	Avg Latency (ms)	p90 (ms)	p99 (ms)	p9999 (ms)
Local	403.67	4.30	4.61	4.71	5.78
TCP	111.85	15.65	25.26	28.94	34.94
IPoIB	401.07	4.36	5.03	6.10	9.02
IB	402.97	4.34	4.63	4.77	6.07

Similar to bandwidth, we next examine the variation in latency with respect to the number of NVMe-oF client and target cores performing I/Os for all the transport types. From the cumulative distribution function (CDF) plot of latencies in Fig. 6 and 7 one can see the latency increases with increase in number of cores irrespective of the transport type and IB has the latency closet to local SSDs for all the cores. RoCE and IPoIB have quite similar latency distribution except p9999 latency of RoCE being unusally high (1146 ms). From Fig. 6c, d, Table 1, and Table 2 we can observe that the tail latency of IPoIB and IB are dependent upon the I/O size. For small and medium sized I/Os IB provides lower tail latency and for larger I/Os IPoIB produces slightly better tail latency.

4.4 CPU Utilization Study

In this experiment, we measure the NVMe-oF client CPU utilization for all four transport types performing 1 MB random read I/O at full subscription using Linux sysstat tools [23]. This helps us measure the efficiency of the various transport types initiating I/O operations at the client. One can see from Fig. 8 that interrupt based TCP and

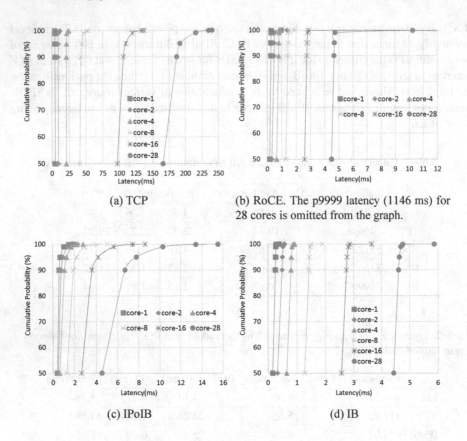

(a) TCP

(b) RoCE. The p9999 latency (1146 ms) for 28 cores is omitted from the graph.

(c) IPoIB

(d) IB

Fig. 6. Latency CDF for various cores for each transport type at 4 KB random read I/O

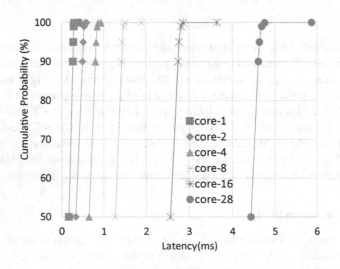

Fig. 7. Latency CDF for various cores for local SSD at 4 KB random read I/O

IPoIB have lower user mode CPU utilization when compared to polling based RoCE and IB. Similar CPU utilization is observed for other workloads too. Table 1 shows us the bandwidth and latency of IPoIB and IB transport for this configuration. Though IB has higher bandwidth when compared to IPoIB, the latencies (p99 and p9999) of IB is slightly higher (1.15×) than IPoIB. This indicates that IPoIB is more efficient at large I/Os despite being an interrupt based network protocol, which may imply that running IB in event based mode could be considered for large I/O sizes rather than polling mode.

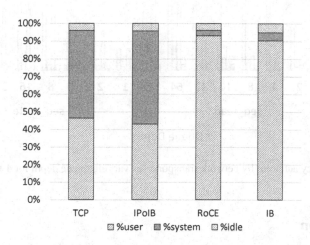

Fig. 8. NVMe-oF client CPU utilization at full subscription for 1 MB random read I/O

4.5   SSD Concurrency Study

To find the parallelism each transport type could achieve, we first measure the throughput or IOPS of local and remote NVMe SSDs for varying queue depth at 4 KB workloads when only 1 CPU core performs I/O operations. The concurrency/parallelism at any queue depth for a specific workload type is calculated by dividing the throughput of that transport type by the throughput of local NVMe SSD at queue depth of 1. For example, the concurrency of an IB transport type for sequential read operations is computed by dividing the each of the IOPS attained by IB transport type for queue depths 1 to 128 by the throughput of a local NVMe SSD for a similar workload at queue depth of 1. Similarly, the concurrency for all network transports and workloads (sequential/random read/write) are calculated. In Fig. 9 and 10 we can see that concurrency for read workloads increases with queue depth whereas write concurrency does not change after queue depth of 8. In terms of network transport, IB is able to reach higher parallelism for both sequential/random read workloads than rest of the transports, followed by RoCE. IPoIB is only able to achieve maximum concurrency of 2.3 for sequential read I/O at a queue depth of 128 which is significantly lower from the maximum concurrencies of IB and RoCE, 6.3 and 4.6 respectively.

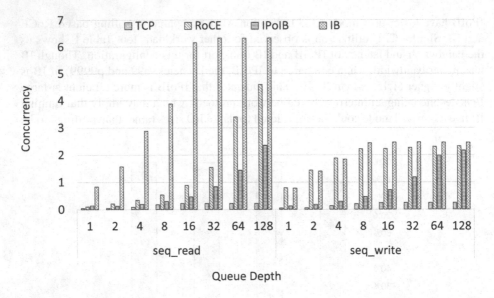

Fig. 9. Concurrency achieved by network transports for varying queue depth for 4 KB sequential workload

5   Discussion

Tradeoffs. Our performance characterization and analysis of user-space NVMe-oF protocol specification is done across four dimensions and various metrics (throughput, latency, CPU utilization, and concurrency). Table 3 provides a summary of the tradeoffs between different transports for evaluated metrics. In terms of throughput/bandwidth and average/tail latencies IB network transport delivers very efficient performance among all the protocols. IB with RDMA was also able to obtain 2.7× higher concurrency than IPoIB transport. IPoIB had better CPU utilization and tail latencies at maximum throughput. There might be two reasons for this. One is that the performance of the tested SSD is limited, which prevents our experiments from achieving higher performance with native RDMA. The achievable performance with IPoIB on IB EDR is sufficient to saturate the SSD's performance. The other reason is that the software implementation in SPDK may not exploit the best configurations with RDMA protocol, which leaves rooms for further performance improvements.

RoCE was similar to IB and IPoIB in terms of bandwidth, concurrency, and average latency but fared slightly worse in terms of tail latency and client CPU utilization. A general trend observed across all network transports was that latency increased as we increased the number of cores performing I/Os. Though IPoIB and IB (RDMA) are faster and have higher performance than RoCE and TCP (ethernet), the current-generation networking infrastructure in datacenters is typically built on top of traditional ethernet. The costs of laying down a new RDMA-capable network would be expensive. To reduce the deployment cost, RoCE could be used on top of the ethernet

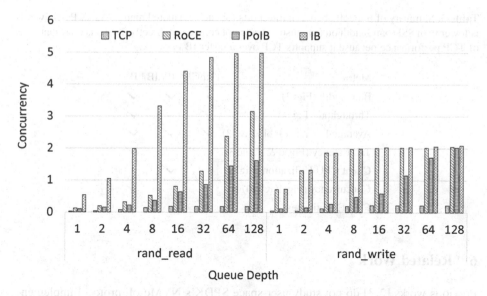

Fig. 10. Concurrency achieved by network transports for varying queue depth for 4 KB random workload

infrastructure by adding specialized NICs to the nodes. Hence, NVMe-over-RoCE may be a good tradeoff between cost and efficiency.

Other Metrics. Despite having a low bandwidth ethernet card (1 Gbps) for NVMe over TCP, the throughput of TCP transport is quite low due to execution of kernel space code during communication. On the contrary, kernel-space based IPoIB (100 Gbps NIC) shows good performance, which implies that kernel overhead is minimal at maximum throughput and when the network bandwidth is high. Although we did not evaluate the kernel NVMe-oF driver, our results indicate that kernel overhead may not have significant impact on throughput, if not latency. We leave a complete evaluation for future work. We also expect the type of SSD to have a profound impact on the metrics across all dimensions due to different driver/controller software and storage technology (NAND flash-based and next generation 3D XPoint [6]). The SSD we evaluated suffers from write amplification effects. Therefore, all networks (except TCP) were able to saturate the SSD write bandwidth, but only IB was able to saturate the read bandwidth. Newer Optane drives do not suffer from garbage collection and write amplification overheads and will thus be harder to saturate for writes. We expect the type of network and its bandwidth to be even more important for such SSDs.

Table 3. Summary of tradeoffs between transports for each evaluated metric. As TCP bandwidth is lower than SSD bandwidth on our cluster, we do not consider it directly. IPoIB is representative of TCP performance because it supports TCP over a faster IB network.

Metric	RoCE	IPoIB	IB
Bandwidth (Fig. 3)	✓	✓	✓
Throughput (Fig. 4)	✓		✓
Average Latency (Table 1 & 3)	✓	✓	✓
Tail Latency (Fig. 6 & Table 3)			✓
Client CPU Utilization (Fig. 8)		✓	
Concurrency (Fig. 9 & 10)			✓
Cost-Effectiveness	✓		

6   Related Work

Previous works [2,3] do not study user-space SPDK's NVMe-oF protocol implementation rather they study NVMe-oF driver present in Linux kernel and compare it with similar protocols like iSCSI [10,11]. Yang et al. [25] showed the inefficiencies present in the Linux kernel NVMe-oF drivers when compared to userspace NVMe-oF drivers. Given that NVMe over TCP is relatively new only two studies [22,26] exist as far as we know which evaluate NVMe/TCP in user-space but no comparison exists with other network tranpsorts. NVMe over TCP is important for the datacenters which currently do not support RDMA-capable networks yet.

Some work which does evaluate disaggregated flash storage in [1–3,9,12,14,15, 17,21,24] only use RoCE/iWARP rather than InfiniBand interconnect. Klimovic et al. in [14,15] implement a software system for remote flash access only over TCP/IP and in [13] describe an architecture for disaggregated flash system that optimizes remote flash access by tuning system settings. [9] evaluates NVMe-oF on ARM SoC whereas our characterization is done on x86 architecture. [24] studies NVMe and NVMe-oF for docker storage drivers and containerized applications. Other than [4], which implement HDFS over Fabric on top of NVMe-oF, none of the previous work extensively evaluate an important networking protocol IPoIB and IB or study various workload types like sequential/random reads/writes or NVMe-oF client CPU utilization.

Our work is first-of-a-kind to comprehensively study and characterize SPDK's user-space NVMe-oF protocol for 4 different networking/transport protocols, namely TCP, IPoIB, RoCE, and IB, across numerous dimensions, including number of cores, I/O size, workloads, concurrency, and client-side CPU utilization.

7   Conclusion and Future Work

In this paper, we present an in-depth analysis of the tradeoffs and performance characteristics of network protocols on storage disaggregation. Our characterization of NVMe-over-Fabrics over Ethernet and RDMA was performed across four dimensions

- networking protocols (TCP, RoCE, IPoIB, and IB), I/O size, number of cores, and I/O pattern. We found that native RDMA with IB was able to deliver the best performance among all tested networking protocols in most experiments. IB with RDMA can typically deliver lower latency and higher throughput whereas IB with IPoIB offers lower CPU utilization. Native RDMA with IB or RoCE can achieve higher SSD concurrency. We believe that our analysis helps gain insight into the deployment implications of NVMeoF in datacenters. In the future, we plan to study additional protocols, such as iWARP and fibre channel, and types of NVMe-SSDs. We also plan to evaluate various transport types on real world applications like key-value stores and distributed filesystems.

References

1. Chelsio Communications. NVM Express over Fabrics (2014). http://www.chelsio.com/wp-content/uploads/resources/NVM_Express_Over_Fabrics.pdf
2. Guz, Z., (Huan) Li, H., Shayesteh, A., Balakrishnan, H.: NVMe-over-Fabrics performance characterization and the path to low-overhead flash disaggregation. In: Proceedings of the 10th ACM International Systems and Storage Conference, SYSTOR 2017 (2017)
3. Guz, Z., (Huan) Li, H., Shayestch, A., Balakrishnan, V.: Performance characterization of NVMe-over-fabrics storage disaggregation. ACM Trans. Storage **14**(4), 1–18 (2018)
4. Han, D., Nam, B.: Improving access to HDFS using NVMeoF. In: 2019 IEEE International Conference on Cluster Computing (CLUSTER), pp. 1–2 (2019)
5. IBM Research - Zurich. Crail (2017). http://www.crail.io/
6. Intel. Intel Optane Memory. https://www.intel.com/OptaneMemory
7. Intel. SPDK NVMe over Fabrics Target (2017). https://spdk.io/doc/nvmf.html
8. Intel. SPDK NVMe over Fabrics Target Programming Guide (2017). https://spdk.io/doc/nvmf.html
9. Jia, Y., Anger, E., Chen, F.: When NVMe over fabrics meets arm: performance and implications. In: 2019 35th Symposium on Mass Storage Systems and Technologies (MSST), pp/ 134–140 (2019)
10. Joglekar, A., Kounavis, M.E., Berry, F.L.: A scalable and high performance software ISCSI implementation. In: Proceedings of the 4th Conference on USENIX Conference on File and Storage Technologies, FAST 2005, vol. 4, p. 20, USA. USENIX Association (2005)
11. Khosravi, H.M., Joglekar, A., Iyer, R.: Performance characterization of iSCSI processing in a server platform. In: 2005 24th IEEE International Performance, Computing, and Communications Conference, PCCC 2005, pp. 99–107 (2005)
12. Kim, J., Fair, D.: How ethernet RDMA protocols iWARP and RoCE support NVMe over fabrics (Ethernet Storage Forum) (2016). https://www.snia.org/sites/default/files/ESF/How_Ethernet_RDMA_Protocols_Support_NVMe_over_Fabrics_Final.pdf
13. Klimovic, A., Kozyrakis, C., Thereska, E., John, B., Kumar, S.: Flash storage disaggregation. In Proceedings of the Eleventh European Conference on Computer Systems, EuroSys 2016 (2016)
14. Klimovic, A., Litz, H., Kozyrakis, C.: ReFlex: remote flash ≈ local flash. In: Proceedings of the Twenty-Second International Conference on Architectural Support for Programming Languages and Operating Systems, ASPLOS 2017, pp. 345–359 (2017)
15. Klimovic, A., Wang, Y., Stuedi, P., Trivedi, A., Pfefferle, J., Kozyrakis, C.: Pocket: elastic ephemeral storage for serverless analytics. In: Proceedings of the 13th USENIX Conference on Operating Systems Design and Implementation, OSDI 2018, pp. 427–444, USA. USENIX Association (2018)

16. Mickens, J., et al.: Blizzard: fast, cloud-scale block storage for cloud-oblivious applications. In: 11th USENIX Symposium on Networked Systems Design and Implementation (NSDI 2014), pp. 257–273 (2014)
17. Dave M., Metz, J.: Under the Hood with NVMe over fabrics. In: Proceedings of the Ethernet Storage Forum (2015)
18. NVM Express (2011). https://nvmexpress.org/
19. NVMe-over-Fabrics Specification (2019). https://nvmexpress.org/developers/nvme-of-speci fication/
20. SPDK NVMe perf Benchmark. https://github.com/spdk/spdk/tree/master/examples/nvme/perf
21. SPDK 20.04 NVMe-oF RDMA Performance Report. https://ci.spdk.io/download/performance-reports/SPDK_rdma_perf_report_2004.pdf
22. SPDK 20.04 NVMe-oF TCP Performance Report. https://ci.spdk.io/download/performance-reports/SPDK_tcp_perf_report_2004.pdf
23. Linux sysstat. https://github.com/sysstat/sysstat
24. Xu, Q., et al.: Performance analysis of containerized applications on local and remote storage. In: International Conference on Massive Storage Systems and Technology (2017)
25. Yang, Z., et al.: SPDK: a development kit to build high performance storage applications. In: 2017 IEEE International Conference on Cloud Computing Technology and Science (Cloud-Com), pp. 154–161 (2017)
26. Yang, Z., Wan, Q., Cao, G., Latecki, K.: uNVMe-TCP: a user space approach to optimizing NVMe over fabrics TCP transport. In: Hsu, C.-H., Kallel, S., Lan, K.-C., Zheng, Z. (eds.) IOV 2019. LNCS, vol. 11894, pp. 125–142. Springer, Cham (2020). https://doi.org/10.1007/978-3-030-38651-1_13

K2RDF: A Distributed RDF Data Management System on Kudu and Impala

Xu Chen, Boyu Qiu, Jungang Xu$^{(\boxtimes)}$, and Renfeng Liu

School of Computer Science and Technology,
University of Chinese Academy of Sciences, Beijing, China
{chenxu18,qiuboyu18,liurenfeng16}@mails.ucas.ac.cn,
xujg@ucas.ac.cn

Abstract. The Resource Description Framework (RDF) has been widely used in various applications or services as a model for displaying, sharing and connecting data. With the increase of RDF data scale, distributed RDF data management system becomes popular, but there are still many problems to be solved. To solve these problems, we proposed a distributed RDF data management system K2RDF based on the Porperty Chain model on the Kudu and Impala platforms. Kudu is a data storage engine that combines OLAP and OLTP scenario and Impala can process SQL queries in real time. The combination of these two platforms provides new options for processing RDF data, making storage more efficient and queries faster. The Property Chain model is derived from the RDF data content. The RDF data is divided into different parts stored in the corresponding attribute table by the class information extracted from RDF schema. In the attribute table, In the attribute table, each column corresponds to a property in the RDF class. This model can increase the data storage density and improve the query processing speed by reducing the number of the join operation. By comparing with the current popular distributed RDF data management systems in some experiments, our system has lower query latency and faster query speed.

Keywords: RDF · SPARQL · Big data · Distributed system · Database

1 Introduction

The Resource Description Framework (RDF) [1] is a set of knowledge representation models proposed by the World Wide Web Consortium (W3C), and it has been widely used in all fields to describe and express the content and structure of network resources abundantly. The basic unit of RDF is called a triple, which is expressed as $<subject, property, object>$. RDF has a schema language called RDF Schema (RDFS) [2], which is used to describe the class to which the resource belongs, the properties of the resource, and the relationship between two resources. The RDF data that has schema can not only provide the information expressed directly by the triples, but also indicate the information that

© Springer Nature Switzerland AG 2021
F. Wolf and W. Gao (Eds.): Bench 2020, LNCS 12614, pp. 57–73, 2021.
https://doi.org/10.1007/978-3-030-71058-3_4

can be inferred based on the RDFS inference rules. The W3C organization has also proposed the RDF data standard query language SPARQL (Simple Protocol And RDF Query Language) [3], which can be used to find the target data and manipulate RDF data, like inserting new triple or deleting unused triple.

RDF data is getting larger and complicated. The Bio2RDF dataset containing human and mouse genomic data has 2.3 billion RDF triples [4], and the US government's open dataset has 6.4 billion triples. The global catalogue of microorganisms organized by Institute of Microbiology, Chinese Academy of Sciences is expected to reach the scale of 10 billion. With the development of technology, the scale of RDF data sets will become larger and larger. However, the huge data set poses a serious challenge to the storage system and the query system. Storage and query processing requirements for large-scale data has exceeded the limitation of the stand-alone system. Therefore, using distributed clusters to process large-scale RDF data has become one of the current research hotspots. At present, there are many researches that uses distributed system to process RDF data, which can be divided into three categories: Systems are based on existing distributed big data systems, such as HadoopRDF [5], SHARD [6], etc.; Some systems are based on graph data partitioning, such as TriAD; And there are some federal distributed RDF data management systems, such as DARQ [8], etc. Each of these three systems have its characteristics and application range [9].

Kudu [10] is an open source distributed storage system developed by Cloudera, which provides both efficient data analysis and low latency random read and write ability. It can been integrated well with other query systems such as Impala [11] and Spark [12]. Most of the application scenarios of RDF data are data analysis. For some domain-specific RDF data, real-time data update capability is also needed. Kudu can provide these two capabilities for RDF data. Impala is an open source massively parallel processing (MPP) SQL execution engine developed by Cloudera for the Hadoop [13] ecosystem, it is for low-latency real-time data query and analysis scenarios. Impala is ahead of other similar systems because of fast query speed, flexibility and scalability.

The excellent performance of Kudu and Impala create a new option for managing RDF data. Kudu provides storage for RDF data, which can achieve efficient RDF data analysis and real-time update capabilities. Impala is responsible for the execution of queries in RDF data, which can provide real-time query speed. Therefore, we built the distributed RDF data management system called K2RDF on the Kudu and Impala. The main contributions are as follows:

- A distributed RDF data management system is built on the Kudu and Impala. RDF data can be stored and queried in a distributed cluster.
- The Property Chain model is used as a mapping between the RDF model and the Kudu table, and which can reduce the amount of join operation on different Kudu table and improve the query efficiency.
- The comparative experiments of K2RDF and other distributed RDF data management systems using RDF benchmark set are conducted. Experiment results show that the K2RDF system has faster query speed.

2   Related Works

2.1   RDF

RDF is composed of a series of statements, each of which can express a property of a resource or a relationship between two resources. A resource can be described by a collection of statements. Similar to human language, a statement contains three elements: subject, property, and object. Because each statement must contain these three parts, it is also referred to as a triple. A triple can be interpreted as that the property of the subject is the object or that the relationship between the subject and the object is the property.

In RDF data, resource is usually represented by a URI (Uniform Resource Identifier). The URI is unique so that the resource can be uniquely identified in Internet. We mark the resource URI as U. When presenting the properties of a resource, the types of expression such as string, integer, etc. are often used. These types are often represented using literal, we mark it as L. In addition, RDF also provides some special expression types to satisfy some special scenarios or make the expression more smooth and natural, such as blank node, which is marked as B. Blank node are often used to represent resources that are not given by a URI or literal, and are also referred to as anonymous resources. The formal definition of the triple is as follows:

A statement, or a triple, can be expressed as $<subject, property, object>$, $triple \quad t = <s, p, o>$. The subject(s) may be a URI or a blank node, $s \in U \cup B$. The property(p) may be a URI or a blank node, $p \in U \cup B$. The object(o) may be a URI, an blank node or literal value, $o \in U \cup B \cup L$. The value space of a triple can be expressed as $(U \cup B) \times (U \cup B) \times (U \cup B \cup L)$.

Table 1 shows an RDF section about the former US president Abraham Lincoln. This collection includes six triples that describe Lincoln's title, place of birth, location of death, and other information. In RDF data, the subject or object can be represented as a node in the graph, and the property is the edge connecting the two nodes of the subject and the object. Therefore, the RDF data can also be considered as a directed graph $G = <V, E, L>$. V denotes the vertex in the RDF data graph. Each vertex is the subject or object in the triple, which can be a URI, blank node or literal value. $E = V \times V$ is the directed edge set in the RDF data graph. Each edge is a statement or a triple in RDF. L is a collection of properties for all edges, and each edge corresponds to an property in the triple. Figure 1 shows the RDF data graph according to the RDF data in Table 1.

2.2   SPARQL

The SPARQL language is the recommended standard proposed by the W3C for quering and manipulating RDF data and it is used widely in RDF data management systems. It is a declarative language that does not require writing processing steps when we want to find something in RDF data. The SPARQL language provides almost all kinds of statements for manipulating RDF data

Table 1. RDF triple example

Subject	Predicate	Object
Abraham Lincoln	Title	president
Abraham Lincoln	bornIn	Hodgenvillel KY
Abraham Lincoln	diedIn	Washington DC
Washington DC	foundingYear	1790
United States	hasCapital	Washington DC
Hodgenvillel KY	locatedIn	United States

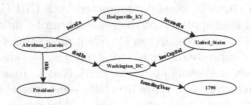

Fig. 1. RDF data graph

and comes in two main categories: querying and updating RDF data. What we concern is the query part of the SPARQL language.

A SPARQL query Q defines a graph pattern P. The query is to find the RDF data that can match P in graph G. By replacing the data what we want to find in the pattern P to a variable, the data represented by the variable can be found by the method of pattern matching. In a SPARQL query, the variable is a string that begins with "?". Variables can appear in any one or more locations of a subject, property, or object. When a subject, property, or object in a triple is replaced by a variable, the triple is called a triple pattern. Formalization is defined as triple pattern $tp = (s', p', o')$, where $s' \in \{s, ?s\}, p' \in \{p, ?p\}, o' \in \{o, ?o\}$. The value space of the triple pattern can be expressed as $(U \cup B \cup V) \times (U \cup B \cup V) \times (U \cup B \cup L \cup V)$, where V is a set of all variables. The BGP (Basic Graph Pattern) is a pattern consisting only of the triple patterns. A SPARQL query can be represented as a directed graph $Q = \,<V^Q, E^Q, L^Q>$. $V^Q = V \cup V_{var}$, V^Q represents that the collection of all vertices and V_{var} vertices are variables. $E^Q = V^Q \times V^Q$ represents the collection of edges, represented by a combination of all vertices. L^Q represents the collection of properties for all edges.

Figure 2(a) is a SPARQL query on the triples of Table 1, which is a BGP query that contains only the triple pattern. It can be interpreted as "find the name of the president who was born in Hodgenvillel KY, USA". Where ?name, ?people are variables. Figure 2(b) is the query graph G corresponding to this SPARQL query. When processing query, the data matching the graph pattern is filtered by graph matching method.

SELECT ?name   WHERE {
?people name ?name.
?people title president.
?people bornIn Hodgenvillel_KY.
Hodgenvillel_KY locatedIn United_States.
}

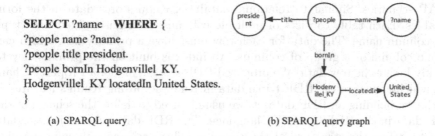

(a) SPARQL query   (b) SPARQL query graph

Fig. 2. SPARQL query example

2.3 Related Systems

The cloud computing systems have been developed for many years and raised of many excellent systems. Based on existing distributed computing systems to develop upper-layer applications can effectively utilize the advantages of existing systems, and developers can focus on the application scenario without dealing with distributed problems. So, the RDF data management system based on existing distributed systems has become one of the popular way to process RDF data.

Hadoop is a widely used open source big data processing platform. There are many RDF data management systems based on Hadoop, such as SHARD [6], HadoopRDF, H2RDF [14] and so on. SHARD combines the triples that have same subject into a single line and stores the lines in a file. When querying, a whole query can be divided into many subqueries and each subquery is iteratively calculated using the MapReduce computing framework. HadoopRDF uses properties to divide RDF data into multiple files. The query method is the same as SHARD, but you can quickly locate the required data through different files. H2RDF uses the key-value system HBase [15] to store all six permutations of triples. For query, H2RDF uses indices to quickly locate data and convert all join operations to merge joins to improve speed. S2RDF [19] uses the Spark system. Based on VP (Vertical Partition) [18] storage structure, it proposed ExtVP (Extended Vertical Partition) structure to accelerate the join operation in the query process. ExtVP uses the principle that join operation can be split into semi-joins, and accelerates the join process by prestoring the semi-join results. There are also many systems based on existing cloud systems, such as Trinity.RDF [21] based on Trinity [20], Sempala [22] based on Parquet and Impala, S2X [24] based on GraphX [23], and so on.

3 Property Chain Model

3.1 Model Definition

Kudu is a distributed storage system that provides low-latency random I/O capabilities and efficient data ayalysis, which can be used in both OLTP and

OLAP scenarios. Similar to relational database, Kudu stores data in the form of tables. Each table consists of multiple columns, each has a fixed data type and column name. The data for each row must have a primary key, which can be one column or a group of columns. An index is built on the primary key to quickly locate the row data. We proposed RDF storage model a Property Chain and which can store the RDF triple data in Kudu according Kudu's features.

Before building an RDF dataset, we usually need to define the schema of the RDF data in the RDFS or OWL language. The RDF data schema is metadata used to define the structure of the contents. These schema languages provide definition statements of resource class, property, literal value, etc., which can be used to build the backbone of the RDF resources. In the relational database, we need to pre-define the relational schema of the data, then create relational table in database. The data is split by relational schema and stored in realtional table. Similarly, the metadata defined by RDFS or OWL is the schema of RDF data. Class describes the properties and relationships that resource in same type has in common. RDFS provides statements like rdfs:Resource, rdfs:Class, rdfs:Literal, etc. to define resource class. Property can be divided into ObjectProperty, DatatypeProperty, etc., which can be used to describe the property value of resource or the relationship between two resources. In addition, RDFS and OWL also provide a series of other statements to describe RDF data more accurately.

The RDF data has schema, and the Kudu table also has schema. Therefore, we propose a model to convert the schema of RDF data into the schema of Kudu table. Entities are instances of class, and triples in RDF are used to describe entities. We divide the triples into different parts according to the class to which the entity belongs. Each part is stored as a table in Kudu.

There are some systems that has been used similar model to store data. Jena (property table implementation) [16] uses the property table to store data. According to the class information in the RDF data, the data is manually divided into different property tables. But this method requires artificial creation of property table and cannot handle arbitrary data. DB2RDF [17] is a DB2-based RDF data management system that stores triples belonging to the same subject in one row of the data table. Each row stores the properties and objects of the same subject and has a different number of columns. This approach does not divide different data into different parts and is not friendly to distributed systems.

We designed a new storage model called Property Chain for the Kudu system. This model divides RDF data according to the class to which the RDF entity belongs. Each class will create a Kudu table to store, and each property in the class is stored in corresponding column in the table. In this way, the RDF data can be stored in a table according to the class to which the subject belongs, and the triples with same subject are stored in one row of the table. Each object in triple is stored in the corresponding column. If the value of the property does not exist, the column is stored as null. The design of the table is shown in Fig. 3. We can see that there are two tables for each class, one is the class table containing all the properties in the class, and the other is the class link table storing the property containing multiple values. The class table is shown in Fig. 3(a). The first column of the table stores the value of the subject. From the second column, each column stores the value of the property. The data stored in the class table is only the subject and the object, and the property is determined by the position of the table. If encountering a property that has multiple values, we create and store an ID in the class table and store all the values in the class link table. In the class link table, each value and the ID to which the value belongs are stored in one row. For query, the class table and the class link table can be joined on the ID if the property has multiple values. We use the subject as the primary key in the class table and use the combination of ID and Value as the primary key in the class link table.

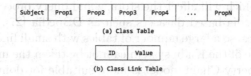

(a) Class Table

(b) Class Link Table

Fig. 3. Property Chain table

3.2   Model Features

The Property Chain model divides and stores RDF data in different data tables according to the class to which the subject belongs. The results of a SPARQL query usually focus on one subset of data. Our model can improve the hit rate of the query, reduce the amount of data read on disk and transferred in the cluster network. Each column of the table stores only data for the same property. For a column storage system such as Kudu, the data compression rate can be increased and the data storage density can be improved. We classify the SPARQL queries into different types according to the BGP graph structure, including line queries, star queries, and snowflake queries. The most used queries are star queries and snowflake queries, while snowflake queries are a combination of multiple star queries. In our model, the data of the same subject is stored in one row, so the star query of the same subject can be proccessed by line scan. And the same for every star structure in a snowflake query. This can reduce the number of join operations and speed up the query processing. Kudu can only create the primary key index. By setting the subject column in the class table as the primary key, we can take advantage of the Kudu primary key index.

Equation (1) is a general formula for the time cost required for distributed query execution [25]. The time cost consists of four parts. The first two parts are the local processing time, including the CPU instruction time and the disk I/O time. The last two parts are the time spent communicating, including the time it takes from the message to be sent to receive the message and the time it takes for the data to travel from one site to another. Kudu's efficient random access ability can reduce the amount of data on disk I/O. Stroring different class data into different table avoids reading unusable data. The reduction of table join operations reduces the amount of data transmitted on the network and time for transmission. So our model can effectively reduce the time cost for distributed query processing.

$$\text{Total time} = T_{cpu} * \#\text{insts} + T_{I/0} * \#I/Os + T_{MSG} * \#msgs + T_{TR} * \#bytes \tag{1}$$

The Property Chain model and Jena (property table implementation) are both content-related models, but our model solves the problem of not being able to process arbitrary data. Compared to DB2RDF, Property Chain model is more suitable for distributed systems. The Property Chain model also has drawbacks. If the number of classes in RDF data is very large, the model will create a large number of tables, which will affect the storage and query processing of the data. For example, wikipedia-based datasets such as DBpedia [27], YAGO [28], etc. contain lots of classes, so a large number of tables with small lines will be created, and the performance of the Kudu system cannot be taken the most advantage of. Therefore, the Property Chain model is more suitable for domain-specific RDF data.

4   System Design

Based on the Property Chain model, we built K2RDF on Kudu and Impala. The system consists of three parts: the data loader, the SPARQL query translater, and the query executor. The data loader is responsible for analyzing the RDF data, converting the RDF schema into a table schema in Kudu, and loading the data into Kudu tables. The query translater can translate the SPARQL query into a SQL query based on the table schema saved by data loader. The query executor is responsible for mapping the tables in query to Kudu tables and executing the converted SQL queries on the Impala.

4.1   Data Loader

The data loader is responsible for importing RDF data into Kudu tables. The import process includes four steps: (1) Analyze the RDF data and construct the table schema according to the data schema. (2) Create data tables in Kudu and Impala according to the table schema. (3) Sort the data according to the table schema. (4) Import the sorted data into the Kudu tables.

We classify RDF data into three categories: RDF data containing RDF-S/OWL schema, RDF data containing rdfs:type property, and RDF data without schema and rdfs:type property. RDF data containing RDFS/OWL schema refers to data that contains RDF data schema defined by RDFS/OWL. Through this schema, we can directly get the classes, properties and other information in data and use this information to create tables. RDF data that does not contain RDFS/OWL schema can be divided into two other categories: data containing rdfs:type property and data not containing rdfs:type property. These two types of data have no explicit class and property information, and the classes and properties of the data need to be summarized by the clustering algorithm to create table schema.

RDF data containing RDFS/OWL schema can obtain the classes and properties from RDFS/OWL schema. We use the OWL API to extract all the classes from the schema and get all the properties of each class. Then, we create a table for each class. Each property in the class is mapped to each column in the table. If there are properties that has multiple values, we create a linked table for this class. The loading algorithm is shown in Algorithm 1.

Algorithm 1. Loading algorithm of RDF data with schema

Input: RDF data;
Output: Table;
 1: ontology = owlapi.load(rdfs or owl file);
 2: classes = ontology.classes;
 3: **for** class in classes **do**
 4:     create table named after class;
 5:     **for** property in class.properties **do**
 6:         create column named after property in table
 7:     **end for**;
 8:     tables.add(table);
 9: **end for**
10: **for** table in tables **do**
11:     create table in Kudu;
12:     create table map in Impala;
13: **end for**

Data that does not contain RDFS/OWL schema needs to be analyzed to obtain class and property information. If the data contains rdfs:type property, we can extract all the classes in the data through rdfs:type property. With the class information, we can use the clustering algorithm to conclude the properties contained in each class. Firstly, we create a collection of properties for each class. The triple data need be sorted by subject, making the triples with same subject appear together. The triple group with same subject must contain a triple that its property is rdfs:type, and the object of this triple is the class to which the triple group's subject belongs. Then add all the properties contained in the triple group to the property collection of the class, and determine the type of each property, the value range of property, and whether the property has multiple values. Finally, we get all the classes and properties in each class, so we can create the class table and class link table in Kudu and Impala. The clustering algorithm is shown in Algorithm 2. If the data has neither RDFS/OWL schema nor rdfs:type property, the class and property information in the data needs to be summarized by the clustering algorithm. We extract the properties of triples with same subject to form a collection of properties. The method of clustering

---

Algorithm 2. Clustering algorithm of RDF data with rdfs:type

Input: RDF data;
Output: table;
 1: select all classes from triples;
 2: sort(rdf) by subject
 3: **for** triple in RDF data **do**
 4:     **if** triple.subject == lastSubject **then**
 5:         **if** triple.property == rdfs:type **then**
 6:             class == triple.object;
 7:         **else**
 8:             class.addProperty(triple.property);
 9:         **end if**
10:     **else**
11:         lastSubject = triple.subject
12:         **if** triple.property == rdfs:type **then**
13:             class = triple.object
14:         **else**
15:             class.addPropertytriple.property)
16:         **end if**
17:     **end if**
18: **end for**
19: create table for classes and properties

---

is to calculate the collections of properties without intersections by merging any two collections if there is common property in these two collections. We treat the collection that has no common property with any other collection as a class. The classes derived from this method deviates from the original class defined by RDFS or OWL schema. This method may split the original class into two classes, and the property that does not appear in the current data cannot be calculated. Therefore, the classes and properties are only valid for the current data. If some triples need to be inserted into current data, the classes and properties should be re-analyzed. Although the schema information has deviations, it is not a problem for the storage and query for data. The result of splitting the original class into two classes is that the data of one class is stored in two tables, but there is no missing or repeated data. Moreover, the table schema is the key for query translater to translate a SPARQL query to SQL query. In the translated SQL query, the two tables derived from one class is joined on subject, so it is not a problem on the query. The classes and properties derived from this method is enough to divide the data into different tables.

After converting the class schema to the table schema, the data loader creates tables in Kudu and table maps in Impala. Then it imports the data into the Kudu tables. Before importing data, the loader divide the triples into different triple group according to the subject. Each triple group will be converted to a row in table and inserted to the belonging table that is determined by comparing the classes and properties between triple group and table schema. The data is imported into the Kudu table. The metadata for the Kudu tables is saved for use by the query translator.

4.2   Query Translater

The Impala system only supports SQL queries. We need to translate SPARQL queries to SQL queries for Impala, which can query the data in Kudu. The process of translating a SPARQL query to a SQL query includes four steps. Firstly, the SPARQL query statement is parsed into the SPARQL syntax tree. Secondly, the SPARQL syntax tree is converted into the SQL syntax tree. Thirdly, the SQL query tree is used to generate the SQL query. Finally, we opimize the generated SQL query.

Firstly, we use Jena ARQ to parse the SPARQL query into the SPARQL syntax tree. Then, convert the SPARQL syntax tree to a SQL syntax tree. In this process, we transform each syntax node in the SPARQL syntax tree into the corresponding SQL syntax node to build the SQL syntax tree. Some syntax between the two query languages is similar and can be mapped directly, such as Order By. For syntax that cannot be directly mapped, such as BGP queries, we create special syntax nodes to handle. After that, we convert each syntax node in the SQL syntax tree into SQL statements and stitch them into a complete SQL query. This step is the key one in translating process and related to the storage schema of the data. We will describe it in detail below.

In Property Chain model, RDF data is divided by class. Therefore, the query statement needs to be translated according to the way the data is divided. In the BGP query, we divide the triples in the query into different triple group according to the subject, and extract the classes and properties in each group. By comparing the classes and properties between the triple group and table's metadata saved during the import process, we can determine which class each group belongs to. If there is a triple's property is rdfs:type in the triple group, the object of this triple is the class. The table triple group belongs to can be inferred by the class. If the object is a variable or the group does not contain rdfs:type property, we should compare the properties in the group with the properties in each table to get a list of candidate tables. If there is only one candidate table, translate this triple group to a subquery on this candidate table. If there are multiple candidate tables, a subquery is generated on each candidate table, and then the multiple subqueries are combined to a query for the triple group. A BGP query contains multiple triple groups and generates multiple subqueries. These subqueries can be combined into one query by the join conditions contained in the triple. Finally, the SQL statements generated by other syntax nodes in the SQL syntax tree, such as the Select statement generated by the Project node, are combined into a complete SQL query.

The join order of multiple subqueries affects the execution efficiency of SQL query, so the order of subqueries needs to be optimized. When sorting subqueries, we take two factors into consider, the size of the table and the size of the subquery results. The size of the table can be obtained from statistical data saved by the data loader, and the size of the subquery results is estimated by the query condition. We believe that the more query conditions, the more accurate the results of the query, the less the number of results. After sorting the join order, we get the final SQL query.

Based on the Property Chain model, the SPARQL query in Fig. 4 is converted to a SQL query as shown in Fig. 5. In SPARQL query, the first two triples belong to a group of properties, and we can infer that the triple group belongs to the taxonnode table by comparing the properties between triple group and table schema. The first subquery in the SQL query is the subquery generated on the first two triples. The last three triples belong to a griple group, the matching table is named taxonname, and the second subquery in the SQL query is the subquery generated on the last three triples. The two triple groups in the SPARQL query are connected by the taxonid variable. In the SQL query, the two SQL subqueries are also joined on the taxonid variable. The condition for the join is $tab0.taxonid = tab1.taxonid$. Finally, we combine the Limit, Select and other statements into the final SQL query.

SELECT ?taxonid ?rank ?nameId **WHERE** {
?taxonid anno:ancestorTaxid taxon:33;
anno:nodeRank ?rank.
?nameId anno:taxid ?taxonid;
anno:nameclass "scientificName";
anno:taxname ?name.
} **LIMIT** 20

Fig. 4. SPARQL query

SELECT tab2.rank **AS** rank, tab2.nameId **AS** nameId, tab2.taxonid **AS** taxonid
FROM (
SELECT tab1.name **AS** name, tab0.rank **AS** rank, tab1.nameId **AS** nameId,
tab0.taxonid AS taxonid   **FROM** (
SELECT _noderank AS rank, _subject AS taxonid   **FROM** _taxonnode
WHERE _ancestortaxid =
'<http://gcm.wdcm.org/data/gcmAnnotation1/taxonomy/33>'
) tab0
JOIN (
SELECT _taxname AS name, _subject AS nameId, _taxid AS taxonid
FROM _taxonname   **WHERE** _nameclass = 'scientificName'
) tab1
ON (tab0.taxonid=tab1.taxonid)   **LIMIT** 20
) tab2

Fig. 5. SQL query

4.3   Query Executor

After translating the SPARQL query to a SQL query, we can use Impala to query the data stored in Kudu. The main function of the query executor is to submit the translated SQL query to Impala and get the result from Impala. Because the table names in Kudu and the mapping table names in Impala has been preprocessed, such as removing special characters, query executor needs to provide a table name mapping for the query to make it execute in Impala. In addition, the query executor provides other auxiliary functions, such as recording query time, providing access API, and so on.

5   Evaluation

5.1   Environment

To evaluate the efficiency of the Property Chain model on Kudu and Impala systems, we conducted experiments in a cluster of five rack servers. Table 2 shows the specific configuration of all machines in the cluster. The Dell R740 server acts as the master node of the cluster, and the other IBM X3650 servers act as slave nodes. All machines are equipped with Ubuntu 16.04 operating system, and big data systems such as Hadoop 2.6.0, Spark 1.6, Kudu 1.7, Impapa 2.12, Hive 1.1 are deployed. GCM-Bench [26] is a benchmark to evaluate the performance of general-purpose RDF data management systems on microorganism RDF data, and we use it to evaluate our system. The size of the data and the number of triples are shown in Table 3.

Table 2. Test environment

Node	Role	CPU	Cores	Memory	Disk
R740	Master	5115*2	20c40t	64 GB	24 TB
X3650	Slave	E5-2620*2	12c24t	32 GB	1.5 TB
X3650	Slave	E5-2620*2	12c24t	32 GB	1.5 TB
X3650	Slave	E5620*2	8c16t	32 GB	1 TB
X3650	Slave	E5620*2	8c16t	32 GB	1 TB

SPARQL queries have different graph structures, and they can be divided into line query, star query and snowflake query. We selected 4 different query statements for each structure, and 12 queries in total. The number of triples included in each query is shown in Fig. 6.

In the experiments, we selected the S2RDF and Sempala systems as baseline systems. S2RDF is a Spark-based RDF data management system that uses its unique ExtVP model to store data in HDFS and uses Spark SQL as the query execution engine. Sempala stores data in a wide table containing all the

Table 3. Test data

Dataset	Triple count	Size
gcm1m	1,001,398	141 MB
gcm10m	10,102,594	1.4 GB
gcm100m	100,818,065	14 GB

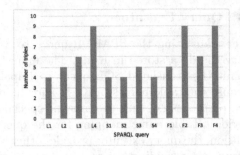

Fig. 6. Triple number in each query

properties and uses Impala as the query execution engine. These two systems has faster query speed than other distributed RDF data managements systems based on existing big data systems. In addition, we implemented the ExtVP model of the S2RDF on the Kudu and Impala systems, and also used as baseline system to verify the performance of the K2RDF system.

5.2 Experimental Results

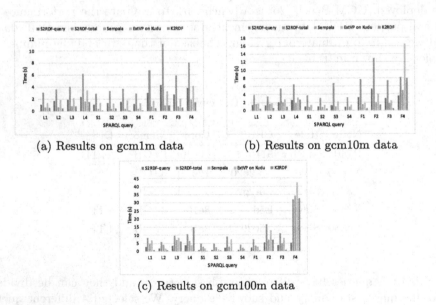

(a) Results on gcm1m data   (b) Results on gcm10m data

(c) Results on gcm100m data

Fig. 7. Experimental Results on gcm1m, gcm10m and gcm100m data.

The S2RDF system uses Spark as the query processing engine, and need to load the table data into memory before executing the query. S2RDF-query refers to the query time that does not include the time spent on loading table data, and

S2RDF-total refers to all the time consumed from the query submitted to results returned. Figure 7(a), Fig. 7(b) and Fig. 7(c) show the time comsumed of the four systems on the three data sets gcm1m, gcm10m, gcm100m.

As can be seen from the three figures, in most of the queries, the K2RDF system is ahead of the other three systems. And the query time can be controlled within 1 second. The total time taken by S2RDF from loading data to completing the query is much more than that of the other three systems. If only the query time is considered, the S2RDF system is very similar to the Sempala and Kudu-based ExtVP system. In the F4 query, these systems consume far more time than the other queries. This is because the F4 query returns a lot of results, and it takes a lot of time to return and write the results. If returning the number of the results by count function, the time spent on the gcm100m data set is reduced to about 10 seconds.

Comparing the number of triple patterns in the query with the query response time, we found that there is a certain correlation between these two metrics. The more the number of triples in the query, the longer time the query will take. This is because there are many subqueries to be joined no matter what storage model is used on translated SQL query. Converting triples to subqueries is a common practice in translating SPARQL query to SQL query. A lot of join operations may consume a lot of time. Therefore, the more join operations in SQL query, the longer the time consuming. The K2RDF system is able to reduce the number of join operations is the most important factor for faster speed.

6   Conclusion and Future Work

In the future, the RDF data will become larger and complicated, and the distributed RDF data management systems will become more important. As can be seen from the experimental results in the previous section, the K2RDF system has faster query speed than other systems. In the SPARQL query translating, we only optimize the order of subqueries, and there is still a lot of optimization space. So we will further optimize the execution speed of SPARQL queries according to the features of Kudu and Impala systems. In addition, the Kudu system has excellent random access performance. With this feature, we will implement the update statement in SPARQL to provide more complete support for RDF data management.

Acknowledgment. This work is supported by the National Key Research and Development Plan of China (Grant No. 2016YFB1000600 and 2016YFB1000601).

References

1. Manola, F., Miller, E., McBride, B.: RDF primer. W3C Recomm. **10**(1–107), 6 (2004)
2. Dan, B., Guha, R.V.: RDF vocabulary description language 1.0: RDF Schema. W3C Recommendation (2004)

3. Eric, P., Andy, S.: SPARQL query language for RDF. W3C Recommendation (2008)
4. Beleau, F., Nolin, M.A., Tourigny, N., et al.: Bio2RDF: towards a mashup to build bioinformatics knowledge systems. J. Biomed. Inform. **41**(5), 706–716 (2008)
5. Du, J.-H., Wang, H.-F., Ni, Y., Yu, Y.: HadoopRDF: a scalable semantic data analytical engine. In: Huang, D.-S., Ma, J., Jo, K.-H., Gromiha, M.M. (eds.) ICIC 2012. LNCS (LNAI), vol. 7390, pp. 633–641. Springer, Heidelberg (2012). https://doi.org/10.1007/978-3-642-31576-3_80
6. Rohloff, K., Schantz, R.E.: High-performance, massively scalable distributed systems using the MapReduce software framework: the SHARD triple-store. In: Proceedings of the Programming Support Innovations for Emerging Distributed Applications, p. 4. ACM (2010)
7. Gurajada, S., Seufert, S., Miliaraki, I., et al.: TriAD: a distributed shared-nothing RDF engine based on asynchronous message passing. In: Proceedings of the 2014 ACM SIGMOD International Conference on Management of Data, pp. 289–300. ACM (2014)
8. Quilitz, B., Leser, U.: Querying distributed RDF data sources with SPARQL. In: Bechhofer, S., Hauswirth, M., Hoffmann, J., Koubarakis, M. (eds.) ESWC 2008. LNCS, vol. 5021, pp. 524–538. Springer, Heidelberg (2008). https://doi.org/10.1007/978-3-540-68234-9_39
9. Özsu, M.T.: A survey of RDF data management systems. Front. Comput. Sci. **10**(3), 418–432 (2016). https://doi.org/10.1007/s11704-016-5554-y
10. Lipcon, T., Alves, D., Burkert, D., et al.: Kudu: Storage for fast analytics on fast data. Apache (2015). https://kudu.apache.org/kudu.pdf
11. Kornacker, M., Behm, A., Bittorf, V., et al.: Impala: a modern, open-source SQL engine for Hadoop. In: Proceedings of the 7th Conference on Innovative Data Systems Research (CIDR), vol. 1, p. 9 (2015)
12. Zaharia, M., Chowdhury, M., Franklin, M.J., et al.: Spark: cluster computing with working sets. HotCloud **10**(10–10), 95 (2010)
13. Shvachko, K., Kuang, H., Radia, S., et al.: The Hadoop distributed file system. In: Proceedings of 2010 IEEE 26th Symposium on Mass Storage Systems and Technologies (MSST). IEEE, pp. 1–10 (2010)
14. Papailiou, N., Konstantinou, I., Tsoumakos, D., et al.: H2RDF: adaptive query processing on RDF data in the cloud. In: Proceedings of the 21st International Conference on World Wide Web, pp. 397–400. ACM (2012)
15. Vora, M.N.: Hadoop-HBase for large-scale data. In: Proceedings of 2011 International Conference on Computer Science and Network Technology, vol. 1, pp. 601–605. IEEE (2011)
16. Wilkinson, K.: Jena property table implementation. In: The Second Workshop on Scalable Semantic Web Knowledge Base Systems, Georgia, USA (2006)
17. Bornea, M.A., Dolby, J., Kementsietsidis, A., et al.: Building an efficient RDF store over a relational database. In: Proceedings of the 2013 ACM SIGMOD International Conference on Management of Data, pp. 121–132. ACM (2013)
18. Abadi, D.J., Marcus, A., Madden, S.R., et al.: Scalable semantic web data management using vertical partitioning. In: Proceedings of the VLDB Endowment, pp. 411–422 (2007)
19. Schtzle, A., Przyjaciel-Zablocki, M., Skilevic, S., et al.: S2RDF: RDF querying with SPARQL on spark. Proc. VLDB Endow. **9**(10), 804–815 (2016)
20. Shao, B., Wang, H., Li, Y.: The trinity graph engine. Technical Report 161291, Microsoft Research (2012)

21. Zeng, K., Yang, J., Wang, H., et al.: A distributed graph engine for web scale RDF data. Proc. VLDB Endow. **6**(4), 265–276 (2013)
22. Schätzle, A., Przyjaciel-Zablocki, M., Neu, A., Lausen, G.: Sempala: interactive SPARQL query processing on Hadoop. In: Mika, P., et al. (eds.) ISWC 2014. LNCS, vol. 8796, pp. 164–179. Springer, Cham (2014). https://doi.org/10.1007/978-3-319-11964-9_11
23. Xin, R.S., Gonzalez, J.E., Franklin, M.J., Stoica, I.: GraphX: a resilient distributed graph system on spark. In: Proceedings of the First International Workshop on Graph Data Management Experiences and Systems, p. 2. ACM (2013)
24. Schätzle, A., Przyjaciel-Zablocki, M., Berberich, T., Lausen, G.: S2X: graph-parallel querying of RDF with GraphX. In: Wang, F., Luo, G., Weng, C., Khan, A., Mitra, P., Yu, C. (eds.) Big-O(Q)/DMAH -2015. LNCS, vol. 9579, pp. 155–168. Springer, Cham (2016). https://doi.org/10.1007/978-3-319-41576-5_12
25. Ösu, M.T., Valduriez, P.: Principles of Distributed Database Systems. Springer, Heidelberg (2011). https://doi.org/10.1007/978-3-030-26253-2
26. Liu, R., Xu, J.: GCM-bench: a benchmark for RDF data management system on microorganism data. In: Ren, R., Zheng, C., Zhan, J. (eds.) SDBA 2018. CCIS, vol. 911, pp. 3–14. Springer, Singapore (2019). https://doi.org/10.1007/978-981-13-5910-1_1
27. Lehmann, J., Isele, R., Jakob, M., Jentzsch, A., et al.: DBpediaa large-scale, multilingual knowledge base extracted from Wikipedia. Semantic Web **6**(2), 167–195 (2015)
28. Suchanek, F.M., Kasneci, G., Weikum, G.: Yago: a large ontology from wikipedia and wordnet. Web Seman.: Sci. Servi. Agents World Wide Web **6**(3), 203–217 (2008)

Artemis: An Automatic Test Suite Generator for Large Scale OLAP Database

Kaiming Mi[✉], Chunxi Zhang, Weining Qian, and Rong Zhang

East China Normal University, Shanghai, China
{mkm,cxzhang}@stu.ecnu.edu.cn, {wnqian,rzhang}@dase.ecnu.edu.cn

Abstract. We design an automatic test suite generation tool **Artemis** for functionality test of Online Analytical Processing Databases (OLAP DBs). This is the first work which accomplishes the work of DB test by integrating three artifacts, i.e., **data generation**, **workload generation** and **oracle generation**, but promises the scalability, effectiveness and efficiency. The key idea of our approach is to design a deterministic random data generation mechanism, based on which we can instantiate the parameterized queries and calculate the oracles simultaneously by resolving the constraint chains along query trees. Since we provide deterministic random functions for data generations corresponding to a predefined schema, repetitive test and data migration become a trivial job. Random workload generation and automatic oracle calculation instead of differential comparison make abundant and massive scale of test possible. We finally provide extensive experiments to show the performance of **Artemis**.

Keywords: Data generation · Query generation · Result verification

1 Introduction

Application-oriented data management stimulates agile development of databases. Constructing thorough test cases is an necessary and efficient way to guarantee the correctness of database management systems (DBMSs). However the complexity of DBMSs makes test cases enumeration impossible. Realizing automatic DB test has been an urgent expectation.

Usually, building a complete test suite for DBMS consists of three artifacts: database generation, workload (query) generation and ground-truth generation. Database generation is a widely studied issue. There are some commercial and academic tools dedicated to this topic [10,20], which usually generate data by analyzing the given database schema to get the specific generation rules, e.g., data distribution. However, this kind of data generation is query-unaware, and executing the workloads on the test database may not return meaningful results, i.e., empty result set. Instead, query-aware database generation [7,14,16] is proposed to generate databases for specific applications, which is suitable for performance benchmarking instead of functionality verification. In order to satisfy the requirement of thorough test coverage for functions, randomized workload

© Springer Nature Switzerland AG 2021
F. Wolf and W. Gao (Eds.): Bench 2020, LNCS 12614, pp. 74–89, 2021.
https://doi.org/10.1007/978-3-030-71058-3_5

generation is preferred [4,19]. It can generate a large number of queries in parallel, which may be syntactically correct but may not run through the deep logic behind codes [18]. The most difficult thing for randomized workload generation is the verification of running results on the synthetical databases. Currently, this process is commonly completed by *differential testing* [19], which compares execution results to the ones from an authoritative database,e.g., Oracle. A few work, e.g., ADUSA [2,12], have proposed to generate orcales along workload generation, but the computation complexity of these tools seriously lows down the usability. Since these three parts of generation work are usually addressed separately, it is not practical or applicable to simply combine them together to launch functionality test on DBMSs [8], which encumbers DB development seriously.

Therefore, in this paper, we propose to design an automatic test suite generation tool **Artemis** for OLAP DBs, which integrates the three parts of generation work organically but promises scalability, effectiveness and efficiency on DB test. *Scalability* is achieved by designing a deterministic database generation mechanism which can generate large scale of data in full parallel while with little memory consumption. It devises a data-sensitive query generation method, which can generate correct and *effective* workloads in a random style, the most useful method for functional testing [19], to promise high test coverage. Oracles are produced along with the generation of workloads in a manner of calculation instead of execution, which guarantees the *efficiency* of DB verification. **Artemis** is dedicated to serving the functional test of DBs to discover potential logic bugs. To the best of our knowledge, it is the first full-fledged work supporting automatic generation of test suite for OLAP databases.

2 Architecture Overview of Artemis

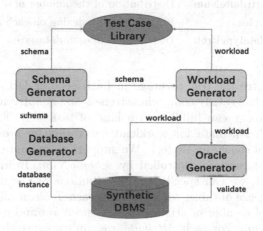

Fig. 1. Overall Architecture of Artemis

The architecture of **Artemis** is divided into four components shown in Fig. 1, which are **Schema Generator, Database Generator, Workload**

Generator and **Oracle Generator**. All the workload cases and database schema together with the corresponding deterministic functions can be put into **Test Case Library**, which can support well for iterative test without the migration of real data in database, but just read the generation functions to import data into the **Synthetic DBMS** and then load the cases to the target DB.

Schema Generator provides a variety of configurable items, and randomly generates a large number of database schemata according to personal needs. **Database Generator** can build a group of deterministic random attribute generators for all non-key attributes in parallel and generate the database instances (DBIs) as needed, given the databases schema. **Workload Generator** generates massive random workloads valid in both semantics and effectiveness considering database schema and random attribute generators. **Oracle Generator** calculates correct results for database verification automatically, given workloads and attribute generators.

3   Database Schema Generation

Table 1. Configuration Knobs for Randomness

Level	Item	Knobs
DB	schemaNum	The number of databases to be generated
DBI	tableNum	Distribution of the number of tables
	tableSize	Distribution of the table size
Table	ForeignkeyNum	distribution of the number of foreign keys
	attributeNum	Distribution of the number of attributes
Attribute	Index	Probability of indexing on each attribute
	datatypeProb	Distribution of each data type

In order to guarantee the test coverage in both code or DB components, the constructed cases shall satisfy comprehensiveness and adaptiveness. Generation-based fuzzy technology can fulfill such a kind of task well [9]. We propose to construct type-rich schemata for workload generation by providing 4-level of randomness control shown in Table 1. We support to generate a random number of databases at runtime controlled by $schemaNum$. Inside each database instance, i.e., DBI, we can specify the distributions of the number of tables $tableNum$ and the size of tables $tableSize$. On each $Table$, it allows to configure the distributions of number of attributes $attributeNum$ and number of foreign keys $foreignkeyNum$. For each $Attribute$, we can configure the indexing probability, together with the existence probability of each data type by $index$ and $datatypeProb$.

The algorithm for generating test database schemata is shown in Algorithm 1. In this algorithm, we describe the generation steps by using the configuration knobs in Table 1. For each database, we randomly generate schema for tables (line 3–24). We can control the number of tables *tableNum* and the size of each table *tableSize* in each database. For each attribute, we assign it a type randomly by *datatypeProb* (line 7). Specifically, for *decimal* and *varchar* types, we need to control the generation precision and length, respectively (line 8–12). Additionally, the number of foreign keys shall be less than the number of tables (line 15–20). Finally, for each attribute, its probability to be indexed is controlled by *index* (line 22).

Algorithm 1: Schema Generator

Input: Schema Configuration Information
Output: Database Schema

```
1  for each database instance do
2  |    Determine the number of tables by randomizing tableNum;
3  |    for each table do
4  |    |    Determine the size of the table by randomizing tableSize;
5  |    |    Determine the number of attributes by randomizing attributeNum;
6  |    |    for each attribute do
7  |    |    |    Determine the type of the attribute by datatypeProb;
8  |    |    |    if datatype is decimal then
9  |    |    |    |    control precision;
10 |    |    |    else if datatype is varchar then
11 |    |    |    |    control length;
12 |    |    |    end
13 |    |    end
14 |    |    Assign foreign key size by randomizing foreighkeyNum;
15 |    |    if the number of generated tables is less than foreighkeyNum then
16 |    |    |    foreignkeyNum= the number of generated tables;
17 |    |    end
18 |    |    for each foreign key do
19 |    |    |    randomly select a table and link to the reference primary key;
20 |    |    end
21 |    |    for each non-key attribute do
22 |    |    |    Determine whether to build the index controlled by index;
23 |    |    end
24 |    end
25 end
```

The overall generation complexity of a database schema is $O(tableNum \cdot (attributeNum + foreignkeyNum))$, decided by the number of tables and the total size of attributes.

4   Data Generation

4.1   Deterministic Random Data Generation

In order to support automatic result verification, we must provide a calculable way generating correct results instead of using comparison databases.

Fig. 2. Attribute generator

Random Function Group for *att* Hit Function is: f(k) = (2k + 1) % 5
$Func_0(k) = k + 2$
$Func_1(k) = 2k - 1$
$Func_2(k) = k^2 + 4$
$Func_3(k) = 3k - 3$
$Func_4(k) = 2k^2 - 2$

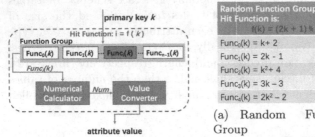

(a) Random Function Group

Seed Set for *att* *Hit Function is:* f(num) = num % 6	
0	2sdvsd78rjbsdij
1	vsd133thberth45
2	dfg356466ndhgwe
3	974jvikmkvnk08t
4	7nsjkjajq823io5
5	nx63bcydjgi872n

(b) Seeds for Varchar

Fig. 3. Example for Varchar typed value generation

We propose to design a deterministic random data generation mechanism for **Artemis**. For each table, the primary keys are generated in order, and other non-primary key attributes are generated deterministically based on primary keys as shown in Fig. 2. For guaranteeing test coverage, we construct a group of random N functions $Func_i()$ ($i < N$) for each attribute, if needed, to generate data on keys, where we can specify the data distribution for each $Func_i()$, e.g., polynomials. For an attribute $attr$ with primary key k and the domain requirement S, it randomizes by a random function, e.g., $f(k) = k\%N$ to select its generation function. Supposing $Func_i(k)$ is selected, it then outputs a seed numerical value $num = Func_i(k)$ which is used as input for our final value converter $coverter()$ according to data type and domain requirements. For a numeric typed $attr$, e.g., int, $coverter()$ may need to satisfy the precision requirement; while for a varchar typed $attr$, $coverter()$ can concate randomized values to a seed string sized L that are generated in advance and satisfy the length distribution requirement.

Let's take an generation example in Fig. 3 for an varchar typed $attr$ with $k = 3$. $attr$ has 5 random functions shown in Fig. 3(a). First we select a random function by $f(k) = (2k + 1)\%5$, which is $Func_2(k)$ with the output 13. We then perform a second random selection on seeds by hit function $f(num) = num\%6$ shown in Fig. 3(b), and we get 1st seed which is **vsd133thberth45**. If $converter()$ is defined to concatecate seeds with the num for $Func_2()$ at both ends, we finally generate the varchar value for $attr$ as 13**vsd133thberth45**13.

4.2 Parallel Data Generation

In order to support to generate a large scale of data, parallel generation is imperative. Data generation based on different database schemata is independent of each other, so we can first implement parallel data generation at the schema level. A database schema generally contains multiple tables. Although there may be referencial dependence represented by primary keys and foreign keys, the generation mechanism of foreign keys does not depend on the generation of referencial primary keys, and then the generation of tables can be completely parallelized.

For even the same table, since the generation of each record is independent, we can divide the primary keys into multiple disjoint intervals, and each interval is assigned to a separate generation thread to achieve parallel data generation, specially:

- First, the generation thread sequentially gets a primary key according to the assigned primary key interval;
- Then, the generation thread calls the attribute generator for the non-key attributes with the primary key as input, and the output of the attribute generator is the value;
- Finally, the generation thread assembles those non-key values corresponding to a specific primary key, which compose a complete record and output to a file asynchronously.

The generation can be totally parallized on each record, if needed, without any storage requirement for any intermediate states. At the same time, in order to avoid conflicts in writing files by multiple threads, each data generating thread will have an independent output file. After the database instance is completely generated, the tables are imported to the target DB in the order of schema referencial topology. So **Artemis** can scale well by parallelizing data generation on multi-nodes and by multi-threads.

5   Workload Generation

We expect to generate large scale of diverse workloads which are valid in semantics and during execution, defined in Definition 1. We take two steps to stochastically generate the valid SQL statements:

1. Generate queries with parametric predicates based on SQL grammar shown in Fig. 4. We generate queries by walking a stochastic parse tree, where the predicates in the queries are parameterized. As shown in Fig. 5, the example query template has 4 constraints with 4 parameters labelled by p_i, $i = 1 - 4$. This step guarantees to generate workloads syntactically and semantically correct.
2. Based on our deterministic data generation mechanism, we can calculate to fill parameters to instantiate queries, which guarantees the validation in workload execution.

Definition 1. *Workload Generation. Given a database schema S and attribute generators, generating a valid workload Q is 1) to make the query satisfy SQL syntax and semantics; 2) fill parameters in predicates which can generate results along the query tree.*

QUERY -> SELECT FROM WHERE GROUP_BY ORDER_BY.
SELECT -> 'SELECT' selectTerm.
selectTerm-> term | aggregate(term).
FROM -> 'FROM' (table | table JOIN table).
WHERE -> 'WHERE' term operator (term | value).
GROUP_BY -> 'GROUP BY' term.
ORDER_BY -> 'ORDER BY' term.
aggregate -> 'MAX' | 'MIN' | 'AVG' | 'COUNT' | 'SUM'.
operator -> '<' | '>' | '<=' | '>=' | '=' | '!='.

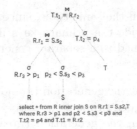

select * from R inner join S on R.r1 = S.s2,T
where R.r3 > p1 and p2 < S.s3 < p3 and
T.t2 = p4 and T.t1 = R.r2

Fig. 4. Example grammar for workload generation

Fig. 5. Query with parametric predicates

5.1 Parameter Instantiation

In grammar-valid SQL templates as shown in Fig. 5, we consider two types of parameters. One is used for range predicates and the other is used for point-value predicates. We have two kinds of range predicates, which are single-sided predicates, e.g., $p_1 < R.r_3$ and double-sided predicates, e.g., $p_2 < S.s_3 < p_3$. For point-value predicates, it includes single value ones, e.g., $T.t_2 = p_4$ and multi-value ones.

We take the quantile-based method to instantiate these parameters. For each parameter, it generates a random quantile s representing its position in the corresponding domain, with $0 \leq s \leq 1$. For example in Fig. 5, we randomize a value $s = 0.5$ for p_1, and p_1 is then instantiate as the median value among current valid values of $R.r_3$. For double-end range parameters, we generate a pair of quantiles and assign the larger quantile to the right end; for multi-value ones, we generate the number of unique quantiles before instantiate parameters along its domain. For each s, we first calculate the maximum max and minimum min values of the involved parameter. By continuously dichotomizing, we generate a new parameter in the candidate space between min and max. And then random sampling is used to validate the correctness of the parameter based on MonteCarlo algorithm [21]. The complexity for each parameter instantiation is $O(log(max - min))$.

6 Oracle Generation

Here we will introduce the final step of oracle generation by traversing the example query "select * from R inner join S on $R.r_1 = S.s_2$, T where $R.r_3 > 3$ and $5 < S.s_3 < 10$ and $T.t_2 = 8$ and $T.t_1 = R.r_2$" on Tables R, S and T shown in Fig. 6. In order to simplify the explanation, each attribute is defined with one generation function, as labeled by $Func$ in Fig. 6(a). For example, Table R has a foreign key r_2 referencing to Table T on t_1, where the generation function for r_2 is $Func2 : k + 1$ with k as the key value for current row. Filter and join predicates in the example workloads control the middle and final results along the query tree. Since we focus on the correctness of queries, we don't care the actual execution process inside DB implementation, such as join order or join types, which does not manipulate the oracles.

We construct the primary-key-based constraint chains for the attributes involved in predicates for oracle generation. There are two kinds of constraints for attributes, which is the local constraints and the global constraint. **Local constraints** represent the value dependency to the primary key of current table itself, e.g. the predicates $R.r_3 > 3$ in n_1 in Fig. 6(b). Since $R.r_3$ has the generation function $Func3 : 2k+3$ based on its primary keys, predicate $R.r_3 > 3$ is then explained as $2k + 3 > 3$, which decides the candidate keys satisfying this constraint. **Global constraints** are caused by the foreign key dependency among tables, and control the selection of rows satisfying the foreign key dependency. Let's take n_4 for example, which has an equal join predicate $R.r_1 = S.s_2$ and $S.s_2$ references to $R.r_1$. Since in n_2, Table S has a local constraint $5 < S.s_3 < 10$, a part of rows satisfy this constraints can be joined to Table R in n_4. $S.s_2$ and $S.s_3$ have generation functions as $Func : 2k + 1$ and $Func : k + 2$ respectively. Considering both R and S, for items transferred to $n4$, they shall satisfy the following constraints on local keys k:

$$Table\ R \begin{cases} 2k_R + 3 > 3, local\ constraints\ from\ n1 \\ k_R \geq 1, S.s_2\ 2k + 1 \geq 1\ from\ n2 \\ k_R\%2 = 1, S.s_2\ shall\ be\ interger\ typed\ from\ n2 \\ 5 < \dfrac{k_R - 1}{2} + 2 < 10.\ local\ constraints\ on\ foreign\ keys\ from\ n2 \end{cases}$$

$$Table\ S \begin{cases} 5 < k_S + 2 < 10, local\ constraints\ from\ n2 \\ 2 \cdot (2 \cdot k_S + 1) + 3 > 3, R.r_3\ 2k + 3 \geq 3\ from\ n1 \end{cases}$$

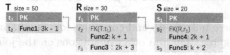

(a) Dependency among Tables R, S and T

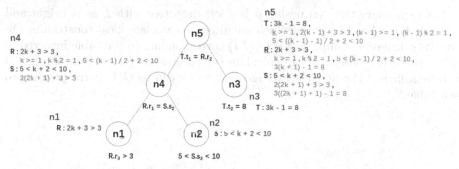

Purple: local constraint; Blue: global constraint from n4; Orange: global constraint from n5

(b) Constraint Chains

Fig. 6. Oracle generation example

The complete oracle generation algorithm is shown in Algorithm 2. We show an example constraints resolving based on Fig. 6(b). First we get all constraints in filter predicates (line 2), which are $2k + 3 > 3$ for Table R in $n1$, $5 < k + 2 < 10$ for Table S in n_2 and $3k - 1 = 8$ for Table T in n_3, colored in purple. We then put two join predicates to $jNodes$ (line 3), which locate in n_4 and n_5. We process these join predicates in a bottom-up way. In n_4 with join predicate JP_1: $R.r_1 = S.s_2$, we add global constraints to both R and S (line 4–9). For example, for S, it inserts a global constraints $2(2k + 1) + 3 > 3$ from n_1 on R for $R.r_3$ together with the original local constraints from n_2 and R will also insert the global constraints from S, colored in blue. In n_5, it has $JP2 : T.t_1 = R.r_2$. $JP2$ will generate global constraints on T, R and S which is caused from R, colored in orange. After we construct all constaints for the query tree, we generate results in a bottom-up way (line 10) and do other operations (line 11), e.g., aggregation, which will not affect the result size along each branch. In such a way, we can construct oracles for each generated workload.

Algorithm 2: Oracle Generation

Input: Query Tree and Data Generators
Output: Orcales

1 Traverse the query tree by breadth first search to get all query nodes into $nodes$;
2 Put filter predicates into $filters$ to get local constraints LC on tables;
3 Traverse the query tree bottom-up and put all join nodes into $jNodes$ in order;
4 **for** each $jn \in jNodes$ between table $table_l$ and $table_r$ **do**
5 | Collect constraints from child nodes for $table_l$ and $table_r$;
6 | Update global constraints based on the reference from $table_r$ for $table_l$;
7 | Update global constraints based on the reference from $table_l$ for $table_r$;
8 | Update global constraints based on previous references from other tables;
9 **end**
10 traverse the query tree bottom-up and construct join results in order;
11 perform selection, aggregation and other operations on the join results;
12 return $results$ in root node;

For each query tree, supposing it is a left deep tree with L as it height and $2^L - 1$ nodes, it has $\lfloor L \rfloor$ leaves which are filters to calculate local constraints. On root, its calculation complexity is $O(\lfloor L \rfloor)$ corresponding to the table involved in leaves. However, each table can calculate the constraints for itself in parallel. If we have sufficient threads, the average complexity can be $O(1)$ corresponding to each table.

7 Experiment

Data configuration																
item	tableNum			tableSize			columnNum			datatype						
range/kind	20-40	40-60	60-80	5w-10w	10w-30w	30w-50w	10-20	20-50	50-100	int	float	double	decimal	datetime	varchar	bool
ratio	0.4	0.3	0.3	0.3	0.3	0.4	0.2	0.3	0.5	0.2	0.1	0.1	0.2	0.1	0.2	0.1

Query configuration				
item	selectedtableNum	predicateNum	groupByNum	orderByNum	aggregationNum
range	1-5	1-5	0-2	0-2	0-3

Fig. 7. Default configuration

Environment. We perform all our experiments on a cluster with 8 nodes. Each node is equipped with 2 Intel Xeon E5-2620 @ 2.0 GHz CPUs, 64 GB memory and 3TB HDD disk configured in RAID-5. The cluster is connected using 1 Gigabit Ethernet. The calculation tool we use for constraint resolving is Mathematica [1].

Input. The input to **Artemis** is the customized configuration file for database schema generation and workload generation, which includes the number of schemata, the number of attributes, distribution of data types, and workload information, example is shown in Fig. 7. According to the configuration,we generate schema and workload randomly. And then we generate the DBIs. We import the database schema and the *DBI* into the target database, i.e. MySQL 5.7.

Setting. The default database schema and workload configurations are shown in Fig. 7, where *range* or *kind* specify the scale or data type of the element, and *ratio* defines the data distribution of the element. Defaultedly each node is configured with the number of threads equal to the kernels.

Since there is no applicable comparison work which can generate data, workloads and oracles as a complete suite but guarantee scalability, effectiveness and efficiency, we evaluate *Artemis* in detail in this part.

7.1 Data Generation

We first randomly generate DBIs with the schema following the default setting defined in Fig. 7. In Fig. 8, it shows the data generation throughputs per node of *Artemis*, i.e., generation rate on each node, as we vary the number of nodes. It keeps a almost stable generation rate on each node, i.e., about 0.49 GB/s; increasing the number of nodes, the generation time decreases linearly. Since we take random generation models, different schema will affect the data generation rate, so there will be slight fluctuations in the generation rate.

Specifically, Fig. 9 shows the data generation time of *Artemis* under different scales (i.e., number of tuples) with three different database schema which follow the statistics requirement of the default schema configuration. All the tuples are generated by only one node. Since we take the totally random way to generate databases, we can only control the generation statistically consistent with the configuration settings. For different complexities of the randomly generated schema, which are the size of attributes and the types of attributes, it may meet

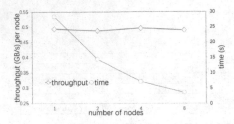

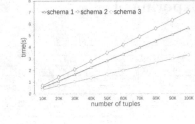

Fig. 8. Multiple nodes   **Fig. 9.** Data scale

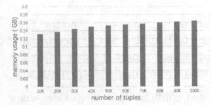

Fig. 10. Memory consumption   **Fig. 11.** Relative error of re^p

different generation time. For example, a table with 10 boolean typed attributes will be much smaller than the one with 10 string typed attributes. As shown in Fig. 9, for three different schema, it takes different time to generate even the same number of tuples. We can also find data generation time always increases linearly with the number of tuples, that is to say, *Artemis* is linearly scalable to data size. For the generation of each tuple is independent and the generated tuples need not be stored in memory, the data generation throughput is always stable. In Fig. 10, we show the average memory consumptions under the three different schema. Our memory is mainly used for java *JVM* and *Artemis* has little pressure in memory requirement.

It can be see that our data generation method is almost linearly scalable, and can be easily configured in parallel, which makes it capable of supporting industrial scale database generation.

7.2 Query Generation

Since we take the random sampling technology for parameter instantiations, it may introduce errors in query parameter generations, which causes unexpected results. In order to demonstrate the effectiveness of our instantiation method, we calculate two kinds of relative errors defined by re^p and re^c. re^p represents the relative error between the expected parameter value p^{exp} and the generated one p^{gen}; re^c represents the relative error between the expected candidate size c^{exp} and the generated one c^{gen}.

$$re^p = \frac{|p^{exp} - p^{gen}|}{p^{exp}} \qquad re^c = \frac{|c^{exp} - c^{gen}|}{c^{exp}}; \qquad (1)$$

Figure 11 shows the *min*, *max* and *avg* re^p for random generated queries sized 50–250, with default configuration. The maximum re^p among these queries is less than 2.2%, and the average re^p is about 0.5%. The maximum re^c among these queries is less than 2.0%, and the average re^c is about 0.4% as shown in Fig. 12.

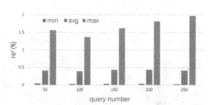

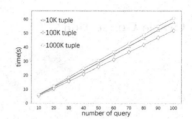

Fig. 12. Relative error of re^c

Fig. 13. The impact of data size on query generation

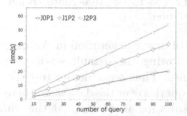

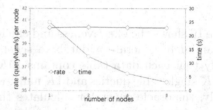

Fig. 14. The impact of query complexity on query generation

Fig. 15. Query generation on multiple nodes

Figure 13 shows the impact of data size to the efficiency of query generation. We generate one database with fifty tables sized $10K, 100K$, and $1000K$ tuples using the default table configuration. We randomly generate 100 queries with default configuration by one thread. As shown in Fig. 13, for different data scales, the query generation speed is almost the same, which proves that our query generation algorithm is scalable for the size of the data. The tiny difference in generation time is affected by parameter types, which lead to different parameter instantiation cost. Figure 14 shows the generation efficiency of queries with different complexities. The complexity of a query in our work is simply defined as the number of joins and the number of parameters, which are used in constraint chains to calculate the size of result set. In Fig. 14, **J** and **P** represent *join* and *parameter* respectively. For example, $J1P2$ refers to a query with 1 join and 2 parameters in predicates. Generally, query generation time is mainly affected by the number of parametric predicates, which can be proved by Fig. 14. So, $J2P3$ generates queries only two times slower than the simplest one $J0P1$ on average, for it has 3 times more parameters to instantiate than $JOP1$. In Fig. 15, we generate $1K$ queries based on the default configuration. It keeps a almost stable generation rate on each node; when increasing the number of nodes from 1 to 8, the generation time decreases linearly.

It can be see that **Artemis** can generate workloads scalably and the parameter instantiation algorithm can guarantee the precision with small bias.

7.3   Oracle Generation

Type	Query Num	Correct Num	Avg. calculate time(ms)
Single-Table	1000	1000	1057.8
Multi-Table	1000	1000	1643.8

Fig. 16. Effectiveness of oracle generation

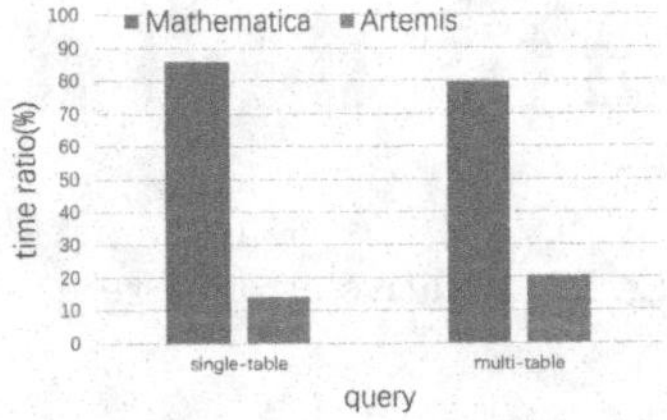

Fig. 17. Calculation time consumption distribution

Figure 16 shows the effectiveness and efficiency of oracle generation in **Artemis**. We randomly generate a database schema following the default setting, and specify that each data table contains $10K$ tuples. Then we generate test data, and $1K$ single table queries and $1K$ multi-table queries over the database schema. Finally, the oracle generator calculates the results for all queries. At the same time, we import the generated test data into MySQL, and execute all queries in MySQL. By Comparing the query results of MySQL with the results of our oracle generator, we find our calculation is correct, as shown in Fig. 16, which proves the correctness in syntax and semantics. The calculate time is a little different for the complexity of queries and the mainly overhead is the call to Mathematica which is used to solve the constraint chain. As shown in Fig. 17, we compare the time consumption of **Artemis** and Mathematica for the single table queries and multi-table queries. It can be seen that around 80% of the time are consumed by Mathematica and our design is efficient. In the future, we may integrate some other more efficient calculation tool to support **Artemis**.

Calculation-based oracle generation and automatic verification has great advantage in improving test efficiency, compared to the usage of authoritative databases, especially for $OLAP$ applications.

8   Related Work

Synthetic data generation, query (workload) and oracle creation are three fundamental artifacts supporting functionality verification of Databases.

For data generation, it mainly covers two categories, which are query-unaware [3,10,20] and query-aware ones [7,14,15]. For Query-unaware ones, they take data characteristics of the target database into consideration for synthesizing data, usually with the requirement of generation scalability. The challenge with these work is that test queries run on synthetic data may not generate meaningful results. It can cause large amount of ineffective effort in testing DBMSs. Query-aware ones are usually application sensitive, with limited number of query templates as one of the inputs for data generation. They devote to generate databases on which executing the test queries can obtain desired intermediate query results as the real workloads do. This kind of workload generation is designed for performance benchmarking instead of functionality verification, and it aims for database comparison/selection or optimization. For it lacks of case diversity, it is not thorough for database testing.

For query generation, RAGS [19] is the earliest known random SQL generator, serving for the testing of Microsoft SQL Server. RAGS can generate a large number of random workloads that satisfy the SQL syntax based on the perdefined schema of the test database. Since the effective workloads are less than 50% in RAGS, GARan [4] designs self-adaptive random testing technologies to find useful test cases. It uses genetic algorithms to improve the case coverage based on the execution feedback of workloads. Both the work mentioned above verify execution by running workloads on multiple database systems, and then judge the correctness by comparing all of the returned result sets line by line. The other type of work is to use the predefined workload templates for workload generation [16,17]. QGen [17] is used by TPC-DS for performance testing. Work in [16] aims to fill the parameters in query templates satisfying the specific requirement in workload characteristics based on an existing database instance. These work can only have a limited number of workloads which is not sufficient for database testing.

For orcale creation, some work [6,12] generate the results along with generating test cases. Both the data generation and workload generation of ADUSA [12] rely on Alloy [11]. However, the complexity of Alloy is too high to support large-scale test database generation. At the same time, the workload types supported by ADUSA are conservative and can not meet the needs of testing. Work in [2,13] propose to improve ADUSA by integrating query generation, data generation and oracle creation into an automated test framework. However, they still have insufficient support for workload types and are unable to support testing on large data sets. Work [6] extends Reverse Query Processing (RQP) technology proposed in [5], generates the queries and the expected results first and then generates the database correspondingly. But the cost of generating database is very expensive, which is not feasible for generating large OLAP databases.

9   Conclusion

We have presented a deterministic random data generation approach supporting automatic and thorough functionality test for OLAP database, based on which we implement a prototype **Artemis** covering all the three artifacts in DB testing. The main advantages of our work includes: 1) data generation is scalable for producing large scale of database. 2) query generation can be exhaustive and guarantee the effectiveness of queries. 3) oracle generation is automatically calculable, which can promise the test efficiency. However, our current design can only process read operations without any write, the performance of our tool is restricted by Mathematica and complex data analysis is not supported, all of which will be left as our future work.

References

1. https://www.wolfram.com/mathematica/
2. Abdul Khalek, S., Khurshid, S.: Automated SQL query generation for systematic testing of database engines. In ASE 2010, pp. 329–332 (2010)
3. Alexandrov, A., Tzoumas, K., Markl, V.: Myriad: scalable and expressive data generation. In: VLDB 2012, vol. 5, issue 12, pp. 1890–1893 (2012)
4. Bati, H., Giakoumakis, L., Herbert, S., Surna, A.: A genetic approach for random testing of database systems. In: VLDB 2007, pp. 1243–1251 (2007)
5. Binnig, C., Kossmann, D., Lo, E.: Reverse query processing. In: ICDE 2007, pp. 506–515 (2007)
6. Binnig, C., Kossmann, D., Lo, E., Saenzbadillos, A.: Automatic result verification for the functional testing of a query language. In: ICDE 2008, pp. 1534–1536 (2008)
7. Binnig, C., Kossmann, D., Lo, E., Özsu, M.T.: Qagen generating query-aware test databases. In: SIGMOD 2007, pp. 341–352 (2007)
8. Hamlin, A., Herzog, J.: A test-suite generator for database systems. In: HPEC 2014, pp. 1–6 (2014)
9. He, S., Manns, G., Saunders, J., Wang, W., Pollock, L., Soffa, M.L.: A statistics-based performance testing methodology for cloud applications. In: ESEC/FSE 2019 (2019)
10. Hoag, J.E., Thompson, C.W.: A parallel general-purpose synthetic data generator. SIGMOD Rec **36**(1), 19–24 (2007)
11. Jackson, D.: Alloy: a lightweight object modelling notation. ACM Trans. Softw. Eng. Methodol. **11**(2), 256–290 (2002)
12. Khalek, S.A., Elkarablieh, B., Laleye, Y.O., Khurshid, S.: Query-aware test generation using a relational constraint solver. In: ASE 2008, pp. 238–247 (2008)
13. Khalek, S.A., Khurshid, S.: Systematic testing of database engines using a relational constraint solver. In: ICST 2011, pp. 50–59 (2011)
14. Li, Y., Zhang, R., Yang, X., Zhang, Z., Zhou, A.: Touchstone: generating enormous query-aware test databases. In: ATC 2018, pp. 575–586 (2018)
15. Lo, E., Cheng, N., Lin, W.W.K., Hon, W.K., Choi, B.: Mybenchmark: generating databases for query workloads. VLDB J. **23**(6), 895–913 (2014)
16. Mishra, C., Koudas, N., Zuzarte, C.: Generating targeted queries for database testing. In: SIGMOD 2008, pp. 499–510 (2008)
17. Poess, M., Stephens, J.M.: Generating thousand benchmark queries in seconds. in: VLDB 2004, pp. 1045–1053 (2004)
18. Rigger, M., Su, Z.: Testing database engines via pivoted query synthesis. arXiv: Databases (2020)
19. Slutz, D.R.: Massive stochastic testing of SQL. In: VLDB 1998, pp. 618–622 (1998)

20. Torlak, E.: Scalable test data generation from multidimensional models. In: SIG-SOFT FSE 2012, p. 36 (2012)
21. Zhou, J., Aghili, N., Ghaleini, E.N., Bui, D.T., Tahir, M.M., Koopialipoor, M.: A Monte Carlo simulation approach for effective assessment of flyrock based on intelligent system of neural network. Eng. Comput. **36**(2), 1–11 (2020). https://doi.org/10.1007/s00366-019-00726-z

OStoreBench: Benchmarking Distributed Object Storage Systems Using Real-World Application Scenarios

Guoxin Kang[1], Defei Kong[2], Lei Wang[1], and Jianfeng Zhan[1,3(✉)]

[1] State Key Laboratory of Computer Architecture, Institute of Computing
Technology, Chinese Academy of Sciences, Beijing, China
{kangguoxin,wanglei,zhanjianfeng}@ict.ac.cn
[2] ByteDance, Beijing, China
kongdefei@bytedance.com
[3] University of Chinese Academy of Sciences, Beijing, China

Abstract. Their hierarchical organization and metadata management limit the traditional file storage systems' scalability. The industry widely uses Distributed Object Storage Systems because they keep the advantages of traditional file storage systems, e.g., data sharing, and alleviate the scalability issue through benefiting from the flat namespaces and integrating the meta-data in the object. However, evaluating and comparing distributed object storage systems remains a significant challenge. The existing DOSS benchmarks provide simple read/write operations without considering the complex workload characteristics in request arrival patterns and request size distribution. This paper presents an Object Storage Benchmark suite, named OStoreBench, which characterizes critical paths of three real-world application scenarios, including online service, big data analysis, and file backup. We evaluate three state-of-the-practice object storage systems using OStoreBench, including Ceph, Openstack Swift, and Haystack. The benchmark suite is publicly available from https://github.com/EVERYGO111/OStoreBench.

Keywords: Object Storage · Benchmark · Real-world application scenarios · QoS

1 Introduction

Object storage systems [1] alleviate the scalability issue that files storage systems [2] face. Specifically, object storage systems adopt a flat namespace organization [3] and an expandable metadata functionality [4], enabling them to deal with massive unstructured data. Object storage systems have been applied to more and more application scenarios and become an essential service of major cloud service providers, such as Amazon S3 [5], Alibaba cloud Object Storage Service (OSS) [6], and Qiniu cloud storage [7].

F. Wolf and W. Gao (Eds.): Bench 2020, LNCS 12614, pp. 90–105, 2021.
https://doi.org/10.1007/978-3-030-71058-3_6

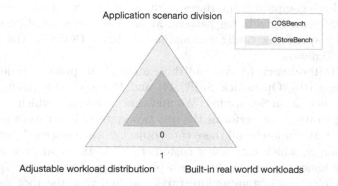

Fig. 1. Why we need OStoreBench? "0" means do not include the feature on the corner, "1" is the opposite.

To promote the development of distributed object storage systems (in short, DOSS), it is necessary to design and implement a benchmark suite evaluating state-of-the-art and state-of-the-practice DOSS. However, there are two main challenges.

First, various DOSS establish no standard interfaces, making the comparison between different DOSS more difficult. Existing benchmarks are principally designed for file storage systems, incompatible with DOSS because the former's POSIX-based workloads include operations on meta-data directories. In contrast, the latter's workloads do not have.

Second, COSBench [8], proposed by Intel, is widely used to evaluate DOSS. It provides simple read/write operations without considering the complex workload regarding request arrival patterns and request size distribution. So the benchmarks like COSBench can't fully represent essential characteristics of real-world workloads, and the evaluation results can not reflect the performances of the storage systems. That is why we need a new object storage benchmark suite, as explained in Fig. 1. As there are numerous application scenarios, it is nontrivial to characterize typical workloads. We propose a benchmark suite for distributed object storage systems, named OStoreBench, which simulates the critical paths [9] of object storage services from query delivering to response receiving. Instead of only focusing on partial stages, e.g., network transferring performance or storage performance, our benchmarks abstract the essential tasks of cloud object storage services [9], comprehensively disclosing the potential performance bottlenecks, and hence they are of great significance for cloud service quality.

We choose three typical workloads from real-world object storage scenarios: online service workloads, big data analytics workloads, and file backup workloads. We include these workloads into OStoreBench with characterizing request distributions, sizes, and types.

To suit for incompatible interfaces of different DOSS, we wrap other interfaces of DOSS with the adapter pattern. Meanwhile, users could customize the workloads by specifying configurations and evaluate DOSS in the concerned application scenarios.

We use OStoreBench to evaluate three state-of-the-practice object storage systems: Ceph [10], Openstack Swift [11] and Haystack [12] (using its opensource implementation Seaweedfs). We find that Seaweedfs, which uses a small file merging strategy, outperforms the rest two systems in terms of latency and throughput. Unfortunately, all these three object storage systems' performances fluctuate sharply, which may lower customer satisfaction and productivity. To address this issue, we first analyze such phenomenon from the perspectives of design principles and system architectures and find that the root cause is the imbalanced distribution of workloads among data nodes.

Our contributions are summarized as follows:

1. We implement OStoreBench, a scenario benchmark suite for distributed object storage systems. OStoreBench wraps different DOSS interfaces with the adapter pattern and provides users with scenario benchmarks that characterize object storage services' critical paths. Using the real workloads, the evaluation results using OStoreBench could represent DOSS performances in real-world applications.
2. We evaluate three state-of-the-practice object storage systems with OStoreBench and find that all these three systems' performances fluctuate sharply.
3. Through extensive experiments, we find that the root cause of the three state-of-the-practice system's performance fluctuation is the unbalanced distribution of requests among data nodes.

2   Related Work

In this section, we introduce the related work about distributed object storage systems and benchmarks for them.

2.1   Mainstream Distributed Object Storage System

The mainstream DOSS includes general distributed storage systems like Ceph [10], Lustre [13], and dedicated storage systems optimized for specific scenarios, such as Haystack [12] and Ambry [14]. The main advantages of DOSS are as follows:

Scalability. Not like traditional file storage systems, of which the lookup operations become a bottleneck when dealing with massive files due to the hierarchical directory structure, DOSS adopt flat address spaces, which makes it easier to locate and retrieve the data across regions. Moreover, DOSS also provide scalable metadata management. Openstack Swift adopts consistency hash [15] and Ceph uses CRUSH which obtains locations of files by calculation [16]. By simply adding nodes, Ceph can scale to petabytes and beyond.

Table 1. Benchmarks for distributed storage system

Benchmark	Configurable request distribution	Built-in real-world workloads	Target system	
			File-oriented system	*Object-oriented storage system*
Fio			✓	
Filebench	✓		✓	
Iozone			✓	
Postmark	✓	✓	✓	
COSBench	✓			✓
OStoreBench	✓	✓		✓

Application-Friendly. Most distributed file systems, which use POSIX protocol, provide interfaces such as open, close, read, write, and lseek. However, the interfaces provided by object storage systems are usually RESTful-
style APIs based on HTTP protocol. Specifically, PUT, GET and DELETE of
HTTP requests are used to upload, download and delete files respectively. Such
RESTful-style interfaces are more friendly to the web and mobile application
developers.

High Availability. Traditional file systems often use RAID to backup data.
DOSS adopt an object-level multiple replication strategy that is much simpler
than block-level redundancy in traditional file systems.

2.2 Benchmarks for Distributed Storage Systems

We list existing benchmarks for storage systems from the perspectives of IO
R/W supports, workloads, and target systems in Table 1. File storage systems
adopt portable operating system interface (POSIX) [17], thus, the benchmarks
for file storage systems are designed with POSIX semantics. Flexible IO Tester
(fio) [18] is mainly used for block devices or file systems while it doesn't consider
the IO access pattern. IOZone [19] is a file system benchmark similar to fio.
Filebench [20] can simulate the IO loads of the application layer according to
user configurations and currently only supports POSIX based file systems. Unlike
Filebench, Postmark [21] provides real traces of workloads such as email services
and online news services. However, traditional POSIX-based benchmarks are
incompatible with distributed object storage systems, because the POSIX-based
workloads include operations on metadata directories while the workloads of
object storage systems don't. Industry primarily uses Cosbench [8] proposed by
Intel to evaluate DOSS. It can evaluate Amazon S3, Ceph and Openstack Swift
but only provides simple read and write operations, so it can't describe the access
pattern of real workloads of the object storage systems. Besides, YCSB (Yahoo!

Cloud Serving Benchmark) [22] and its extented versions [23,24] are designed for nosql databases.

2.3 Workloads Behavior and Storage Access Patterns

In order to guarantee the response time, the online service workloads are usually allocated with the resources (CPU, Memory, and Disk) required by the peak load. But in fact the resource usage of the online service workloads are very low [25]. And big data analysis workloads are mostly throughput-oriented [3]. Therefore, our app-level workloads are not only of great significance for co-located workload research [25,26], but also for real-time data analysis research directly in the object storage system [27,28]. Grant's backup workloads characterization study [29] focuses on comparison the different characteristics between backup and primary storage systems. The size and access pattern of Store and Retrieve data streams received by Dropbox has been explored in this study [30]. Glauber [31] analyzes the characteristics of the workload from the perspective of the Dropbox client, and models the behavior of the client.

3   Benchmark Building

In this section, we first list the requirements for building the benchmark of DOSS, then introduce how we design and implement the benchmark.

3.1   Requirements

Unlike the benchmarks for traditional file storage systems, there are three different requirements when building a general benchmark for DOSS:

Scalability. As distributed object storage systems are applied on large-scale storage clusters, the evaluation tool should be scalable enough to generate large-scale workloads, such that the bottlenecks of DOSS could be recognised.

Compatibility. Unlike file systems which have a standard POSIX interface, there is no unified interface standard for object storage systems. To compare the performances between different object storage systems, the benchmark should be compatible with different interfaces.

Typical Workloads. The workloads of the benchmark for traditional file storage system contain operations on metadata directories, so these workloads are incompatible with object storage systems. To evaluate the performance of DOSS precisely, the benchmark should provide typical open-loop workloads which are abstracted from real-world application scenarios of DOSS.

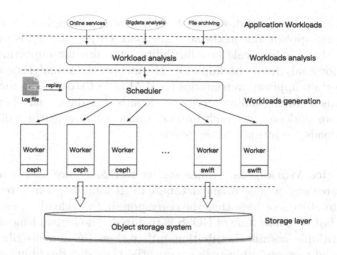

Fig. 2. OStoreBench design.

3.2   The Design of OStoreBench

We propose a methodology for constructing the DOSS benchmark which consists of 5 steps: (1) Investigate the application scenarios and future development trends of the object storage systems, (2) Classify the application scenarios
according to the characteristics of the application workloads, (3) Analyze the
workloads of different application scenarios and build the load model, (4) Simulate the workloads of object storage systems based on the established load model,
(5) Build object storage system evaluation tools based on the simulations and
different software stacks.

Under the guidance of our proposed methodology, we design and implement
OStoreBench. Figure 2 shows the structure of OStoreBench which consists of
four layers: application workloads, workloads modeling, workloads generation
and storage systems. In the first two layers, we classify the workloads based
on the investigation of cloud services and model the typical workloads. In the
third layer, we generate the workloads and deliver them to the storage systems.
OStoreBench uses the Master/Slave architecture to ensure the scalability. The
scheduler (master) generates specific loads according to the user configurations
and allocates them to the workers (slave), then the workers deliver requests
to DOSS. The number of workers is specified by the user and the workers are
created by the scheduler. If the loads become heavier, the scheduler will create
workers on the new physical nodes. Besides, we leverage coroutine technology
in Golang [32] to make full use of the multi-core resources. We also adopt the
adapter pattern to make OStoreBench compatible with different interfaces of
DOSS.

The workloads of DOSS have different features in different scenarios. Through
our investigation, we find that the online service (such as Google) and the big
data analysis (such as Hadoop) are two kinds of the most important applica-

tions in the computing cloud, the file backup (such as Dropbox) is one of the most important applications in the storage cloud. Object storage is suitable for applications that require scale and flexibility, and also for importing existing data stores for analytics or backup [33]. Meanwhile, data analysis and backup are two important application scenarios for IBM object storage. So three typical real workloads including online service workloads, big data analysis workloads and file backup workloads are built into OStoreBench. The features of the three typical workloads are introduced as follows.

Online Service Workloads. Online service workloads are mainly abstracted from web search engines and online database in ACloud [34], which require real-time access to objects or files, thus the corresponding workloads are sensitive to latency and fast response time of DOSS is required. The arrival time of requests follows logarithmic normal distribution rather than Poisson distribution [35]. The size of read requests subjects to exponential Gaussian distribution and 98% of the sizes of those files are less than 400KB [34]. The size of write requests subjects to Zipf distribution and 93% of the sizes of those files are less than 400KB. These observations are similar to [36]. There are more read requests than write requests.

Big Data Analysis Workloads. Big data analysis workloads are abstracted from the Hadoop clusters at Yahoo!, which dedicates to supporting a mix of data-intensive MapReduce jobs like processing advertisement targeting information [37]. Big data analysis applications aim to analyze the data stored in object storage systems and then store the results in the storage systems. The analyzing procedure usually consists of sequential phases like data preprocessing, statistics and mining operations, with the output of current phase is taken as the input of the next phase. Temporary files generated in the intermediate phases will be deleted and only the results of the last phase will be stored. The arrival time of requests is random. The size of 20% files are zero and 80% of the remaining files are more than 10G in size [37]. The read, write and delete operations are frequent and periodic.

File Backup Workloads. File backup workloads are abstracted from Dropbox system [30]. A typical file backup scenario is the cloud disks such as Dropbox, where users back up files through the client and rarely download files from it. The client periodically detects file changes and continuously uploads new files to the cloud storage service [31]. The size of 40%– 80% requests is less than 100 KB. There are more read requests than write requests.

3.3   The Implementation of OStoreBench

The workloads generation layer in Fig. 1 mainly consists of two parts: the scheduler and the worker. The scheduler receives user configuration2 and replays log

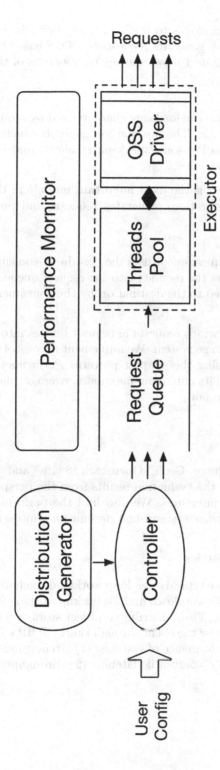

Fig. 3. OStoreBench components.

files, then allocates the workloads to workers. The worker is a key part of our workloads generation, which generates requests to DOSS based on the loads allocated by the scheduler. Figure 3 shows the key components of the worker which are introduced as follows.

Distribution Generator. The loads are characterized by request distribution, request size and request type. The distribution generator includes a variety of distribution models such as Poisson, Zipf, logarithmic normal.

Controller. The controller is the most important module in the worker. Controller receives user configurations, generates requests and puts requests into request queues.

Request Queue. The request queue uses the "producer-consumer model". The producer (controller) places the requests into the request queue. The requests in request queues are delivered to the destination by the consumer (worker).

Executor. The executor wraps requests in request queues into HTTP requests and sends them to the storage system. We implement drivers of different **O**bject **S**torage **S**ystem (OSS) using the adapter pattern. *Performance monitor* The performance monitor exhibits minimum, maximum, average, and 99th percentile latencies as well as throughput.

4 Evaluation

In this section, we evaluate Ceph, Openstack Swift, and Seaweedfs with OStoreBench and analyze the evaluation results from the perspectives of design principles and system architectures. We also find the performance fluctuation problem of these three storage systems and present an approach to address it.

4.1 Approach and Metrics

OStoreBench provides three typical open-loop workloads including online service workloads, big data analysis workloads and file backup workloads to Ceph, Openstack Swift, and Seaweedfs. These distributed object storage systems accept the remote procedure call sent by the client through the TCP/IP socket. We use two metrics to measure the performance of systems: (1) latency, including minimum, average, maximum, and 99th percentile latency; (2) throughput.

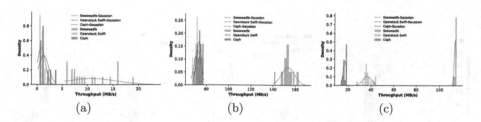

(a)   (b)   (c)

Fig. 4. (a) The variation of throughput under the online service workloads; (b) The variation of throughput under the big data analysis workloads; (c) The variation of throughput under the file archiving workloads.

4.2 Experimental Setup

Our experimental environment is a cluster consisting of 4 storage nodes and a master/proxy node with three data replication. The server includes one Intel Xeon E5310 @ 1.6 GHz CPU with 4 core (8 hyper threads), a DRAM of 4 GB and a disk of 8TB. The machines run an Ubuntu 16.04 distribution with the Linux kernel version 4.4. All machines are configured with Intel 82573E 1GbE NICs. We use Seaweedfs version 1.87, OpenStack Swift version 3.0 and Ceph version 13.2.10. We remain the default configurations of these three storage systems. Though the performance of the three object storage systems mentioned above will increase or change in their future releases, our results of experiments are still meaningful because they demonstrate the value of OStoreBench in facilitating performance comparison and system optimization.

4.3 Experimental Results

The Evaluation for Online Service Workloads. The arrival time of requests in online service workloads satisfies the log-normal distribution. The request size satisfies Zipf distribution and is less than 64 MB. Figure 4(a) shows the probability density function of the throughput under online service workloads. Seaweedfs achieves the highest average throughput which is 10.8 MB per second. Ceph's average throughput is 1.3 MB per second and Swift's average throughput is 0.9 MB per second. The dashed line is a curve of Gaussian distribution fitting to the histogram. Figure 4(a) shows that the throughput of online service workloads fluctuates sharply. The latency of Seaweedfs is regarded as a baseline and the latency of the other systems is depicted based on their multiples of the baseline. The unit of latency is milliseconds. In this paper, such processing is used for all latency evaluations. Figure 5 shows the read and write latencies under the online service workloads. It is apparent that the average latency of Openstack Swift is more 30 times than Seaweedfs. Although Ceph is much better than Openstack, its latency is still more 20 times than Seaweedfs in the worst case. The latency distributions of Seaweedfs and Openstack Swift are relatively plain. But the latency of Ceph fluctuates sharply, and the read latency increases abruptly at some points.

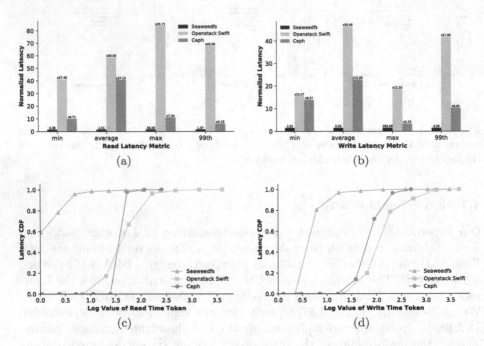

Fig. 5. Read and write latencies under the online service workloads. (a) Read request latency, (b) Write request latency, (c) Logarithmic read latency CDF, (d) Logarithmic write latency CDF.

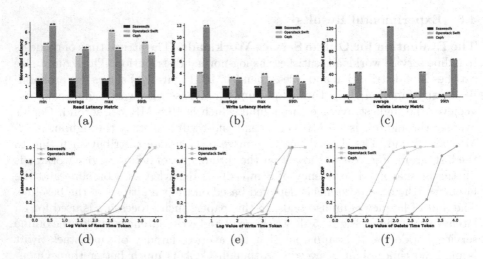

Fig. 6. Read, write and delete latencies under the big data analysis workloads. (a) Read latency; (b) Write latency; (c) Delete latency; (d) Logarithmic read latency CDF; (e) Logarithmic write latency CDF; (f) Logarithmic delete latency CDF.

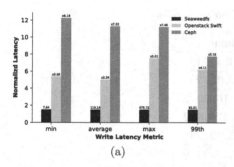
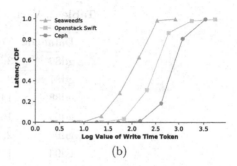

(a)   (b)

Fig. 7. Write latency under the file backup workloads. (a) Write latency; (b) Logarithmic write latency CDF.

The Evaluation of Big Data Analysis Workloads. The OStoreBench's built-in big data analysis workloads simulate multi-stage loads including a lot of read, write and delete operations. Figure 4(b) shows the probability density function of the throughput under the big data analysis workloads. What stands out in Fig. 4(b) is that the throughput of Seaweedfs is higher than others. And the average throughput of Seaweedfs reaches 153.4 MB/s. Ceph and Swift have a similar distribution of throughput. Their average throughput is 73.2 MB/s and 71.8 MB/s respectively. However, the throughput fluctuations of these three systems are significant.

Figure 6 shows the read, write and delete latencies under the big data analysis workloads. As we can see, Seaweedfs achieves the lowest minimum, maximum, average and 99th percentile latencies. The minimum and average read latency of Openstack Swift is lower than Ceph, but the maximum and 99th percentile are higher than Ceph. Openstack Swift's minimum write latency is much smaller than Ceph, and the average, maximum and 99th percentile are close to Ceph. It is obvious that Ceph and Swift have similar performance. Openstack Swift's delete latency is better than Ceph in minimum average, maximum and 99th percentile. The most interesting aspect of Fig. 6(d) is that there are two intersection of Ceph and Swift. For 20% of the read requests, Ceph's delay is lower than Swift. The same phenomenon also exists in Fig. 6(e).

The Evaluation of File Backup Workloads. OStoreBench simulates the operations of the client and periodically writes files to the cloud storage system. In each period, 10 to 100 requests are generated randomly and the upload interval is 5 s. The size of generated requests is 64 MB at most. Figure 4(c) shows the probability density function of the throughput under the file backup workloads. It can be seen that the throughput of Seaweedfs is significantly higher than those of the other two systems. On average, the throughput of Seaweedfs reaches 113 MB/s, but only 17 MB/s and 37 MB/s for Ceph and Swift respectively. Figure 7 shows the write latency under the file backup workloads. The latency of Seaweedfs is significantly better than the other two systems. From the evaluation

Table 2. Volumes on datanodes

Datanode	Volume
gd86	3, 4, 12, 19
gd87	8, 9, 10, 22
gd88	14, 15, 20, 23
gd89	16, 17, 18, 21
gd92	2, 5, 13, 24
gd94	1, 6, 7, 11

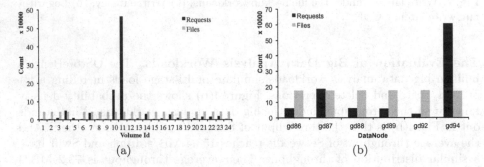

(a)   (b)

Fig. 8. The distribution of workloads among different data nodes. (a) Files and Requests received by each volume, (b) Files and Requests received by each data node.

results, we can see that under the file backup workloads Seaweedfs still has better performance than Ceph and Openstack Swift, and the performance of Ceph is slightly worse than Openstack Swift.

Performance Fluctuation Analysis. From above experimental results, we find that the performance of all these three object storage systems fluctuates violently, so we further conduct comprehensive experiments to analyze the performance fluctuation problem. The experiments are conducted on a cluster consisting of five data nodes and one master node. Relationships between volumes and data nodes are displayed in Table 2. We evaluate Seaweedfs with the online service workloads and make a statistic of the received requests of each data node to analyze the performance fluctuation problem. The request size is set to be no more than 100 KB and 2 million files are written to Seaweedfs at first. Then we send 1 million read requests to the cluster. Figure 8 shows the distribution of workloads among different data nodes. We can see that the numbers of requests received by different nodes are seriously unbalanced even though the static files are fairly well-distributed. So we conclude that the main cause of the performance fluctuation is the unbalanced distribution of loads among the data nodes which is the result of the existence of hotspots in data access. Overall, from the views of the design principles and system architectures, these evaluation results indicate:

1. The performance of Seaweedfs is the best in three typical scenarios compared to Ceph and Swift. Seaweedfs adopts a "small file merging" strategy so that the performance of Seaweedfs is most stable than the others. The authentication services of both Ceph and Openstack Swift use third-party services. Two times of network transmissions are required for each authentication. In a production environment, swift's authentication uses Keystone. Ceph's authentication is provided by radosgw [38]. Seaweedfs integrates authentication internally so that the requests latency is less.
2. Ceph's performance has a slight advantage compared to Swift. The performance of Swift is slightly worse than Ceph almost in all scenarios. This difference may be because Ceph is implemented in C++ and Swift is implemented in Python.
3. The performance of all DOSS fluctuates greatly. The source of performance fluctuations is that the load is unbalanced among nodes of the cluster. The essential reason for the imbalance of load is that there are hotspots in data access.

5   Conclusion

This paper presents a scenario benchmark suite (OStoreBench) for distributed object storage systems. OStoreBench provides users with scenario benchmarks that characterize critical paths of cloud object storage services. Through using the real workloads, the evaluation results of OStoreBench could represent the performances of DOSS in real-world applications. Using OStoreBench, We evaluate three representative object storage systems, i.e., Ceph, Openstack Swift and Seaweedfs, in various scenarios. We find that Seaweedfs performs better in all three scenarios and Oepnstack Swift has the worst performance. However, for all of these systems, the performance is unstable in every scenario. We conduct a more detailed evaluation of the object storage systems with the online service workloads and find that the distribution of loads among different data nodes is unbalanced even though the distribution of static files is uniform at the beginning.

6   Future Work

This paper explores the evaluation and optimization of object storage systems. In the future, we will conduct the research from two aspects:

1. With the increment of application scenarios of cloud services, we plan to add more workloads in OStoreBench to comprehensively compare the performance between different DOSS. We will also conduct the experiments on a larger cluster.
2. We plan to predict the hotspots by machine learning algorithms such that the data migration could be performed before the nodes become overloaded.

References

1. Factor, M., Meth, K., Naor, D., Rodeh, O., Satran, J.: Object storage: the future building block for storage systems. In: 2005 IEEE International Symposium on Mass Storage Systems and Technology, pp. 119–123. IEEE (2005)
2. Satyanarayanan, M.: A survey of distributed file systems. Ann. Rev. Comput. Sci. **4**(1), 73–104 (1990)
3. Tang, H., Byna, S., Dong, B., Liu, J., Koziol, Q.: Someta: scalable object-centric metadata management for high performance computing. In: 2017 IEEE International Conference on Cluster Computing (CLUSTER), pp. 359–369. IEEE (2017)
4. Mesnier, M., Ganger, G.R., Riedel, E.: Object-based storage. IEEE Commun. Mag. **41**(8), 84–90 (2003)
5. Amazon. Amazon s3. https://s3.amazonaws.com
6. Alibaba. Alibaba OSS. https://www.alibabacloud.com/zh/product/oss
7. Qiniu. Qiniu cloud storage. https://www.qiniu.com
8. Zheng, Q., Chen, H., Wang, Y., Zhang, J., Duan, J.: COSBench. In: The ACM/SPEC International Conference, New York, NY, USA, pp. 199–210. ACM Press (2013)
9. Gao, W., et al.: Aibench: Scenario-distilling ai benchmarking, arXiv preprint arXiv:2005.03459 (2020)
10. Weil, S.A., Brandt, S.A., Miller, E.L., Long, D.D., Maltzahn, C.: Ceph: a scalable, high-performance distributed file system. In: Proceedings of the 7th Symposium on Operating Systems Design and Implementation, pp. 307–320. USENIX Association (2006)
11. Openstack. Openstack swift. https://www.openstack.org
12. Beaver, D., Kumar, S., Li, H.C., Sobel, J., Vajgel, P., et al.: Finding a needle in haystack: Facebook's photo storage. In: OSDI, vol. 10, pp. 1–8 (2010)
13. Schwan, P., et al.: Lustre: building a file system for 1000-node clusters. In: Proceedings of the 2003 Linux Symposium, vol. 2003, pp. 380–386 (2003)
14. Noghabi, S.A., et al.: Ambry: Linkedin's scalable geo-distributed object store. In: Proceedings of the 2016 International Conference on Management of Data, pp. 253–265. ACM (2016)
15. Swift. Consistent hashing. https://docs.openstack.org/swift/latest/ring_backgroun d.html
16. Weil, S.A., Brandt, S.A., Miller, E.L., Maltzahn, C.: Crush: controlled, scalable, decentralized placement of replicated data. In: Proceedings of the 2006 ACM/IEEE conference on Supercomputing, p. 122, ACM (2006)
17. Wikipedia. Posix. https://zh.wikipedia.org/wiki/POSIX
18. Linux. Flexible i/o tester. https://linux.die.net/man/1/fio
19. iozone. Iozone filesystem benchmark. http://www.iozone.org
20. Tarasov, V., Zadok, E., Shepler, S.: Filebench: a flexible framework for file system benchmarking. Login: USENIX Mag. **41**(1), 6–12 (2016)
21. Katcher, J.: Postmark: a new file system benchmark, Technical report, Technical Report TR3022, Network Appliance (1997)
22. Cooper, B.F., Silberstein, A., Tam, E., Ramakrishnan, R., Sears, R.: Benchmarking cloud serving systems with YCSB. In Proceedings of the 1st ACM Symposium on Cloud computing, pp. 143–154. ACM (2010)
23. Patil, S., et al.: YCSB++: benchmarking and performance debugging advanced features in scalable table stores. In: Proceedings of the 2nd ACM Symposium on Cloud Computing, p. 9. ACM (2011)

24. Dey, A., Fekete, A., Nambiar, R., Röhm, U.: YCSB+T: benchmarking web-scale transactional databases. In: 2014 IEEE 30th International Conference on Data Engineering Workshops, pp. 223–230. IEEE (2014)
25. Iorgulescu, C., et al.: Perfiso: performance isolation for commercial latency-sensitive services. In: 2018 {USENIX} Annual Technical Conference ({USENIX}{ATC} 18), pp. 519–532 (2018)
26. Ousterhout, A., Fried, J., Behrens, J., Belay, A., Balakrishnan, H.: Shenango: achieving high {CPU} efficiency for latency-sensitive datacenter workloads. In: 16th {USENIX} Symposium on Networked Systems Design and Implementation ({NSDI} 19), pp. 361–378 (2019)
27. Alibaba. Hadoop-Aliyun module: Integration with Aliyun web services (2017)
28. Athena, A.: Amazon athena. https://aws.amazon.com/cn/athena
29. Wallace, G., et al.: Characteristics of backup workloads in production systems. In: FAST, vol. 12, p. 4 (2012)
30. Drago, I., Mellia, M., Munafo, M.M., Sperotto, A., Sadre, R., Pras, A.: Inside dropbox: Understanding personal cloud storage services. In: Proceedings of the 2012 Internet Measurement Conference, IMC 2012, New York, NY, USA, pp. 481–494. ACM (2012)
31. Gonçalves, G., Drago, I., Da Silva, A.P.C., Vieira, A.B., Almeida, J.M.: Modeling the dropbox client behavior. In: 2014 IEEE International Conference on Communications (ICC), pp. 1332–1337. IEEE (2014)
32. Golang. Golang. https://golang.org
33. Obrutsky, S.: Cloud storage: advantages, disadvantages and enterprise solutions for business. In: Conference: EIT New Zealand (2016)
34. Ren, Z., Shi, W., Wan, J.: Towards realistic benchmarking for cloud file systems: early experiences. In: 2014 IEEE International Symposium on Workload Characterization (IISWC), pp. 88–98. IEEE (2014)
35. Ross, S.M., et al.: Stochastic processes, vol. 2, (1996)
36. Breslau, L., Cao, P., Fan, L., Phillips, G., Shenker, S.: Web caching and Zipf-like distributions: evidence and implications. In: INFOCOM 1999. Proceedings of the IEEE Eighteenth Annual Joint Conference of the IEEE Computer and Communications Societies, vol. 1, pp. 126–134. IEEE (1999)
37. Abad, C.L., Roberts, N., Lu, Y., Campbell, R.H.: A storage-centric analysis of mapreduce workloads: file popularity, temporal locality and arrival patterns. In: 2012 IEEE International Symposium on Workload Characterization (IISWC), pp. 100–109. IEEE (2012)
38. Ceph. Ceph rados gateway. http://docs.ceph.com/docs/master/radosgw/

ConfAdvisor: An Automatic Configuration Tuning Framework for NoSQL Database Benchmarking with a Black-box Approach

Pengfei Chen[✉], Zhaoheng Huo, Xiaoyun Li, Hui Dou, and Chu Zhu

School of Data and Computer Science, Sun Yat-sen University, Guangzhou, China
chenpf7@mail.sysu.edu.cn,
{huozhh,lixy223,douhui,zhuch9}@mail2.sysu.edu.cn

Abstract. Nowadays, the widely used NoSQL databases play a fundamental role for big data storage, processing and analysis. However, NoSQL databases usually consume a large amount of computing resources and always run in a low performance state, which seriously impacts the end-to-end quality of service. Therefore, tuning the performance of NoSQL databases via benchmarking tools becomes a critical issue. Unfortunately, it is non-trivial to solve this problem because there exists a considerable number of performance-related configuration parameters from both the databases (application-specific) and the operating system kernel (kernel-specific), and manually tuning methods only consider a small subset of the whole candidate configuration parameters space, leading to a sub-optimal performance. To address this challenge, we design *ConfAdvisor*, an automatic configuration tuning framework for NoSQL database benchmarking. Specifically, *ConfAdvisor* treats the database performance as a black-box function of configuration parameters and leverage an online learning method to search the best configurations. Experimental results based on several popular NoSQL databases show that: 1) Through only tuning the kernel-specific parameters can improve database performance by up to 30%, which is often overlooked in previous studies. 2) *ConfAdvisor* is able to achieve well-tuned configurations with a very few trials, even in a high-dimension configuration space. And compared with default configurations, the well-tuned parameters can improve database performance by up to 88%.

Keywords: NoSQL database · Configuration optimization · Bayesian Optimization · YCSB benchmark

1 Introduction

Today, we have stepped into a big data era. In this big data era, a tremendous amount of data is generated every second, which requires IT service providers to have a solid database infrastructure. To help users store and manage such a large

© Springer Nature Switzerland AG 2021
F. Wolf and W. Gao (Eds.): Bench 2020, LNCS 12614, pp. 106–124, 2021.
https://doi.org/10.1007/978-3-030-71058-3_7

volume of data, most cloud service providers have provided NoSQL database services such as Amazon S3 [1], IBM Cloudant [3] and so on. Generally, each NoSQL database owns a large number of performance-related configuration parameters from both the database (application-specific) and the operating system kernel (kernel-specific). Unfortunately, current NoSQL databases only provide default and static configurations which are only suitable for general use cases and therefore, tuning configuration parameters for better performance is necessary to further improve the quality of NoSQL databases.

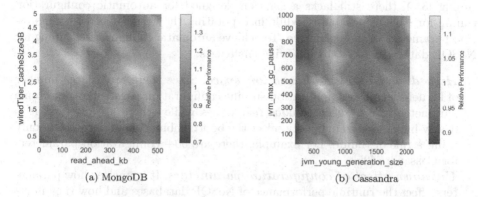

(a) MongoDB   (b) Cassandra

Fig. 1. Performance improvements for different configurations on MongoDB and Cassandra

According to [11], current NoSQL databases usually run under a low-performance state due to their default configuration parameters. In general, the performance of a well-tuned databases can be even hundreds of times better than poorly tuned ones. However, previous methods such as [7–10,18,34,35,37,38] only focus on the application-specific configurations while ignoring the kernel-specific ones, which leads to a sub-optimal performance. As illustrated in Fig. 1, our experiments[1] based on a local cluster show that both kernel-specific and application-specific can significantly impact the performance of MongoDB and Cassandra. In detail, the yellow area in the heat maps represents the parameter combinations that could achieve high performance, while the blue area represents a lower performance. In Fig. 1(a), tuning application-specific parameter *wiredTiger_cacheSize* and kernel-specific parameter *read_ahead* in MongoDB can improve the performance over default by up to 30%. Similar conclusion can also be found in Fig. 1(b) for Cassandra. As a result, in order to further improve the quality of NoSQL databases, it is necessary to take both kernel-specific and application-specific configuration parameters into account.

However, configuration tuning for NoSQL databases is actually a quite complex task due to hundreds of tunable configuration parameters from both application and kernel. To provide better databases with the same computing resources,

---

[1] The experiment settings will be introduced in detail in Sect. 5.

it is necessary to tune configuration parameters for different business scenarios and different hardware infrastructures. Unfortunately, most DB administrators still have to rely an empirical approach: They choose two or three tunable parameters (usually application-specific) by their own experience, and then evaluate the effectiveness of each parameter with only a small number of values, which leaves a considerable number of possible parameter combinations unexplored. Although there are already some studies on automatic configuration tuning for different methods (e.g. model-based methods [7,21,25,38], search-based methods [23]) and different scenarios (e.g. database configuration tuning [17], buffer tuning [31]), there still lacks a solution designed for automatic configuration tuning for NoSQL databases, while incorporating the kernel-specific configuration parameters in the meantime. To achieve automatic configuration tuning for NoSQL databases faces the following challenges:

- **High dimensional configuration space.** Since there are a large number of kernel-specific and application-specific configuration parameters, and some parameters can take continuous real values while others are discrete, it is nearly impossible to manually select the best combination of parameters only using a rule of thumb. For example, there are 50+ configuration parameters for Cassandra [25].
- **Unknown effect of configuration parameters.** It is unclear how parameters affect the runtime performance of NoSQL databases and how they interact with each other. Moreover, it is validated in [11] that the relationship between the performance and configuration parameters are non-linear, which makes automatic configuration tuning more challenging.
- **Constrained configuration updating times.** To obtain the database performance under a new generated configuration, a reliable evaluation requires a certain test time to wait for configuration updating, database warming up and benchmarking. Considering the strict requirement of quality of DBaaS, automatic configuration tuning must be finished under the constrained configuration updating times.

To address above challenges, we propose *ConfAdvisor*, an automated configuration tuning framework for NoSQL databases. The basic idea of *ConfAdvisor* is treating the database performance as a black-box function of its configuration parameters. In order to solve the black-box optimization problem, *ConfAdvisor* is now able to support most black-box optimization algorithms such as Grid Searching (GS), Random Searching (RS), Simulated Annealing (SA) [20] and Bayesian Optimization (BO) [28]. Specifically, we use BO by default in *ConfAdvisor* because it is able to find a configuration that is close to the optimum with a small number of observations. By modeling the sequential configuration tuning process as a stochastic process [24], *ConfAdvisor* is able to give suggestions on the next best configuration to be evaluated. As more configurations are evaluated, *ConfAdvisor* improves its knowledge on the function. Experimental results based on NoSQL databases such as MongoDB, Cassandra and HBase show that: 1) Through only tuning the kernel-specific parameters can improve database performance by up to 30%, which is often overlooked in previous studies. 2) *ConfAdvisor* is able to achieve well-tuned configurations with a very few trials, even in a high-dimension configuration space. And compared with default configurations, the well-tuned parameters can improve database performance by up to 88%.

In summary, this paper makes the following contributions:

- We design *ConfAdvisor*-an automatic configuration tuning framework for NoSQL database services. In order to solve the black-box optimization problem, we also add support for several black-box optimization algorithms in *ConfAdvisor*.
- Experiments with *ConfAdvisor* prove that kernel-specific parameters can impact NoSQL databases significantly. *ConfAdvisor* is able to find the optimal or sub-optimal application-specific and kernel-specific configuration parameters with an online learning approach.
- Considering the black of validations of BO with different acquisition functions in configuration tuning, we leverage *ConfAdvisor* to compare their effectiveness on MongoDB.

This paper is organized as follows. Section 2 formulates the optimization problem. Section 3 introduces the design and optimization algorithm of *ConfAdvisor*. Section 4 describes the experimental setups and Section 5 analyzes the experimental results. Section 6 presents the related work. In Sect. 7, we conclude this paper and discuss the future work.

2 Problem Statement

In this paper, we focus on how to automatically tune configurations for NoSQL database by database benchmarking. In detail, we select the average throughput including insert, update, delete, and read operations to represent the objective performance of a NoSQL database. Let X_i be the i-th tunable configuration parameters of the database and $Y \in \mathbb{R}$ be the throughput (i.e., ops/sec). In general, a configuration parameter is either numerical or categorical. In the latter case, we let X_i indicate the index of the categorical option. Now, every X_i has a finite domain $Dom(X_i)$ and the configuration space $\mathbb{X}$ can be denoted as: $\mathbb{X} = \prod_{i=1} Dom(X_i)$. The performance of a database under certain configurations can be denoted as a function $f : \mathbb{X} \to \mathbb{R}$. Our target is to find the optimal configuration x^* that maximizes the average throughput of the database:

$$x^* = \arg\max_{x \in \mathbb{X}} f(x)$$

However, the true performance function f is unknown and evaluating the value of $f(x)$ under each configuration x is costly. Thus, we treat f as a black-box function and *ConfAdvisor* aims at finding the optimal configuration x^* with the constrained configuration updating times UT. Now we can obtain the following black-box optimization problem:

$$x^* = \arg\max_{x \in \mathbb{X}} f(x) \tag{1a}$$

$$\text{s.t.} \quad configuration \quad updating \quad times \leqslant UT \tag{1b}$$

In order to solve above black-box optimization problem, we adopt several black-box optimization algorithms such as Grid Searching (GS), Random Searching (RS), Simulated Annealing (SA) and Bayesian Optimization (BO) in *ConfAdvisor* for configuration tuning. Specifically, we use BO by default in *ConfAdvisor* because it has been demonstrated to outperform other black-box optimization algorithms when the evaluation is expensive and the number of configuration updating is low.

3 System Design

3.1 System Overview

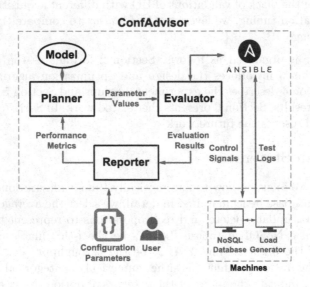

Fig. 2. The framework of *ConfAdvisor*

The design of *ConfAdvisor* is illustrated in Fig. 2. Once the DB for optimization (i.e., the target DB) and the related parameters for tuning are specified, *ConfAdvisor* is ready to launch, including automatic deployment and test. *ConfAdvisor* will continuously report the best configuration it finds. The core of *ConfAdvisor* is a Planning-Evaluation-Report loop shown in Fig. 2.

Planner. In the planning stage, *ConfAdvisor* needs to find the next best configuration x^* and feed it to the **evaluator**. Intuitively, this configuration should be likely to beat the best configuration found so far, or at least be likely to help improve the knowledge of the black-box function f to be optimized. Therefore, it helps the search in the subsequent iterations. Towards this target, we add an optimizer function in *ConfAdvisor* to support most black-box optimization algorithms and set BO as default due to its effectiveness. We will introduce BO in a detailed manner in Sect. 3.2.

Evaluator. In the evaluation stage, *ConfAdvisor* needs to: (i) deploy a new database instance for testing using the given configuration, and (ii) carry out repeated independent tests to measure the performance of the database instance. The tests are repeated to reduce noises because of the uncertainty in performance evaluation.

Reporter. After the evaluation stage, multiple tests are finished and the overall performance is also measured. Then, the reporter receives the performance reports generated by the evaluator. The reporter parses the reports and calculates (if needed) to get the observed value of $f(x)$, denoted as y. y is compared with the performance of the best configuration so far. If the new configuration beats the old one, it is reported to the user. And no matter whether a better configuration is found, the evaluated configuration x, along with the performance result y, is reported back to the optimizer as a new observation of f. After the report stage, a full planning-evaluation-report iteration is done, *ConfAdvisor* starts a new iteration, seeking for better configurations.

Automation. *ConfAdvisor* incorporates *Ansible* [2] to automates its operations including deploying, testing, result fetching, etc. *Ansible* is an open-source, simple and agent-less IT automation tool. *Ansible* leverages a YAML-structured file *storybook* to describe the tasks. With the help of *Ansible playbook*, the evaluator (shown in Fig. 2) is able to carry out the evaluation procedure on other machines automatically.

3.2 Bayesian Optimization

The main idea of BO is that it builds a probabilistic model of target black-box function f, and adopts this model to determine the point $x \in \mathbb{X}$ for next observation. There are two key points in BO. First, we need to specify the *prior function*, which is used by BO to express assumptions about the target function. Second, we need to select an *acquisition function* as the utility function for determining the best point to evaluate. In this paper, we choose the widely-used *Gaussian Process* (GP) [24] as the prior function and we will validate the effectiveness of multiple popular choices of acquisition functions.

Gaussian Process. GP is used as the prior distribution of target function. It is a kind of prior distribution over functions of the form $f : \mathbb{X} \to \mathbb{R}$, and is defined by a mean function $\mu : \mathbb{X} \to \mathbb{R}$ and a positive definite covariance function (also called *kernel*) $\kappa : \mathbb{X} \times \mathbb{X} \to \mathbb{R}$. In GP, for a series of points $x_{1:t}$ in $\mathbb{X}$, the function value $f(x_{1:t})$ accords to a multivariate normal distribution, that is,

$$f(x_{1:t}) \sim \mathcal{N}(\mu(x_{1:t}), \mathcal{K}(x_{1:t}, x_{1:t})) \tag{2}$$

where $\mathcal{K}(x_{1:t}, x_{1:t})_{i,j} = \kappa(x_i, x_j)$ represents the covariance matrix.

Suppose we have n observations of f, and want to estimate the value of a new point x. Then we can let $t = n+1$, $x_{n+1} = x$, and the prior over these $n+1$ points, $[f(x_{1:t}), f(x)]^T$, is given by Eq. 2. And the posterior distribution of $f(x)$ can be computed using Bayes' theorem as,

$$f(x)|f(x_{1:n}) \sim \mathcal{N}(\mu_n(x), \sigma_n^2(x)) \tag{3}$$

according to which, for a series of observations $\{x_i, y_i\}_{i=1}^n$, we can calculate the posterior distribution of f at any point $x \in \mathbb{X}$, in the form of $f(x) \sim \mathcal{N}(\mu_x, \sigma_x^2)$.

Acquisition Function. The role of acquisition function is the utility function for determining whether a point $x \in \mathbb{X}$ is suitable as the next observation point. It has the form $a : \mathbb{X} \to \mathbb{R}^+$ and its value represents the degree to which a point x is suitable for improving the model. The maximum point of acquisition function, $x_{next} = \arg\max a(x)$, will be used as the next point of f for evaluation.

For convenience, we denote the cumulative distribution function of standard normal distribution as $\Phi(\cdot)$. $\mu(x)$, $\sigma(x)$ represent the posterior mean and variance of point x. Popular acquisition function options include *Expected Improvement* [28] (EI), *Probability of Improvement* [28] (POI) and *Upper Confidence Bound* [28] (UCB):

POI. By considering the utility as the probability of getting a better value of f, the utility of x can be computed as $a_{POI}(x) = \Phi(\frac{f(x_{best}) - \mu(x)}{\sigma(x)})$.

EI. Similarly, when the expected improvement of the best value is used, the acquisition function is calculated as $a_{EI}(x) = E(\max\{f(x) - f(x_{best}), 0\})$.

UCB. One can also use the upper confidence bound with certain confidence level to measure the degree of goodness, $a_{UCB}(x) = \mu(x) - \theta\sigma(x)$, in which θ is used to adjust the level of confidence.

In Sect. 5.3, we will compare the effectiveness of BO with these acquisition function.

Example. BO runs in an iterative manner. With several initial observed points, BO is able to build a GP model in the first iteration. These initial points are usually randomly sampled from $\mathbb{X}$, with a number from 2 to 10. During each iteration, BO finds the maximum point x^* of the acquisition function and evaluate $y^* = f(x^*)$. After evaluation, BO adds (x^*, y^*) into the point set H and re-construct the GP model. An example of BO is illustrated in Fig. 3. With given observations, BO calculates the values of the acquisition function, denoted by the purple line. The yellow star is selected as the next point to evaluate because it is the optimum of the acquisition function. Therefore, it is considered to be the greatest potential gain. The more observations, the better BO knows about the target function, and the confidence intervals shrink as well.

4 Experiment Settings

4.1 NoSQL Databases and Benchmarks

In order to evaluate the performance of *ConfAdvisor*, we choose a set of NoSQL databases that are widely used including MongoDB, Cassandra, HBase, and Elasticsearch (ES), each with a set of application-specific parameters. The versions of MongoDB, Cassandra, HBase, and ES used in our experiments are 4.0, 2.0, 3.11 and 6.5, respectively.

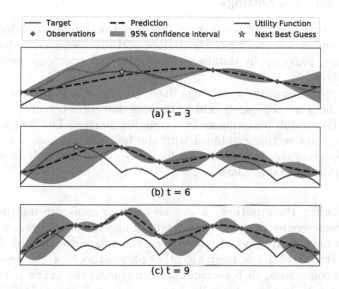

Fig. 3. An example of BO process

ConfAdvisor adopts *Yahoo! Cloud System Benchmark* (YCSB) [5] as the load generator and benchmarking tool for MongoDB, Cassandra and HBase. And we use Rally [4] to test Elasticsearch as YCSB does not support Elasticsearch yet. For YCSB, we defined a workload with mixed operations and uses the average operation throughput as the performance metric. The workload contains 4 types of operations, namely read (5%), read_modify_write (40%), update (35%) and insert (20%). YCSB uses *zipfian* distribution when selecting the records to operate on. In addition, the number of concurrent clients in YCSB is configured to be 1,024 and the CPU usage can be as high as 50% under this setting of concurrent clients. As for Rally, we choose the *gconame* track and uses the throughput of index operation as the performance metric. These load generators are configured for keeping databases under heavy load to differentiate the effectiveness of different configurations. In our experiments with Rally, the CPU usage is around 50%.

4.2   Hardware Platforms

ConfAdvisor is evaluated within a cluster connected with LAN, all with Intel(R) Core(TM) i7-7700, 16 GB RAM, running Ubuntu 18.04 LTS. During the experiments, *ConfAdvisor* is hosted exclusively on one machine and *ConfAdvisor* launches its optimization task on two other machines, one for the database and the other for the load generator. The database and the load generator are separated to avoid interference.

4.3   Configuration Settings

ConfAdvisor tunes a set of parameters that could be roughly divided into two groups: (i) application specific configurations and (ii) operating system specific configurations, provided by database documents and operating system documents respectively.

During the optimization process, both groups of parameters are tuned together, rather than separately. This is because that these two groups of parameters affect the overall performance in a complex manner. The best application specific parameter setting combined with the best OS parameter setting does not certainly gives the best overall performance. Even worse, it is possible to result in performance degradation.

Kernel-Specific Parameters. Users are able to configure multiple system runtime parameters by changing the content of files in `/proc/sys/` of linux OS, which contains a wide range of parameters, covering network, disk I/O, CPU scheduling, etc. In addition, there are other parameters that can be configured with certain commands, such as `mount` for configuring the `atime` parameter for mounted disks. As database generally consumes a large amount of CPU, memory, disk and network resources, we selected a set of parameters that are likely to affect the database performance in these aspects, listed in Table 1.

Application-Specific Parameters. Parameters of application configuration vary from one to another, it is very hard to find the intersections of tunable parameters among databases. As MongoDB, Cassandra, HBase and ES are chosen for test, we selected a set of parameters from the configuration files respectively. These parameters are listed in Table 2, Table 3, Table 4 and Table 5 respectively. Note that these are not the the complete parameters but the most common ones.

Since Cassandra, HBase and Elasticsearch run in Java Virtual Machine (JVM), the parameters passed to JVM may have impact on the performance as well [12]. In fact, all these three databases provide interfaces to configure JVM parameters upon launching. So we consider JVM parameters while tuning the performance. The JVM parameters are listed in Table 6.

Table 1. Operating system specific parameters

Name	Description
swapiness	How aggressive the kernel will swap memory pages
somaxconn	The maximum listen backlog
numa_balancing	Enables NUMA blancing
dirty_ratio	The number of pages at which a process generating disk writes will itself start writing out dirty data
dirty_background_ratio	The number of pages at which the background kernel flusher threads will start writing out dirty data
dirty_expire_centisecs	When dirty data is old enough to be eligible for writeout
netdev_max_backlog	Maximum number of packets queued on input side
rmem_max	Maximum receive socket buffer size
wmem_max	Maximum send socket buffer size
tcp_max_syn_backlog	Maximum number of remembered connection requests waiting for ack
tcp_slow_start_after_idle	Congestion window size of a connection after it has been idled
tcp_tw_reuse	Whether to reuse TIME-WAIT sockets for new connections
tcp_abort_on_overflow	Whether to reset listening service when it's too slow to accept new connection
rq_affinity	Whether to migrate request completions to the original CPU group
I/O_scheduler	Request scheduler for disks
nr_requests	How many requests may be allocated in the block layer for r/w requests
read_ahead_kb	Maximum number of kilobytes to read-ahead
disk_atime	Whether to maintain atime attribute for files

5   Experimental Results

5.1   Impact of Operating System Parameters

In order to evaluate the impact of kernel-specific parameters on different NoSQL databases, we leave all the application-specific parameters as default and tune the kernel-specific parameters for MongoDB, Cassandra, HBase and Elasticsearch

Table 2. Application specific parameters: MongoDB

Name	Description
storage_engine	Storage engine for the database
syncPeriodSecs	Amount of time that can pass before MongoDB flushes data to the data files via fsync
journal_commitIntervalMs	Maximum amount of time that the mongod process allows between journal operations
mmapv1_smallFiles	Whether to use a smaller default file size
cacheSizeGB	The size of the WiredTiger internal cache
journalCompressor	Type of compression to use to compress WiredTiger journal data
blockCompressor	Type of compression to use to compress collection data
prefixCompression	Whether to use prefix compression for index data

Table 3. Application specific parameters: Cassandra

Name	Description
trickle_fsync	Whether to force the OS to flush the dirty buffers at the set interval
trickle_fsync_interval	Size of the fsync
rpc_server_type	Options for the RPC server
rpc_max_threads	Maximum number of concurrent requests in the RPC thread pool
thrift_framed_transport	Frame size (maximum field length) for Thrift
concurrent_compactors	Number of concurrent compaction processes allowed to run simultaneously on a node
compaction_throughput	Throttles compaction to the specified value
concurrent_reads	Number of active reads that can run simultaneously
concurrent_writes	Number of active writes that can run simultaneously
commitlog_sync	Determines the method Cassandra uses to acknowledge writes in milliseconds
commitlog_sync_period	How often the commit log is synchronized to disk
commitlog_sync_batch	Maximum length of time that queries may be batched together
compression_chunk	Chunk length of table compression

using *ConfAdvisor* with the Random Search algorithm. The results are shown in Fig. 4. Since the observed performances vary with database types [30] and

Table 4. Application specific parameters: HBase

Name	Description
hbase_heapsize	Maximum Java heap size for HBase master
hbase_offheapsize	Amount of off-heap memory to allocate to HBase

Table 5. Application specific parameters: Elasticsearch

Name	Description
max_merge_thread	Maximum number of threads on a single shard that may be merging at once
index_buffer_size	Size of memory used as the indexing buffer
threadpool_index_size	Number of threads in thread pool for index operation
threadpool_index_queue	Size of the queue of pending index requests
threadpool_write_size	Number of threads in thread pool for write operation
threadpool_write_queue	Size of the queue of pending write requests
refresh_interval	The frequency of refreshes

Table 6. JVM parameters

Name	Description
min_heap_size	Initial heap size
max_heap_size	Maximum heap size
young_generation_size	Size of the heap for the young generation
use_g1gc	Whether to use Hotspot garbage-first collector
max_gc_pause	Expected peak pause time
g1_rset_update_pause	Percentage of the time taken by the Update RS phase
par_gc_thread	Number of threads used during parallel phases of garbage collectors
conc_gc_thread_ratio	Number of threads for concurrent garbage collectors

hardware configurations, we normalize all the performance results with respect to the default performance in order to focus on the relative performance change for each database. After normalization, the default performance is marked as 1. We sort the performances with different OS configurations in ascending order, with the worst case first. And the error bar is given by calculating the upper and lower bounds of the 95% confidence intervals.

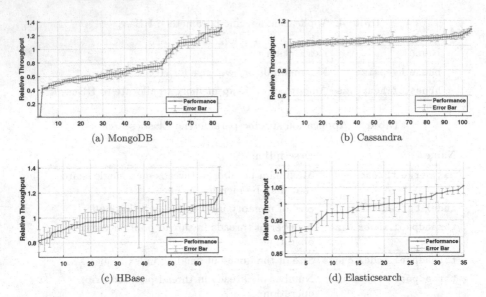

Fig. 4. Performance with kernel-specific parameters tuned, normalized with respect to the default performance

It is shown clearly in Fig. 4a that kernel-specific parameters have a significant impact on the performance of MongoDB. The throughput of the best point is approximately 3 times larger than the worst point. And compared to the default performance, there is an increase of around 30% for the best point. It should be noted that there are two points whose performances are close to zero in Fig. 4a. In this case, we regard these points as outliers due to database malfunctioning which shows that a badly-tuned OS can even makes databases fail and omit them for a more reasonable result.

Figure 4b, 4c and 4d show relatively less impact on performances of Cassandra, HBase and Elasticsearch. However, there are still notable gap between the maximum and the minimum. The maximums are 2.41, 1.47, 1.15 times larger than the minimums for Cassandra, HBase and Elasticsearch, respectively. Compared to the default performance, there are improvements of 13%, 19% and 5% for Cassandra, HBase and Elasticsearch respectively. Considering the uncertainty during performance evaluation, there is no significant improvement for these three databases with only kernel-specific parameters tuned, especially for Elasticsearch. We conjecture that JVM takes over the resource managements of these databases, while the OS kernel is decoupled from them to some extent.

5.2   Performance Improvement

The set of tunable configuration parameters determines the possible upper and lower bounds of database performance. To evaluate the effectiveness of tuning both application-specific and kernel-specific configuration parameters, in this

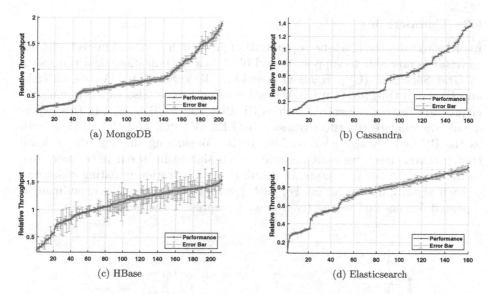

(a) MongoDB   (b) Cassandra

(c) HBase   (d) Elasticsearch

Fig. 5. The throughput with all parameters normalized with respect to the default throughput

experiment, we use random search in *ConfAdvisor* to draw samples from the configuration space. The results are listed in Fig. 5. As mentioned in Sect. 5.1, we also normalize all the performance results with respect to the default performance and sort the results with different configurations in an ascending order.

Figure 5a–5c shows that the selected parameters have drastic influences on the database performance. The well-tuned databases outperform the badly-tuned ones by around ten, or even hundreds of times. For MongoDB, Cassandra and HBase, the gaps between the best performance and the default performance are 88%, 40% and 54%, respectively. These improvements imply that taking both application-specific and kernel-specific parameters into consideration can affect the performance significantly. It is worth noting that in Fig. 5c, a large part of the points shows relatively higher uncertainty with the same number of repetitions, compared to those in Fig. 5a, 5b, 5d. This shows that the configurations can not only affect the performance, but also the performance stability in some scenarios.

On the other hand, in Fig. 5d, we observe that while there is a significant gap between the best point and the worst point, the optimal performance is very close to the default. Besides, the improvement is very similar with only tuning kernel-specific parameters as shown in Fig. 4d. We can conclude that the default configuration shipped with Elasticsearch is good enough and fits well with our test environment, and taking kernel-specific parameters into account can indeed help further improve the database performance.

5.3   Comparisons

In order to solve the black-box optimization problem formulated in Sect. 2, *ConfAdvisor* is now able to support several black-box optimization algorithms such as Grid Searching (GS), Random Searching (RS), Simulated Annealing (SA) and Bayesian Optimization (BO). Besides, *ConfAdvisor* also supports multiple acquisition functions involved such as EI, POI and UCB in BO. In this experiment, we validate the effectiveness of BO_EI, BO_POI and BO_UCB, as well as the RS and SA algorithm on MongoDB. Considering the high dimensional configuration space, we omit the grid search algorithm in our experiment due to the unacceptable time costs. In detail, the configuration undating constraint of each algorithm is set as 50. For each iteration, the evaluation experiment is repeated 5 times and we use the average to represent the performance.

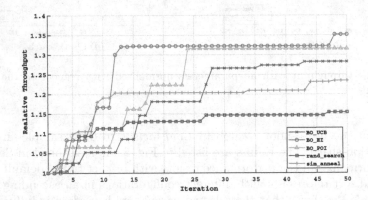

Fig. 6. Comparing BO effectiveness on MongoDB, with different acquisition functions

The results of above algorithms are illustrated in Fig. 6. The current best performance of each iteration is normalization to the default. As shown in Fig. 6, BO_EI is able to achieve the best result when optimizing the performance of MongoDB, both in terms of the final performance and the optimizing speed. With BO_EI, *ConfAdvisor* finds a configuration that is 32% better than the default configuration with only 13 iterations, and finally improve the performance by 35% compared with the default at the end of 50 iterations. Following BO_EI, BO_POI and BO_UCB achieves a final improvement of 32% and 28%, respectively. Next to BO, simulated annealing converges at 23% improvement. And not surprisingly, the random search algorithm only found a configuration that is 15% better than the default configuration.

6   Related Work

In recent years, the automatic tuning of configuration parameters have been extensively studied. Compared to previous work, our approach takes both of the application-specific and kernel-specific parameters of NoSQL databases into account. Moreover, we compare different versions of Bayesian Optimization with different acquisition functions utilizing *ConfAdvisor*. The detailed related work is introduced as follows.

System Performance Modeling. Due to a low time cost, performance prediction has attracted lots of attention recently. Ernest [33] presented a performance prediction framework using a parametric probabilistic models. Paragon [14], Quasar [15], ProteusTM [16] profile key performance metrics using Collaborative Filtering. Similar to them, PARIS [36] and Selecta [22] predict system performance with the training data for different user-specified metrics. Differently, our approach can learn the performance impacts of configurations online in a black-box way.

Automatic Configuration Tuning. Nowadays, developers manually select configurations based on their own experiences. Many studies e.g., [29] on storage system configuration auto-tuning is conducting now. CherryPick [6] is a system to unearth the best cloud configuration. Selecta [22] recommends near-optimal configurations of cloud compute and storage resources for data analytic workloads. iTuned [17] is a tool that automates the task of identifying a good setting for database system. And other studies [11,32] focuses on file storage system automated configuration. However, they do not take the kernel-specific parameters into account.

Heterogeneous Optimization Algorithms. To address the optimization issue, many mathematical algorithms have been proposed recently. Simulated Annealing [20] is the typical method to deal with the large combinational optimization problem. VCONF [26] proposed a reinforcement learning to automate the VM configuration process. Due to the large-scale configuration space, Bayesian Optimization [28] is suitable to select the best configurations. BOAT [13] proposed structured Bayesian optimization as a black-box auto-tuner. Cherrypick [6] leverages Bayesian Optimization to build performance model for various applications. Some researches [19,27] were conducted using evolutionary algorithms to track dependencies of configurable parameters and then selected the best configurations. Recently, some researchers [11,32] have done a comparative analysis between heterogeneous optimization algorithms. We add support for several black-box optimization algorithms in *ConfAdvisor* and these studies can provide a strong reinforcement and complement for our work.

7 Conclusion

This paper presents *ConfAdvisor*, a novel framework to automatically find the optimal configuration for NoSQL databases by tuning both application parameters and OS parameters with an online learning approach. We evaluate *ConfAdvisor* with several popular NoSQL databases and demonstrate experimentally that both application and OS parameters have significant impact on the performance on NoSQL databases. Moreover, with well-tuned configurations, *ConfAdvisor* can achieve a desirable improvement for most of the selected NoSQL databases. *ConfAdvisor* can locate a configuration that is close to the optimum within a very few trials. As a future work, we will use methods of multi-objective optimization and accelerate the optimization procedure in parallel.

Acknowledgement. This work was supported by the Key-Area Research and Development Program of Guangdong Province (2020B010165002), in part by the National Natural Science Foundation of China under Grant (61802448, U1811462), in part by the Basic and Applied Basic Research of Guangzhou (202002030328), and in part by the Natural Science Foundation of Guangdong Province (2019A1515012229).

References

1. Amazon s3. https://aws.amazon.com/s3/?nc1=h_ls
2. Ansible. https://www.ansible.com/
3. Ibm cloudant. https://www.ibm.com/cloud/cloudant
4. Rally. https://github.com/elastic/rally
5. Ycsb. https://github.com/brianfrankcooper/YCSB
6. Alipourfard, O., Liu, H.H., Chen, J., Venkataraman, S., Yu, M., Zhang, M.: CherryPick: adaptively unearthing the best cloud configurations for big data analytics. In: 14th {USENIX} Symposium on Networked Systems Design and Implementation ({NSDI} 17), pp. 469–482 (2017)
7. Bao, L., Liu, X., Xu, Z., Fang, B.: BestConfig: tapping the performance potential of systems via automatic configuration tuning, pp. 29–40 (2018)
8. Bei, Z., Yu, Z., Liu, Q., Xu, C., Feng, S., Song, S.: MEST: a model-driven efficient searching approach for MapReduce self-tuning. IEEE Access **5**(1), 3580–3593 (2017)
9. Bei, Z., et al.: RFHOC: a random-forest approach to auto-tuning Hadoop's configuration. IEEE Trans. Parallel Distrib. Syst. **27**(5), 1470–1483 (2016)
10. Bu, X., Rao, J., Xu, C.Z.: A reinforcement learning approach to online web systems auto-configuration. In: IEEE International Conference on Distributed Computing Systems, pp. 2–11 (2009)
11. Cao, Z., Tarasov, V., Tiwari, S., Zadok, E.: Towards better understanding of black-box auto-tuning: a comparative analysis for storage systems. In: 2018 {USENIX} Annual Technical Conference ({USENIX} {ATC} 18), pp. 893–907 (2018)
12. Carpen-Amarie, M., Marlier, P., Felber, P., Thomas, G.: A performance study of java garbage collectors on multicore architectures. In: Proceedings of the Sixth International Workshop on Programming Models and Applications for Multicores and Manycores, pp. 20–29. ACM (2015)
13. Dalibard, V., Schaarschmidt, M., Yoneki, E.: BOAT: building auto-tuners with structured bayesian optimization. In: Proceedings of the 26th International Conference on World Wide Web, pp. 479–488. International World Wide Web Conferences Steering Committee (2017)
14. Delimitrou, C., Kozyrakis, C.: Paragon: QoS-aware scheduling for heterogeneous datacenters. ACM SIGPLAN Not. **48**, 77–88 (2013)
15. Delimitrou, C., Kozyrakis, C.: Quasar: resource-efficient and QoS-aware cluster management. ACM SIGPLAN Not. **49**(4), 127–144 (2014)
16. Didona, D., Diegues, N., Kermarrec, A.M., Guerraoui, R., Neves, R., Romano, P.: ProteusTM: abstraction meets performance in transactional memory. ACM SIGOPS Oper. Syst. Rev. **50**(2), 757–771 (2016)

17. Duan, S., Thummala, V., Babu, S.: Tuning database configuration parameters with iTuned. Proc. VLDB Endow. **2**(1), 1246–1257 (2009)
18. Heinze, T., Roediger, L., Meister, A., Ji, Y., Jerzak, Z., Fetzer, C.: Online parameter optimization for elastic data stream processing. In: Proceedings of the Sixth ACM Symposium on Cloud Computing (SoCC 2015), pp. 276–287. ACM (2015)
19. Jaderberg, M., et al.: Population based training of neural networks. arXiv preprint arXiv:1711.09846 (2017)
20. Jeon, Y.J., Kim, J.C., Kim, J.O., Shin, J.R., Lee, K.Y.: An efficient simulated annealing algorithm for network reconfiguration in large-scale distribution systems. IEEE Trans. Power Deliv. **17**(4), 1070–1078 (2002)
21. Johnston, T., Alsulmi, M., Cicotti, P., Taufer, M.: Performance tuning of MapReduce jobs using surrogate-based modeling. Proc. Comput. Sci. **51**, 49–59 (2015)
22. Klimovic, A., Litz, H., Kozyrakis, C.: Selecta: heterogeneous cloud storage configuration for data analytics. In: 2018 {USENIX} Annual Technical Conference ({USENIX} {ATC} 18), pp. 759–773 (2018)
23. Li, L., Jamieson, K., DeSalvo, G., Rostamizadeh, A., Talwalkar, A.: Hyperband: a novel bandit-based approach to hyperparameter optimization. arXiv preprint arXiv:1603.06560 (2016)
24. MacKay, D.J.: Introduction to Gaussian processes. NATO ASI Ser. F Comput. Syst. Sci. **168**, 133–166 (1998)
25. Mahgoub, A., Wood, P., Ganesh, S., Mitra, S., et al.: Rafiki: a middleware for parameter tuning of NoSQL datastores for dynamic metagenomics workloads. In: Proceedings of the 18th ACM/IFIP/USENIX Middleware Conference (Middleware 2017), pp. 28–40. ACM (2017)
26. Rao, J., Bu, X., Xu, C.Z., Wang, L., Yin, G.: VCONF: a reinforcement learning approach to virtual machines auto-configuration. In: Proceedings of the 6th International Conference on Autonomic Computing, pp. 137–146. ACM (2009)
27. Saboori, A., Jiang, G., Chen, H.: Autotuning configurations in distributed systems for performance improvements using evolutionary strategies. In: The 28th International Conference on Distributed Computing Systems, pp. 769–776. IEEE (2008)
28. Snoek, J., Larochelle, H., Adams, R.P.: Practical Bayesian optimization of machine learning algorithms. In: Advances in Neural Information Processing Systems, pp. 2951–2959 (2012)
29. Strunk, J.D., Thereska, E., Faloutsos, C., Ganger, G.R.: Using utility to provision storage systems. In: FAST, vol. 8, pp. 1–16 (2008)
30. Tang, E., Fan, Y.: Performance comparison between five NoSQL databases. In: 2016 7th International Conference on Cloud Computing and Big Data (CCBD), pp. 105–109. IEEE (2016)
31. Tran, D.N., Huynh, P.C., Tay, Y.C., Tung, A.K.: A new approach to dynamic self-tuning of database buffers. ACM Trans. Storage (TOS) **4**(1), 3 (2008)
32. Van Aken, D., Pavlo, A., Gordon, G.J., Zhang, B.: Automatic database management system tuning through large-scale machine learning. In: Proceedings of the 2017 ACM International Conference on Management of Data, pp. 1009–1024. ACM (2017)
33. Venkataraman, S., Yang, Z., Franklin, M.J., Recht, B., Stoica, I.: Ernest: efficient performance prediction for large-scale advanced analytics. In: {NSDI}. pp. 363–378 (2016)

34. Wang, S., Li, C., Hoffmann, H., Lu, S., Sentosa, W., Kistijantoro, A.I.: Understanding and auto-adjusting performance-sensitive configurations. In: Proceedings of 2018 Architectural Support for Programming Languages and Operating Systems (ASPLOS 2018), pp. 154–168. ACM (2018)
35. Xiong, W., Bei, Z., Xu, C., Yu, Z.: ATH: auto-tuning HBase's configuration via ensemble learning. IEEE Access 5(1), 13157–13170 (2017)
36. Yadwadkar, N.J., Hariharan, B., Gonzalez, J.E., Smith, B., Katz, R.H.: Selecting the best VM across multiple public clouds: a data-driven performance modeling approach. In: Proceedings of the 2017 Symposium on Cloud Computing, pp. 452–465. ACM (2017)
37. Yu, Z., Bei, Z., Qian, X.: Datasize-aware high dimensional configurations autotuning of in-memory cluster computing. In: Proceedings of the Twenty-Third International Conference on Architectural Support for Programming Languages and Operating Systems (ASPLOS 2018), pp. 564–577. ACM (2018)
38. Zhu, Y., Liu, J., Guo, M., Bao, Y., et al.: BestConfig: tapping the performance potential of systems via automatic configuration tuning. In: Proceedings of the 2017 Symposium on Cloud Computing, pp. 338–350 (2017)

Supercomputing

Optimization of the Himeno Benchmark for SX-Aurora TSUBASA

Akito Onodera[1]($\boxtimes$), Kazuhiko Komatsu[2], Soya Fujimoto[2,3], Yoko Isobe[2,3], Masayuki Sato[1], and Hiroaki Kobayashi[1]

[1] Graduate School of Information Sciences, Tohoku University, Sendai, Japan
akito.onodera.r2@dc.tohoku.ac.jp
[2] Cyberscience Center, Tohoku University, Sendai, Japan
[3] NEC Corporation, Minato-ku, Japan

Abstract. This paper focuses on optimizing the Himeno benchmark for the vector computing system SX-Aurora TSUBASA and analyzes its performance in detail. The Vector Engine (VE) of SX-Aurora TSUBASA achieves a high memory bandwidth by High Bandwidth Memory (HBM2). The Himeno benchmark solves Poisson's equation using the Jacobi iteration method. The kernel performs 19-point stencil calculations in the 3D domain, which is known as a memory-intensive kernel. This paper introduces four optimizations in a single VE or multiple VEs for the Himeno benchmark. First, for a single VE, to exploit the high bandwidth of the last-level cache (LLC) in the VE, the highly reusable array elements are stored in the LLC with the highest priority. Second, the computational domain is decomposed by considering the architecture of the VE so that this optimization can achieve a high LLC hit ratio and a long vector length. Third, to alleviate the loop overhead that tends to be large for vector computation, loop unrolling is applied to the kernel. Fourth, for multiple VEs, the optimization to improve the sustained MPI communication bandwidth is applied. The process mapping is optimized by considering different types of communication mechanisms of SX-Aurora TSUBASA. The evaluation results show that the optimizations contribute to the long vector length, the high LLC hit ratio, and the short MPI communication time of the Himeno benchmark. As a result, the performance and the power efficiency are improved due to efficient vector processing through the optimizations.

Keywords: Performance optimization · Performance analysis · Vector computing · Himeno benchmark

1 Introduction

Recent computers are hard to improve its performance by increasing the operating frequency of processors. To further increase the peak performance, vector computers have attracted attention. The vector computers employ vector processing technology, which allows us to process a large amount of data by one instruction.

© Springer Nature Switzerland AG 2021
F. Wolf and W. Gao (Eds.): Bench 2020, LNCS 12614, pp. 127–143, 2021.
https://doi.org/10.1007/978-3-030-71058-3_8

Moreover, a recent vector processor is equipped with a high-bandwidth memory subsystem, which effectively supports vector processing. Because of these reasons, the vector computers can accelerate memory-intensive applications that require high memory bandwidth to handle large amounts of data, in particular, in fields of computational fluid dynamics and physical simulations.

This paper optimizes the Himeno benchmark [1] for a vector computing system SX-Aurora TSUBASA [4, 20], which has vector engines (VEs) specially designed for vector computing with an extremely high memory bandwidth. The Himeno benchmark is a general fluid analysis code and requires a high memory bandwidth. This paper shows four optimizations in a single VE and multiple VEs executions for the performance improvement of the Himeno benchmark on SX-Aurora TSUB-ASA. For a single VE execution, two optimizations to mainly exploit the cache bandwidth are applied to the Himeno benchmark. First, the LLC is utilized to save the memory bandwidth. Second, the computational domain is carefully decomposed to maximize both the vector length and the LLC hit ratio for parallel processing by multiple cores in a single VE. In addition, loop overhead is reduced by loop unrolling for the improvement of throughput. For multiple VEs execution, another optimization to exploit the sustained MPI communication bandwidth is applied to the Himeno benchmark. SX-Aurora TSUBASA has multi-level inter-process communication mechanisms: among cores in the same VE, among different VEs in the same PCIe switch, and among different VEs in different PCIe switches. Process mapping is tuned considering these interprocess communication mechanisms in the case of MPI parallel processing by multiple VEs.

This paper consists of five sections. Section 2 shows an overview of SX-Aurora TSUBASA and the Himeno benchmark. Section 3 discusses the optimizations of the Himeno benchmark for SX-Aurora TSUBASA. Section 4 shows the evaluation results of a single VE and multiple VEs. Moreover, this section shows the comparisons among various processors in terms of performance and power consumption. Section 5 reviews the related work. Section 6 concludes this paper with future work.

2   Target Systems and Benchmark

2.1   Overview of SX-Aurora TSUBASA

SX-Aurora TSUBASA consists of Vector Hosts (VHs) and Vector Engines (VEs). A VH is an x86 processor and is responsible for OS-related tasks like system calls. A VE is a high-performance vector processor. Figure 1-(a) shows an overview of a VE. The VE is responsible for the major calculations of applications. One VE has eight vector cores, each of which has a powerful vector processing capability. The maximum vector length is 256. The eight cores share a total of a 16 MB Last Level Cache (LLC), connected by a two-dimensional mesh network. In addition, six 8 GB High Bandwidth Memory (HBM2) modules are mounted on an interposer with a VE to configure the main memory. Thus, to accelerate memory-intensive applications on SX-Aurora TSUBASA, it is necessary to exploit the LLC bandwidth.

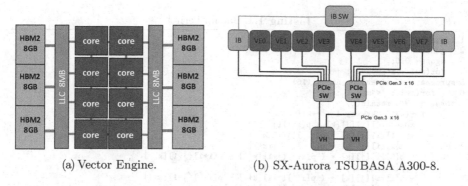

(a) Vector Engine.   (b) SX-Aurora TSUBASA A300-8.

Fig. 1. Overview of SX-Aurora TSUBASA.

Figure 1-(b) shows an overview of the SX-Aurora TSUBASA A300-8. Eight VEs are grouped into two, and each group is connected to one of two VHs via PCI Express Gen.3 x16 (PCIe). The peak bandwidth of the PCIe is 15.75 GB/s. When doing parallel processing by multiple VEs, each VE can communicate via PCIe. In addition, communications among VEs in different PCIe switches should be handled via PCIe or Infiniband (IB), a high-speed communication interconnect. Because of such a system configuration, SX-Aurora TSUBASA has three-level interprocess communication mechanisms: among cores in the same VE, among different VEs in the same PCIe switches, and among VEs in different PCIe switches. Therefore, to improve the sustained MPI communication bandwidth, it is important to consider the three-level interprocess communication mechanisms when allocating MPI processes to multiple VEs.

On the SX-Aurora TSUBASA system, the applications are basically executed on the VEs [16]. Only operations that cannot be done by the VEs, such as system calls, are offloaded to the VHs. On the VHs, the processes based on a software stack called VEOS are always running, and the offloaded operations from VEs are executed through the processes of VEOS.

One of the advantages of SX-Aurora TSUBASA is that the amount of data transfer for an application is less than that of a general CPU-GPU system, in which the applications are partially offloaded from CPU to GPU [18]. In addition, it is not necessary to explicitly describe the kernel and data transfer to be executed on VEs in the source code. An existing program can easily be executed by only compiling the source code for a VE.

2.2 Overview of the Himeno Benchmark

The Himeno benchmark is widely used for measuring the computing performance of computers [1]. The Himeno benchmark measures the processing time of the main loop solving Poisson's equation for incompressible fluid by the Jacobi iteration method. Listing 1.1 shows the Jacobi kernel. The kernel performs the stencil calculation for all 19 points by discretizing the 3D calculation domain in a grid

Listing 1.1. Jacobi kernel

```
1 for(n=0 ; n<nn ; ++n){
2   gosa = 0.0;
3   wgosa= 0.0;
4   for(i=1 ; i<imax-1 ; ++i)
5 #pragma _NEC outerloop_unroll(16)
6     for(j=1 ; j<jmax-1 ; ++j)
7 #pragma _NEC retain(p)
8       for(k=1 ; k<kmax-1 ; ++k){
9         s0 = a[0][i][j][k] * p[i+1][j  ][k  ]
10        + a[1][i][j][k] * p[i  ][j+1][k  ]
11        + a[2][i][j][k] * p[i  ][j  ][k+1]
12        + b[0][i][j][k] * ( p[i+1][j+1][k  ] - p[i+1][j-1][k  ]
13        - p[i-1][j+1][k  ] + p[i-1][j-1][k  ] )
14        + b[1][i][j][k] * ( p[i  ][j+1][k+1] - p[i  ][j-1][k+1]
15        - p[i  ][j+1][k-1] + p[i  ][j-1][k-1] )
16        + b[2][i][j][k] * ( p[i+1][j  ][k+1] - p[i-1][j  ][k+1]
17        - p[i+1][j  ][k-1] + p[i-1][j  ][k-1] )
18        + c[0][i][j][k] * p[i-1][j  ][k  ]
19        + c[1][i][j][k] * p[i  ][j-1][k  ]
20        + c[2][i][j][k] * p[i  ][j  ][k-1]
21        + wrk1[i][j][k];
22
23        ss = ( s0 * a[3][i][j][k] - p[i][j][k] ) * bnd[i][j][k];
24        wgosa += ss*ss;
25
26        wrk2[i][j][k] = p[i][j][k] + omega*ss;
27      }
```

pattern and updating the current values using the values of 18 adjacent grid points. This research uses the MPI static allocate version of the Himeno benchmark. The outermost loop in Line 4 is parallelized by MPI, and the innermost loop in Line 8 is vectorized.

3 Optimization of the Himeno Benchmark

3.1 Optimizations for a Single VE

First, to clarify a guideline for optimizations, the bottleneck of the Himeno benchmark is analyzed by the method of Komatsu et al. [13]. The analysis uses four types of the Byte/Flop (B/F) ratio, the Memory B/F ratio, the LLC B/F ratio, the Required B/F ratio, and the Actual B/F ratio. The Memory B/F ratio is calculated as a ratio of the peak main memory bandwidth to the peak computing performance. The LLC B/F ratio is calculated as a ratio of the peak LLC bandwidth to the peak computing performance. The Required B/F ratio is calculated as a ratio of the bytes specified by load and store instructions to the computing performance [8]. The Actual B/F ratio is calculated as a ratio of bytes of memory access by vector load and store instructions to the computing performance. The numbers of memory accesses and floating operations are obtained by the profiler of SX-Aurora TSUBASA.

Table 1 shows the characteristic classification of the applications by each B/F ratio. As shown in Table 1, the bottleneck of an application can be determined

Table 1. Characteristic classification of the programs by B/F ratio.

B/F ratio	Actual < Memory	Actual > Memory
Required < LLC	Computation-bound	Memory BW-bound
Required > LLC	LLC BW-bound	Memory or LLC bound

in detail by comparing these four B/F ratios. Furthermore, the application is classified as LLC-bound or memory-bound by the following equation.

$$Actual\ B/F * (LLC\ BW\ /\ Memory\ BW) \qquad (1)$$

If the value of Eq. (1) is lower than the Required B/F, the application can be considered LLC-bound. If the value of Eq. (1) is higher than the Required B/F, the application can be considered memory-bound. In the case of single-precision operations on VE Type 10B, the peak computational performance, the peak memory bandwidth, and peak LLC bandwidth are 4.30 Tflop/s, 1.22 TB/s, and 2.66 TB/s, respectively. Thus, the Memory B/F ratio and the LLC B/F ratio become 0.28 and 0.62, respectively. On the other hand, the Required B/F ratio of the Himeno benchmark is 3.96. The Actual B/F ratio is 2.11, which is measured by executing the original version of the Himeno benchmark on the VE. From Table 1, it is considered that the Himeno benchmark is a memory-bound or LLC-bound program. In addition, the value of Eq. (1) is $2.11 * (2.66/1.22) = 4.60$, which is higher than the Required B/F ratio. The result confirms that the Himeno Benchmark is a memory-bound application.

In conclusion, to optimize the Himeno benchmark in a single VE, it is necessary to increase the data reuses in the LLC and exploit the potential of the LLC bandwidth. The LLC is utilized to make up for the memory bandwidth. Domain decomposition is tuned considering the effective use of the LLC as well as an increase in vector length. In addition, loop unrolling is applied to reduce loop overhead.

Utilization of the LLC. In the 19-point stencil calculation in the Jacobi kernel shown in Listing 1.1, array p of the pressure term is referenced 19 times in the triple-nested loop calculation in the i, j, and k directions. Then, by storing array p in the LLC as much as possible, the utilization of the LLC increases, resulting in an improvement in a sustained memory bandwidth.

To store array p in the LLC of the VE with a high priority, compiler directive "#pragma _NEC retain(array-name)" [7] is inserted as shown in Line 7 in Listing 1.1. As a result, array p is retained in the LLC with a high priority in innermost loop k. Therefore, the LLC bandwidth can be exploited.

Reducing the Loop Overhead. In the Himeno benchmark, the larger the calculation size becomes, the larger the number of loop iterations becomes. As a result, the loop overhead for judging the loop-end conditions increases, and the loop overhead might degrade the sustained performance, especially in vector computers.

To reduce the loop overhead, this paper applies loop unrolling [10,17]. Because the VE has more registers than general processors, it is possible to expand the loop body by increasing the unroll times. However, if the unroll time is too large, the performance can be degraded by register spilling. Therefore, the number of the unrolls should be as large as possible, as long as register spill does not occur.

To apply loop unrolling, compiler directive "#pragma _NEC outerloop_unr oll(n)" is inserted as shown in Line 5 in Listing 1.1. As a result, the j-loop is unrolled. In this paper, the unroll time, n, is set to 16 that is selected in a range from 2^0 to 2^6.

Tuning the Domain Decomposition. In the MPI version of the Himeno benchmark, it is necessary to specify the number of the computational domains for parallel processing. For example, the case that the domain decomposition parameter is $(i, j, k) = (2, 32, 1)$ means that the i direction is decomposed in two subdomains, the j direction is decomposed in 32 subdomains, and the k direction is not decomposed.

This paper tunes the decomposition parameters of the computational domain for MPI parallel processing. In the case of MPI execution on a single VE, data transfers can be performed as memory copies. To achieve efficient parallel processing, it is important to decide the degree of decomposition for a VE carefully. For example, when decomposing a vectorized loop k, the vector length may become short. The following two points are important for achieving high performance by domain decomposition.

- Reduce the degree of decomposition in the k direction, which is the innermost loop, to achieve a long vector length.
- Increase the degree of decomposition in the j direction compared with the i direction to achieve a high LLC hit ratio.

It is important to keep the vector length as long as possible, close to 256 in each of the decomposed computational domains to use the VE effectively. Because the innermost loop k of the kernel is vectorized, the decomposition parameters are specified so that the number of iterations in loop k is at least 256 per domain. In addition, by increasing the degree of decomposition in the j direction rather than the i direction, the number of array elements in the j-k plane can be reduced. As a result, the reuse of array elements in the outermost loop i can be increased, resulting in an increase in the LLC hit ratio.

3.2 Optimizations for Multiple VEs

As a preliminary evaluation, the network bandwidth is measured using the Point-to-Point MPI benchmark of the OSU Micro-Benchmarks 5.6.3 [3]. SX-Aurora TSUBASA A300-8 equipped with Infiniband FDR for data transfers between

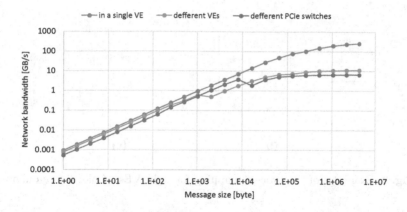

Fig. 2. Network bandwidth of SX-Aurora TSUBASA A300-8.

different PCIe switches is used for this evaluation. The peak bandwidth of Infiniband FDR is 6.8 GB/s. Figure 2 shows the network bandwidth of SX-Aurora TSUBASA A300-8. The bandwidth among cores in a single VE is around 254 GB/s, which is much faster than the other data transfers among different VEs in the same PCIe switch or different PCIe switches. This is because its data transfer can be performed as memory copies. The bandwidth of data transfer among different VEs in the same PCIe switch is around 11 GB/s. This is because its data transfer can be limited by the bandwidth of PCIe. The bandwidth of data transfer among different VEs in different PCIe switches is around 6.5 GB/s. This is because its data transfer can be limited by the bandwidth of IB FDR.

In this way, SX-Aurora TSUBASA A300-8 uses multiple levels of the network bandwidth depending on the MPI process mapping. Therefore, to optimize the Himeno benchmark for multiple VEs, it is necessary to tune the process mapping to maximize the sustained MPI communication bandwidth.

Tuning the Process Mapping. The jacobi kernel requires the communication of the halo area among the processes. As the number of processes increases, the ratio of the communication time to the execution time increases, and it can harmfully affect the performance. The process mapping is one of the important optimizations for efficient MPI parallel processing. As shown in Fig. 2, the communications among different VEs through PCIe switches have relatively low bandwidths, and these can easily become a bottleneck.

Therefore, it is essential to assign processes to cores by considering the different levels of communications. The process mapping is based on the domain decomposition proposed in Sect. 3.1. The following three points are important for process mapping to exploit the network bandwidth in SX-Aurora TSUBASA.

- The processes to calculate adjacent domains should be assigned to the cores in the same VE as many as possible.
- The amounts of data transfer among different VEs in different PCIe switches should be reduced as much as possible.

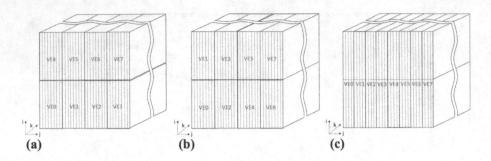

Fig. 3. Examples of the process mapping for eight VEs. (Color figure online)

- To distribute the load of data transfers, the processes should be assigned so that multiple VEs communicate with the other VEs in different PCIe switches.

The processes should be assigned preferentially considering the first and the second points. This is because the effect of the third point on performance is relatively small.

Figure 3 shows three examples of the process mapping for eight VEs in the case where the domain decomposition parameter is $(i, j, k) = (2, 32, 1)$. The red boxes indicate the VEs connected to one PCIe switch. The blue boxes indicate the VEs connected to the other PCIe switch. In Fig. 3-(a), the data transfers among different VEs in different PCIe switches occur in the i direction. The data transfers among cores in a single VE or among different VEs in the same PCIe switch occur in the j direction. In Fig. 3-(b), the data transfers among different VEs in the same PCIe switch occur in the i direction. The data transfers among cores in a single VE, among different VEs in the same PCIe switch, or among different VEs in different PCIe switches occur in the j direction. In Fig. 3-(c), the data transfers among cores in a single VE occur in the i direction. The data transfers among different VEs in the same PCIe switch or among different VEs in different PCIe switches occur in the j direction. In these three examples, the processes to calculate adjacent domains are assigned to the same VE. These examples have the same total amount of data transfer. In addition, these examples have the same amounts of data transfer among different VEs in different PCIe switches. However, the number of VEs that communicate among different VEs in different PCIe switches is different. All the VEs in Fig. 3-(a), four VEs in Fig. 3-(b), and two VEs in Fig. 3-(c) communicate with the other VEs in different PCIe switches. According to the points of the process mapping shown above, Fig. 3-(a) is expected to achieve the highest performance among the three examples.

4 Evaluation

4.1 Experimental Environment

For evaluation, five systems, Aurora1, Aurora2, Aurora8, Xeon, and V100, are used as shown in Table 2. Each of the systems is equipped with one or two sockets of Intel Xeon Gold 6126 [2] as hosts. In addition, Aurora1, Aurora2, and Aurora8 are equipped with one or more VEs. V100 is equipped with NVIDIA V100 [5]. Table 3 shows the specifications of NEC VE Type 10B, Intel Xeon Gold 6126, and NVIDIA V100, respectively.

In these experiments, the MPI static allocate version of the Himeno benchmark 3.0 in C language is used for Aurora1, Aurora2, Aurora8, and Xeon. The Fortran version of the Himeno benchmark with OpenACC directives is used for V100. The computation domain is XL ($512 \times 512 \times 1024$). For the Xeon system, the tuning of the domain decomposition is applied. For V100, system parameters are tuned. For the innermost loop of the first loop body in the Jacobi kernel, directive "!$acc loop vector(512) reduction(+:gosa)" is inserted so that the number of threads in a thread block is set to 512 that achieves the best performance

Table 2. Overview of systems.

System	Host	Accelerator
Aurora1	Xeon Gold 6126 × 1	VE Type 10B × 1
Aurora2	Xeon Gold 6126 × 1	VE Type 10B × 2
Aurora8	Xeon Gold 6126 × 2	VE Type 10B × 8
Xeon	Xeon Gold 6126 × 1	–
V100	Xeon Gold 6126 × 1	V100 × 1

Table 3. Specification of processors.

	NEC VE Type 10B	Intel Xeon Gold 6126	NVIDIA Tesla V100
Performance (SP)	4.30 Tflop/s	883.2 Gflop/s	14 Tflop/s
Memory bandwidth	1.22 TB/s	128 GB/s	900 GB/s
LLC bandwidth	2.66 TB/s	N/A	N/A

Table 4. Compilers and compile options.

Compilers	Compile options
NEC C/C++ Compiler version 3.0.6	-O4, -msched-block
NEC MPI version 2.7.0	-mretain-none
Intel compiler 19.1.1.217	-O3, -xCORE-AVX512
Intel MPI version 2019 Update 7	-qopt-zmm-usage = high, -mcmodel = large
PGI compiler version 19.10	-O3, -acc, -Minfo = all
	-ta = tesla, cuda10.1, cc70
	-mcmodel = medium, -Mlarge_arrays

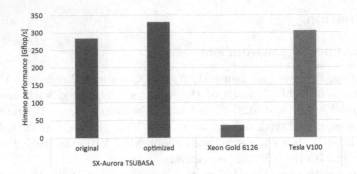

Fig. 4. Performance of a single VE, Xeon, and V100.

from a range from 2^5 to 2^{10} [12]. In the same way, for the innermost loop of the second loop body in the Jacobi kernel, directive "!$acc loop vector(256)" is inserted so that the number of threads in a thread block is set to 256. The number of thread blocks in each loop is set to 64,770 by the compiler.

Table 4 shows the compilers and compile options. The profiling of the VEs is performed using FTRACE, a profiler used to obtain performance information. To measure the power, three tools are used; Supermicro IPMICFG for the overall systems, Vector Engine MMM-Command for the VEs, and NVIDIA-SMI for the V100 GPU.

To improve the performance of a single VE, utilization of the LLC and loop unrolling are applied at first, and then the domain decomposition is tuned. In multiple VEs, utilization of the LLC and loop unrolling are applied in the same way as a single VE at first. Then, in each number of processes, the domain decomposition is tuned. Moreover, in each number of processes, the process mapping is tuned. The Himeno benchmark is executed 10 times for each experiment to measure the average performance.

4.2   Evaluation of a Single VE

Figure 4 shows the performance of a single VE of Aurora1, Xeon, and V100. By utilizing the LLC with the "retain" directive, the LLC hit ratio improves from 44.3% to 49.5%. This is because the LLC bandwidth can be exploited by allocating array p preemptively to the LLC. In addition, further performance improvement is achieved by loop unrolling. Due to loop unrolling, the average vector length is slightly increased from 253.3 to 255.2. This is because the amount of the loop condition evaluation that cannot be vectorized is reduced. The performance of the original Himeno benchmark with a single VE is 283.4 Gflop/s. On the other hand, the performance of the optimized Himeno benchmark is 329.5 Gflop/s, and SX-Aurora TSUBASA achieves a 1.16× performance improvement.

By applying the optimizations, Xeon and V100 achieve 1.05× and 1.50× higher performances than those of the original versions, respectively. As a result,

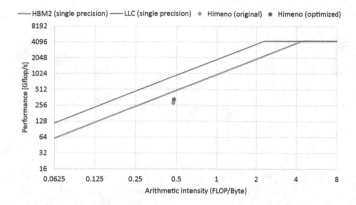

Fig. 5. Roofline model of the Himeno benchmark on SX-Aurora TSUBASA.

SX-Aurora TSUBASA achieves 9.16x and 1.08x higher performance than those of Xeon and V100, respectively. This is because the memory bandwidth can be exploited by the optimizations, resulting in efficient vector processing. The execution efficiencies of the original version on a single VE, the optimized versions on a single VE, Xeon, and V100 are 6.6%, 7.7%, 4.1%, and 2.2%, respectively.

Furthermore, in order to analyze the effects of the proposed optimizations, a roofline model [19] on a VE Type 10B is used. Figure 5 shows the roofline model of the VE. The vertical axis represents the attainable performance (Gflop/s), and the horizontal axis represents the arithmetic intensity (Flops/Byte) that is a ratio of the number of floating-point calculations to the amount of data loaded from the main memory. To determine the roof due to the memory bandwidth, the Triad kernel of the STREAM benchmark [6] is used.

Figure 5 shows that the Himeno benchmark is a memory-bound application because the plot of the Himeno benchmark is on the left of the ridge point. Due to the optimizations, the arithmetic intensity is slightly increased, and the performance is improved almost linearly compared with the original Himeno benchmark. This shows that the memory bandwidth can be exploited by the optimizations. Therefore, the optimizations proposed in this paper are effective for SX-Aurora TSUBASA.

4.3 Evaluation of Multiple VEs

In Aurora8, the Himeno benchmark is executed using eight VEs. A single process is mapped to a single core of the VE. Therefore, up to 64 processes are assigned to eight VEs of Aurora8.

Figure 6 shows the effect of domain decomposition by the box plot. The optimizations except tuning process mapping are also applied. The vertical axis represents the performance (Gflop/s), and the horizontal axis represents the number of processes. The sample minimum, the lower quartile or first quartile, the median, the upper quartile or third quartile, and the sample maximum are

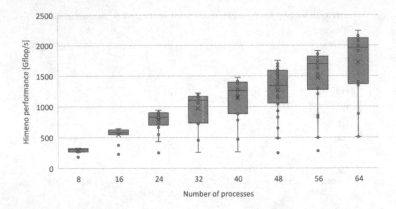

Fig. 6. Effects of domain decomposition tuning on performance.

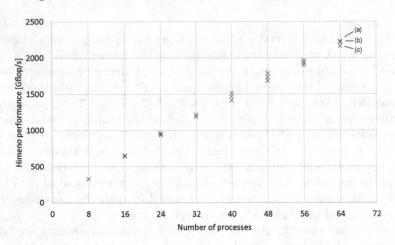

Fig. 7. Effects of the process mapping on performance.

shown in the box plot. The average value is plotted as the cross mark. In the graph, the minimum performance of each process is due to the shortening of the vector length that is caused by the decomposition of the innermost loop. In most cases where the degree of decomposition in the k direction is small, especially it is one or two, the higher performance is achieved than the average value. Furthermore, a high LLC hit ratio is basically achieved by increasing the degree of decomposition in the j direction compared with the i direction. However, that case does not necessarily achieve better performance than the case where the degree of decomposition in the i is larger than the j direction. This is because domain decomposition can also affect interprocess communication. Therefore, it may be possible to obtain higher performance by combining the tuning domain decomposition and the tuning process mapping.

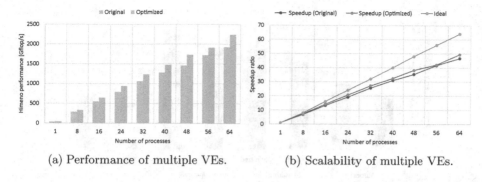

(a) Performance of multiple VEs.   (b) Scalability of multiple VEs.

Fig. 8. Evaluation of multiple VEs

Figure 7 shows the effect of the process mapping on the performance. Different plots mean different process mapping patterns based on the number of processes. The parameters of domain decomposition that achieve the highest performance are used in each number of processes. The other optimizations are also applied. According to the optimization points shown in Sect. 3.2, this experiment performs three candidates of mapping patterns that are expected to achieve high performance in each number of processes. The effect of the process mapping on the performance is noticeable in the cases of 40 or more processes, and there are about 50–100 Gflop/s performance differences among process mappings. This is because of a larger communication time for the data transfers among different VEs in different PCIe switches in such cases. Even though the difference in performances due to the process mapping is in less than 3–5% in the case of the Himeno benchmark, those in real applications become large. In 64 processes, the process mapping shown in Fig. 3-(a) achieves the highest performance among the three examples. On the other hand, the process mapping shown in Fig. 3-(c) is the lowest performance among the three examples. This is because MPI communication time and MPI communication idle time of Fig. 3-(a) are the shortest. In the other cases, the process mappings that follow the points shown in Sect. 3.2 also achieve the highest performance. As a result, to exploit a high bandwidth by memory copies, the processes to calculate adjacent domains should be assigned to the cores in the same VE at first. Second, the amounts of data transfer among different VEs in different PCIe switches should be reduced. Moreover, the processes should be assigned so that multiple VEs communicate with the other VEs in different PCIe switches.

Figures 8-(a) and 8-(b) show the performance and scalability of multiple VEs with all the optimizations, respectively. Each horizontal axis represents the number of processes. From Fig. 8-(a), it is shown that the optimized Himeno benchmark achieves higher performance than that without optimizations in each number of processes. The vertical axis of Fig. 8-(b) represents the speedup ratio to the performance of a single process. The ideal shows the ideal speedup ratio. From Fig. 8-(b), it is shown that the scalability improves compared with no optimizations. In 64 processes, SX-Aurora TSUBASA achieves 49.3× of the

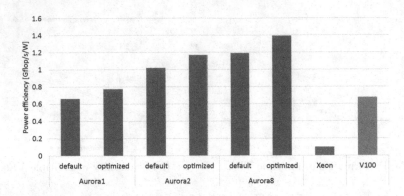

Fig. 9. Power efficiency of Aurora1, Aurora2, Aurora8, Xeon, and V100.

speedup ratio compared with the performance in a single process. The parallelization efficiency is 77.1%. This is due to the effect of the optimizations of domain decomposition and process mapping.

4.4 Power Efficiency

This subsection discusses the power efficiency of each system. The Himeno benchmark runs 10 min to fully consider the effects of changes in power, and the average power consumption per unit is measured. The power efficiency is derived by dividing the sustained performance by the average power consumption.

Figure 9 shows the power efficiencies of Aurora1, Aurora2, Aurora8, Xeon, and V100. From Fig. 9, it is shown that the proposed optimizations improve the power efficiency of Aurora1 by 17 %. Since the optimizations do not affect the power consumption, the power efficiency directly reflects the improvement of the performance. Therefore, the proposed optimizations are effective even for improving the power efficiency.

In addition, Fig. 9 shows that Aurora1, Aurora2, and Aurora8 achieve about 0.77, 1.17, 1.39 Gflop/s/W, respectively. By comparing the power efficiency among Aurora systems, Aurora8 achieves the highest power efficiency although Aurora8 has two sockets of Xeon, two power units, ten fans, and other equipment. This is because even if the number of VEs increases in Aurora8, the power consumption of the VHs does not change significantly. For this reason, the power of the VH per the VE becomes small relatively as the number of VEs increases. Thus, the power efficiency improves due to the performance improvement by increasing the number of VEs.

In addition, Aurora1 achieves 7.65× and 1.15× power efficiency compared with Xeon and V100. This is because the efficient vector processing of SX-Aurora TSUBASA is realized by the optimizations.

5   Related Work

Many optimizations for the Himeno benchmark on GPUs using CUDA and OpenACC have been proposed [11,14,15]. These papers discuss various optimizations such as appropriate domain decomposition and thread usage, optimization of data transfers, optimization of memory accesses, and so on. By these optimizations, the computing performance and memory bandwidth of the GPU can be utilized. However, optimizations of the Himeno benchmark for the latest vector architectures such as SX-Aurora TSUBASA have not yet been proposed.

In recent years, research on vector architectures, e.g., SX-Aurora TSUBASA, has been actively conducted. Afanasyev et al. analyzed SIMD-processing and computational characteristics in the architecture of SX-Aurora TSUBASA and NVIDIA GPU (Pascal, Volta) [9]. Komatsu et al. evaluated the performance of SX-Aurora TSUBASA using multiple benchmark programs, including the Himeno benchmark [13].

This paper optimizes the Himeno benchmark by deeply considering the architecture of SX-Aurora TSUBASA, especially in the differences in network bandwidth among VEs. Higher computing performance can be obtained by multiple optimizations.

6   Conclusions

This paper introduces the optimizations of the Himeno benchmark for the vector computer SX-Aurora TSUBASA to consider its architecture characteristics. In a single VE, optimizations in order to exploit the LLC bandwidth such as utilization of the LLC and tuning of the domain decomposition are applied to the Himeno benchmark. Loop unrolling is also applied to perform efficient vector processing. In multiple VEs, process mapping is tuned considering three-levels interprocess communication mechanisms in order to improve the sustained MPI communication bandwidth. By the optimizations, a single VE achieves 1.16x performance improvement. Furthermore, a single VE achieves 9.16x and 1.08x performance improvement compared with Xeon and V100, respectively. In multiple VEs, a good scalability is achieved by performing suitable domain decomposition and process mapping. Loop unrolling and tuning of the domain decomposition are relatively effective out of the four optimizations. The proposed optimizations also improve the power efficiency of each system configuration of SX-Aurora TSUBASA. In the future, larger-scale systems than Aurora8 are evaluated with a more detailed analysis of the process mapping.

Acknowledgments. This research was partially supported by MEXT Next Generation High-Performance Computing Infrastructures and Applications R&D Program, entitled "R&D of A Quantum-Annealing-Assisted Next Generation HPC Infrastructure and its Applications". The authors also would like to acknowledge HPC Solutions for providing Infiniband products.

References

1. Himeno benchmark. http://i.riken.jp/en/supercom/documents/himenobmt/. Accessed 10 Aug 2020
2. Intel Xeon Gold 6126 Processor. https://www.intel.com/content/www/us/en/products/processors/xeon/scalable/gold-processors/gold-6126.html. Accessed 10 August 2020
3. MVAPICH: MPI over InfiniBand, Omni-Path, Ethernet/iWARP, and RoCE. http://mvapich.cse.ohio-state.edu/benchmarks/. Accessed 12 Aug 2020
4. NEC SX-Aurora TSUBASA. https://www.nec.com/en/global/solutions/hpc/sx/index.html. Accessed 12 Aug 2020
5. NVIDIA V100 TENSOR CORE GPU. https://www.nvidia.com/en-us/data-center/v100/. Accessed 10 Aug 2020
6. STREAM: Sustainable Memory Bandwidth in High Performance Computers. https://www.cs.virginia.edu/stream/. Accessed 10 Aug 2020
7. SX-Aurora TSUBASA C/C++ Compiler User's Guide. https://www.hpc.nec/documents/sdk/pdfs/g2af01e-C++UsersGuide-018.pdf. Accessed 15 Aug 2020
8. SX-Aurora TSUBASA PROGINF/FTRACE User's Guide. https://www.hpc.nec/documents/sdk/pdfs/g2at03e-PROGINF_FTRACE_User_Guide_en.pdf. Accessed 15 Aug 2020
9. Afanasyev, I.V., Voevodin, V.V., Voevodin, V.V., Komatsu, K., Kobayashi, H.: Analysis of relationship between SIMD-processing features used in NVIDIA GPUs and NEC SX-Aurora TSUBASA vector processors. In: Malyshkin, V. (ed.) PaCT 2019. LNCS, vol. 11657, pp. 125–139. Springer, Cham (2019). https://doi.org/10.1007/978-3-030-25636-4_10
10. Davidson, J.W., Jinturkar, S.: Aggressive loop unrolling in a retargetable, optimizing compiler. In: Gyimóthy, T. (ed.) CC 1996. LNCS, vol. 1060, pp. 59–73. Springer, Heidelberg (1996). https://doi.org/10.1007/3-540-61053-7_53
11. Hart, A., Ansaloni, R., Gray, A.: Porting and scaling OpenACC applications on massively-parallel, GPU-accelerated supercomputers. Eur. Phys. J. Spec. Top. **210**, 5–16 (2012). https://doi.org/10.1140/epjst/e2012-01634-y
12. Komatsu, K., Kishitani, T., Sato, M., Kobayashi, H.: An appropriate computing system and its system parameters selection based on bottleneck prediction of applications. In: 2019 IEEE International Parallel and Distributed Processing Symposium Workshops (IPDPSW), pp. 768–777 (2019)
13. Komatsu, K., et al.: Performance evaluation of a vector supercomputer SX-aurora tsubasa. In: Proceedings of the International Conference for High Performance Computing, Networking, Storage, and Analysis, SC 2018. IEEE Press (2018)
14. Matsuoka, S., Aoki, T., Endo, T., Nukada, A., Kato, T., Hasegawa, A.: GPU accelerated computing-from hype to mainstream, the rebirth of vector computing. J. Phys.: Conf. Ser. **180**, 012043 (2009). https://doi.org/10.1088/1742-6596/180/1/012043
15. Phillips, E.H., Fatica, M.: Implementing the himeno benchmark with CUDA on GPU clusters. In: 2010 IEEE International Symposium on Parallel Distributed Processing (IPDPS), pp. 1–10 (2010). https://doi.org/10.1109/IPDPS.2010.5470394
16. Pietrzyk, J., Habich, D., Damme, P., Lehner, W.: First investigations of the vector supercomputer SX-aurora TSUBASA as a co-processor for database systems. In: Meyer, H., Ritter, N., Thor, A., Nicklas, D., Heuer, A., Klettke, M. (eds.) BTW 2019 - Workshopband, pp. 33–50. Gesellschaft für Informatik, Bonn (2019). https://doi.org/10.18420/btw2019-ws-03

17. Sarkar, V.: Optimized unrolling of nested loops. In: Proceedings of the 14th International Conference on Supercomputing, ICS 2000, pp. 153–166. Association for Computing Machinery, New York (2000). https://doi.org/10.1145/335231.335246
18. Van Werkhoven, B., Maassen, J., Seinstra, F.J., Bal, H.E.: Performance models for CPU-GPU data transfers. In: 2014 14th IEEE/ACM International Symposium on Cluster, Cloud and Grid Computing, pp. 11–20 (2014)
19. Williams, S., Waterman, A., Patterson, D.: Roofline: an insightful visual performance model for multicore architectures. Commun. ACM **52**(4), 65–76 (2009). https://doi.org/10.1145/1498765.1498785
20. Yamada, Y., Momose, S.: Vector engine processor of NEC's brand-new supercomputer SX-aurora TSUBASA. In: Proceedings of A Symposium on High Performance Chips, Hot Chips, vol. 30, pp. 19–21 (2018)

Benchmarking on GPU

Parallel Sorted Sparse Approximate Inverse Preconditioning Algorithm on GPU

Qi Chen[1], Jiaquan Gao[1(✉)], Xinyue Chu[1], and Guixia He[2]

[1] School of Computer and Electronic Information, Nanjing Normal University, Nanjing 210023, China
springf12@163.com
[2] Zhijiang College, Zhejiang University of Technology, Hangzhou 310024, China

Abstract. In this study, we present an efficient thread-adaptive sparse approximate inverse preconditioning algorithm on GPU, called GSPAI-Adaptive. For GSPAI-Adaptive, there are three novelties: (1) a thread-adaptive allocation strategy is presented for each column of the preconditioner, (2) a parallel framework of constructing the sparse approximate inverse preconditioner is proposed on GPU, (3) each component of the preconditioner is computed in parallel inside a thread group of GPU. Experimental results show that GSPAI-Adaptive is effective, and is advantageous over the popular preconditioning algorithms in two public libraries, and a latest parallel sparse approximate inverse preconditioning algorithm.

Keywords: Sparse approximate inverse · Preconditioning · GPU

1 Introduction

Sparse approximate inverse (SPAI) preconditioners can efficiently accelerate the convergence rate of Krylov subspace methods, such as the generalized minimal residual method (GMRES) [1] and the biconjugate gradient stabilized method (BiCGSTAB) [2], and thus have attracted considerable attention [3–6].

In recent years, graphic processing units (GPUs) have become an important resource for scientific computing, and have been used for high-performance computation in many fields [7–9]. Given that the cost of constructing SPAI preconditioners is generally very expensive for large-scale problems, some researchers have attempted to accelerate them on GPU and have developed many parallel preconditioning algorithms [10–13].

In this paper, we focus on accelerating to construct a kind of static SPAI preconditioner based on Frobenius norm minimization on GPU due to the high

The research has been supported by the Natural Science Foundation of China under grant number 61872422, and the Natural Science Foundation of Zhejiang Province, China under grant number LY19F020028, and the Natural Science Foundation of Jiangsu Province, China under grant number BK20171480.

F. Wolf and W. Gao (Eds.): Bench 2020, LNCS 12614, pp. 147–156, 2021.
https://doi.org/10.1007/978-3-030-71058-3_9

parallelism of static SPAI and its simple operations. As mentioned above, there has been some work on accelerating static SPAI preconditioners on GPU. In these existing work, SPAI-Adaptive that is proposed in [13] is a representative because it is better than other existing static preconditioning algorithms on GPU. However, we observe that its adaptability is effective only when the number of nonzero entries in each column of the preconditioner is the same or little difference. Otherwise, it may be worse than the one that uses a constant warp number.

Inspired by these observations, here we further investigate how to parallelize the static SPAI preconditioner highly on GPU, and propose an efficient parallel preconditioning algorithm (denoted by GSPAI-Adaptive) by presenting a new thread-adaptive allocation strategy. In GSPAI-Adaptive, the number of threads for computing columns of the preconditioner on each thread block can be different. Thus, it can alleviate the drawback of the thread allocation strategy proposed in [13]. Experimental results show that the proposed GSPAI-Adaptive is effective, and is advantageous over the popular incomplete LU factorization preconditioner in CUSPARSE [14], and a static sparse approximate inverse algorithm in ViennaCL [15], and the latest SPAI-Adaptive [13].

The main contributions in this paper are summarized as follows.

(1) An efficient thread-adaptive allocation strategy is presented. Utilizing this strategy, the thread-group size in each block is the same, and may be different among blocks.
(2) A parallel framework of constructing the SPAI preconditioner is proposed on GPU.
(3) Based on (1) and (2), an efficient SPAI algorithm on GPU, called GSPAI-Adaptive, is proposed.

The rest of this paper is organized as follows. In the second section, the SPAI algorithm is described. In the third section, the GSPAI-Adaptive is presented on GPU. Experimental analysis and evaluation are presented in the fourth section. The fifth section contains conclusions and points to our future research directions.

2   SPAI Algorithm

The basic idea of the SPAI procedure [6] is described as follows: Use a sparse matrix M to approximate the inverse of A, and M is computed by the following formula:

$$\min ||AM - E||_F^2. \tag{1}$$

Owing to the independence of the columns of M, the equation mentioned above can be separated into the following n independent least squares problems

$$\min_{m_k} ||Am_k - e_k||_2^2, \quad k = 1, 2, \cdots, n, \tag{2}$$

where e_k is the kth column of the identity matrix and m_k represents column k in matrix M. For a description of the implementation details of SPAI, we refer to the literature [13].

3   Parallel SPAI on GPU

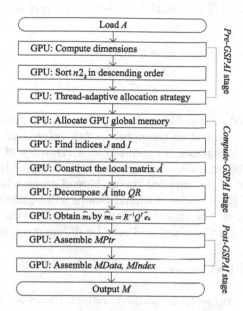

Fig. 1. Parallel framework of GSPAI-Adaptive

We present a thread-adaptive sparse approximate inverse preconditioning algorithm on GPU, called GSPAI-Adaptive. The parallel framework of GSPAI-Adaptive is shown in Fig. 1, which includes the following three stages: *Pre-GSPAI* stage, *Compute-GSPAI* stage, and *Post-GSPAI* stage.

3.1   Pre-GSPAI Stage

In this paper, we prescribe the sparsity of M in advance with the method in [13]. $M(i, j)$ is considered a nonzero if

$$|A(i, j)| > (1 - \tau) \max_j |A(i, j)|, \quad 0 \leqslant \tau \leqslant 1, \tag{3}$$

is satisfied, where τ is a user defined tolerance parameter (the main diagonal is always included).

Next, A is stored in memory using the CSC storage format, and M is also stored in columns. The dimensions of local submatrices $(n1_k, n2_k)$ are usually distinct for different k, $(k = 1, 2, \cdots, n)$. To simplify the accesses of data in memory and enhance the coalescence, the dimensions of all local submatrices are uniformly defined as $(n1max, n2max)$, where $n1max = \max_k\{n1_k\}$ and $n2max = \max_k\{n2_k\}$.

Finally, we present a new thread-adaptive allocation strategy, which includes the following steps:

(1) Sort $n2_k$ (number of nonzero entries of m_k) values in descending order, and use the SC array to map the naive column indices.

(2) For each $n2_k$, $k = 1, 2, \cdots, n$, the number of threads z_k is computed by the following formulas:

$$z_k = \min(2^l, nt), \tag{4}$$

$s.t.$

$$2^{l-1} < n2_k \leqslant 2^l. \tag{5}$$

Here nt is a fixed thread block size. z_k threads are grouped into a thread group, which is assigned to compute the kth column of M. Note that the compute gird in this paper is organized as a 1D array of the thread blocks, and the thread block is also organized as a 1D array of threads.

(3) If each column of M is computed via one thread group whose size is obtained by Eqs. (4) and (5), the size of thread groups will be likely different inside a block. Therefore, we fine tune the thread-group size so that the thread-group size in each block is the same, and may be different among blocks.

3.2 Compute-GSPAI Stage

Table 1. Arrays used in SPAI-Adaptive

Array	Size	Type	Array	Size	Type
$AData$	nonzeros	Double	$\widehat{m}$	$ns \times n2max$	Double
$AIndex$	nonzeros	Integer	$\widehat{A}$	$ns \times n1max \times n2max$	Double
$APtr$	n	Integer	R	$ns \times n2max \times n2max$	Double
SC	n	Integer	I	$ns \times n1max$	Integer
$atomic$	n	Integer	$iPTR$	ns	Integer
WS	$blocks$	Integer	J	$ns \times n2max$	Integer
BS	$blocks$	Integer	$jPTR$	ns	Integer

In the *Compute-GSPAI* stage, the allocations of GPU global memory are shown in Table 1, and transfer A, SC, BS, and WS values to global memory. Then, the following steps are implemented to compute M. In each step, the thread-group size $warpSize$ is first obtained for each block.

Find J: For each block, leting each thread group ($warpSize$ threads) to compute one of subsets of J assigned to the block. Furthermore, parallelism is also exploited inside each thread group, and the threads find indices satisfying Eq. (3) in parallel, and save them to shared memory sJ using the atomic operations. Next, the indices of sJ are sorted in ascending order inside one thread group, and then are written to a subset of J in parallel.

Find I: According to J, each block computes subsets of I assigned to the block in parallel.

Construct the Local Submatrix: Using I and J obtained above, the local submatrix, e.g., $\widehat{A}_k$, inside a thread group is constructed on global memory by loading columns indexed in J_k and matching them to I_k in parallel.

Decompose the Local Submatrix Into QR: This step is used to decompose the local submatrix into QR using modified Gram-Schmidt method. Each thread group is responsible for decomposing a local submatrix into QR. For a description of its detailed implementation, please refer to the literature [13].

Solve the Upper Triangular Linear System: The values of $\widehat{m}_k = R_k^{-1} Q_k^T \widehat{e}_k$ are computed in this step. For each block, we first obtain the thread-group size *warpSize* and then let each thread group in the block to compute one $\widehat{m}_k$. In a thread group, computing values of $\widehat{m}_k$ includes two steps. In the first step, all threads inside a thread group compute $Q_k^T \widehat{e}_k$ in parallel and save values to shared memory xE. In the second step, the values of $\widehat{m}_k$ are obtained by solving the upper triangular linear system, $R_k \widehat{m}_k = xE$, in parallel using shared memory.

Table 2. Descriptions of test matrices

Name	Kind	Dimension	Nonzeros	avg	max	min
cbuckle	Structural	13,681 × 13,681	676,515	49.4	600	26
gyro_m	Duplicate model reduction	17,361 × 13,681	340,431	19.6	120	4
imagesensor	Semiconductor device	118,758 × 118,758	1,446,,96	12.2	21	2
majorbasis	Optimization	160,000 × 160,000	1,750,416	10.9	18	4
Fault_639	Structural	638,802 × 638,802	27,245,944	42.7	267	1
t2em	Electromagnetics	921,632 × 921,632	4,590,832	5.0	5	1
G3_circuit	Circuit simulation	1,585,478 × 1,585,478	7,660,826	4.8	6	2

3.3   Post-GSPAI Stage

The *Post-GSPAI* stage is to assemble M in the CSC storage format, and store it to $MPtr$, $MIndex$, and $MData$ arrays. The *Post-GSPAI* stage includes the following steps: (1) Restore it to the original indices using the SC array; and (2) Assemble $MPtr$ using $jPTR$; and (3) Assemble $MData$ and $MIndex$ utilizing $MPtr$ and SC arrays. Each thread group is responsible for assembling one $\widehat{m}_k$ to $MData$ and one J_k to $MIndex$ in parallel.

4   Evaluation and Analysis

We evaluate the performance of GSPAI-Adaptive in this section. NVIDIA GTX1070 and TITANXp GPUs both are used in the performance evaluation. The test matrices in Table 2 are selected from the University of Florida Sparse Matrix Collection [16]. The source codes are compiled and executed using the CUDA toolkit 10.1 [17].

4.1 Effectiveness Analysis

We first take $\tau = 1.0$ and GTX1070 to test the effectiveness of GSPAI-Adaptive. For each test matrix, GPUBICGSTAB (without the preconditioner) and GPUP-BICGSTAB (with the preconditioner) are called to solve $Ax = b$, where all elemental values of b are 1 and the produced M is used as the preconditioner. They stop when the residual error is less than $1e^{-7}$ or the number of iterations exceeds 10,000. Table 3 shows the results. The time unit is second (s). Note that "/" means that the execution time of the algorithm is not counted because its number of iterations exceeds 10,000.

From Table 3, we can observe that without the preconditioner, for imagesensor, Fault_639, and G3_circuit, GPUBICGSTAB cannot converge in 10,000 iterations while GPUPBICGSTAB can converge under 1226 iterations. For cbuckle, gyro_m, majorbasis, and t2em, GPUBICGSTAB can terminate upon reaching a relative residual of less than $1e^{-7}$, but the number of iterations declines dramatically using the preconditioner. Furthermore, GPUPBICGSTAB has smaller execution time than GPUBICGSTAB.

Second, we take GTX1070 to investigate the effect of increasing τ on the execution time of GSPAI-Adaptive and GPUPBICGSTAB with GSPAI-Adaptive. Table 4 shows the execution time of GSPAI-Adaptive and GPUPBICGSTAB on GTX1070. For each matrix and any given τ, the first and second rows are the execution time of GSPAI-Adaptive and GPUPBICGSTAB, respectively, and the third row is the sum of the first two row time. GPUPBICGSTAB stops while the residual error is less than $1e^{-7}$. The time unit is s, and the minimum values of the second and third rows for each matrix both are marked in the red font.

Table 3. Iterations and execution time of two algorithms on GTX1070

Matrix	GPUBICGSTAB		GPUPBICGSTAB	
	Iterations	Execution time	Iterations	Execution time
cbuckle	8330	3.096	96	2.326
gyro_m	7565	2.109	180	0.635
imagesensor	>10000	/	52	0.596
majorbasis	114	0.821	20	0.643
Fault_639	>10000	/	1226	51.86
t2em	1581	3.861	755	2.790
G3_circuit	>10000	/	468	3.074

Table 4. Execution time of GSPAI-Adaptive and GPUPBICGSTAB

Matrix	$\tau = 0.5$	$\tau = 0.6$	$\tau = 0.7$	$\tau = 0.8$	$\tau = 0.9$	$\tau = 1.0$
cbuckle	0.279	0.264	0.271	0.327	0.463	1.998
	0.591	0.442	0.401	0.392	0.384	0.328
	0.870	0.706	0.672	0.719	0.847	2.326
gyro_m	0.035	0.040	0.044	0.078	0.139	0.311
	0.418	0.374	0.343	0.329	0.323	0.324
	0.453	0.414	0.387	0.407	0.462	0.635
imagesensor	/	/	/	/	/	0.287
	/	/	/	/	/	0.309
	/	/	/	/	/	0.596
majorbasis	0.050	0.050	0.048	0.066	0.090	0.347
	0.300	0.300	0.300	0.300	0.287	0.286
	0.350	0.350	0.348	0.366	0.377	0.643
Fault_639	2.092	2.336	2.692	3.217	5.483	41.813
	12.408	13.087	9.542	9.009	7.304	10.047
	14.500	15.423	12.234	12.226	12.787	51.860
t2em	0.038	0.038	0.041	0.080	0.080	0.091
	4.506	4.499	4.528	2.684	2.682	2.701
	4.544	4.537	4.569	2.764	2.762	2.792
G3_circuit	0.085	0.101	0.110	0.144	0.158	0.195
	4.923	6.828	4.008	3.573	3.356	2.879
	5.008	6.929	4.118	3.717	3.514	3.074

We observe for the total time of GSPAI-Adaptive and GPUPBICGSTAB, at first, as τ increases, it in general decreases although the execution time of GSPAI-Adaptive increases, and then beyond a certain threshold, the increase of τ can have a reverse effect on it. The main reason is that after τ reaches a certain threshold, the decrease of the GPUPBICGSTAB execution time cannot offset the increase of the GSPAI-Adaptive execution time with the increasing τ. This indicates that when constructing the preconditioner, we should pay attention not only to the quality of the preconditioner, but also to the time of constructing the preconditioner. In all our test cases, a large τ is almost well chosen.

4.2 Performance Comparison

We test the GSPAI-Adaptive performance by comparing it with CSRILU0 in CUSPARSE (denoted by CSRILU) [14], the static sparse approximate inverse preconditioning algorithm in ViennaCL (denoted by SSPAI-VCL) [15], and a latest sparse approximate inverse preconditioning algorithm (denoted by SPAI-Adaptive) [13]. Tables 5 and 6 show the comparison results on two GPUs,

Table 5. Execution time of all preconditioning algorithms and GPUPBICGSTAB on GTX1070.

Matrix	CSRILU+ GPUPBICGSTAB	SSPAI-VCL+ GPUPBICGSTAB	SPAI-Adaptive+ GPUPBICGSTAB	GSPAI-Adaptive+ GPUPBICGSTAB
cbuckle	0.731	N/A	8.281	1.998
	2.349	N/A	0.339	0.328
	154	N/A	96	96
	3.080	N/A	8.620	2.326
gyro_m	0.459	N/A	0.868	0.311
	1.506	N/A	0.325	0.324
	125	N/A	180	180
	1.965	N/A	1.193	0.635
imagesensor	/	/	0.338	0.287
	/	/	0.316	0.309
	>10000	>10000	52	52
	/	/	0.654	0.596
majorbasis	1.104	17.380	0.408	0.347
	0.067	0.052	0.295	0.296
	6	14	20	20
	1.171	17.432	0.703	0.643
Fault_639	/	N/A	198.297	41.813
	/	N/A	10.048	10.047
	>10000	N/A	1226	1226
	/	N/A	208.345	51.860
t2em	24.440	N/A	0.089	0.091
	2657.638	N/A	2.708	2.701
	409	N/A	755	755
	2682.078	N/A	2.797	2.792
G3_circuit	4.881	/	0.161	0.195
	14.114	/	2.871	2.879
	303	>10000	468	468
	18.995	/	3.032	3.074

respectively. For each matrix and the preconditioner, the first row is the execution time of the preconditioning algorithm, the second and third rows are the execution time and iterative number of GPUPBICGSTAB when the residual error is less than $1e^{-7}$, respectively, and the fourth row is the sum of execution time of the preconditioning algorithm and GPUPBICGSTAB.

From Tables 5 and 6, we discover that on two GPUs, the total time of GSPAI-Adaptive and GPUPBICGSTAB with GSPAI-Adaptive is the smallest among all algorithms for all matrices except for G3_circuit. This indicates that GSPAI-Adaptive is advantageous over CSRILU and SSPAI-VCL, and significantly improves the performance of SPAI-Adaptive.

Table 6. Execution time of all preconditioning algorithms and GPUPBICGSTAB on TITANXp.

Matrix	CSRILU+ GPUPBICGSTAB	SSPAI-VCL+ GPUPBICGSTAB	SPAI-Adaptive+ GPUPBICGSTAB	GSPAI-Adaptive+ GPUPBICGSTAB
cbuckle	1.097	N/A	6.806	1.811
	2.539	N/A	0.667	0.653
	154	N/A	96	96
	3.637	N/A	7.473	2.464
gyro_m	0.915	N/A	0.649	0.245
	1.648	N/A	0.709	0.710
	125	N/A	180	180
	2.563	N/A	1.358	0.955
imagesensor	/	/	0.240	0.213
	/	/	0.712	0.704
	>10000	>10000	50	50
	/	/	0.952	0.917
majorbasis	1.409	14.254	0.277	0.244
	0.072	0.087	0.688	0.619
	6	14	20	20
	1.481	14.341	0.965	0.863
Fault_639	/	N/A	118.944	29.669
	/	N/A	6.118	6.095
	>10000	N/A	1149	1149
	/	N/A	125.062	35.764
t2em	61.793	N/A	0.069	0.072
	3044.115	N/A	2.063	2.028
	427	N/A	824	824
	3105.908	N/A	2.132	2.100
G3_circuit	5.030	/	0.131	0.182
	11.575	/	2.061	2.044
	264	>10000	472	472
	16.605	/	2.192	2.226

5   Conclusion

We present a thread-adaptive implementation of sparse approximate inverse preconditioner on GPU in this paper, called GSPAI-Adaptive. In the proposed GSPAI-Adaptive, a thread-adaptive allocation strategy is used to assign the optimal thread number for each column of the preconditioner, and a parallel framework of SPAI on GPU is embraced. The experiments validate the high effectiveness of our proposed GSPAI-Adaptive.

References

1. Saad, Y., Schultz, M.H.: GMRES: a generalized minimal residual algorithm for solving nonsymmetric linear systems. SIAM J. Sci. Stat. Comput. **7**, 856–869 (1986)
2. Van der Vorst, H.A.: Bi-CGSTAB: a fast and smoothly converging variant of Bi-CG for the solution of nonsymmetric linear systems. SIAM J. Stat. Comput. **13**(2), 631 (1992)
3. Kolotilina, L.Y., Yeremin, A.Y.: Factorized sparse approximate inverse preconditionings I: theory. Soc. Ind. Appl. Math. **14**, 45–58 (1993)
4. Benzi, M., Meyer, C.D., Tuma, M.: A sparse approximate inverse preconditioner for the conjugate gradient method. SIAM J. Sci. Comput. **17**, 1135–1149 (1996)
5. Grote, M.J., Huckle, T.: Parallel preconditioning with sparse approximate inverses. Soc. Ind. Appl. Math. **18**, 838–853 (1997)
6. Chow, E.: A priori sparsity patterns for parallel sparse approximate inverse preconditioners. SIAM J. Sci. Comput. **21**(5), 1804–1822 (2000)
7. Li, K., Yang, W., Li, K.: A hybrid parallel solving algorithm on GPU for quasi-tridiagonal system of linear equations. IEEE Trans. Parallel Distrib. Syst. **27**(10), 2795–2808 (2016)
8. Gao, J., Zhou, Y., He, G., Xia, Y.: A multi-GPU parallel optimization model for the preconditioned conjugate gradient algorithm. Parallel Comput. **63**, 1–16 (2017)
9. He, G., Gao, J., Wang, J.: Efficient dense matrix-vector multiplication on GPU. Concurr. Comput.: Pract. Exp. **30**(19), e4705 (2018)
10. Gao, J., Wu, K., Wang, Y., Qi, P., He, G.: GPU-accelerated preconditioned GMRES method for two-dimensional Maxwell's equations. Int. J. Comput. Math. **94**(10), 2122–2144 (2017)
11. Lukash, M., Rupp, K., Selberherr, S.: Sparse approximate inverse preconditioners for iterative solvers on GPUs. In: Proceedings of the 2012 Symposium on High Performance Computing, pp. 1–8. Society for Computer Simulation International (2012)
12. Dehnavi, M.M., Fernandez, D.M., Gaudiot, J.L., Giannacopoulos, D.D.: Parallel sparse approximate inverse preconditioning on graphic processing units. IEEE Trans. Parallel Distrib. Syst. **24**(9), 1852–1862 (2012)
13. He, G., Yin, R., Gao, J.: An efficient sparse approximate inverse preconditioning algorithm on GPU. Concurr. Comput.: Pract. Exp. **32**(7), e5598 (2020)
14. Cusparse library, v10.1. https://docs.nvidia.com/cuda/cusparse/index.html
15. Rupp, K., et al.: ViennaCL–linear algebra library for multi-and many-core architectures. SIAM J. Sci. Comput. **38**(5), S412–S439 (2016)
16. Davis, T.A., Hu, Y.: The university of Florida sparse matrix collection. ACM Trans. Math. Softw. (TOMS) **38**(1), 1–25 (2011)
17. CUDA C programming guide, v10.1. https://docs.nvidia.com/cuda/cuda-c-programming-guide

ComScribe: Identifying Intra-node GPU Communication

Palwisha Akhtar$^{(\boxtimes)}$ ⓘ, Erhan Tezcan ⓘ, Fareed Mohammad Qararyah ⓘ,
and Didem Unat ⓘ

Department of Computer Science and Engineering, Koç University, Istanbul, Turkey
{pakhtar19,etezcan19,fqararyah18,dunat}@ku.edu.tr

Abstract. GPU communication plays a critical role in performance and scalability of multi-GPU accelerated applications. With the ever increasing methods and types of communication, it is often hard for the programmer to know the exact amount and type of communication taking place in an application. Though there are prior works that detect communication in distributed systems for MPI and multi-threaded applications on shared memory systems, to our knowledge, none of these works identify intra-node GPU communication. We propose a tool, COMSCRIBE that identifies and categorizes types of communication among all GPU-GPU and CPU-GPU pairs in a node. Built on top of NVIDIA's profiler *nvprof*, COMSCRIBE visualizes data movement as a communication matrix or bar-chart for explicit communication primitives, Unified Memory operations, and Zero-copy Memory transfers. To validate our tool on 16 GPUs, we present communication patterns of 8 micro- and 3 macro-benchmarks from NVIDIA, Comm|Scope, and MGBench benchmark suites. To demonstrate tool's capabilities in real-life applications, we also present insightful communication matrices of two deep neural network models. All in all, COMSCRIBE can guide the programmer in identifying which groups of GPUs communicate in what volume by using which primitives. This offers avenues to detect performance bottlenecks and more importantly communication bugs in an application.

Keywords: Inter-GPU communication · Multi-GPUs · Profiling

1 Introduction

Graphical Processing Units (GPUs) are increasingly becoming common and vital in compute-intensive applications such as deep learning, big data and scientific computing. With just a single GPU and exceeding working sets, memory becomes a bottleneck, inevitably shifting the trend towards multi-GPU computing. Currently, a variety of single node multi-GPU systems are available such as NVIDIA's TU102, V100-DGX2 and DGX A100 with varying number of GPUs ranging from 2 to 16, connected via NVLink based interconnects [15,19,20,26]. Traditionally, multiple GPUs in a node are interconnected via PCIe such as in DGX1 with PCIe Gen3 [19]. A balanced tree structure is formed by the

© Springer Nature Switzerland AG 2021
F. Wolf and W. Gao (Eds.): Bench 2020, LNCS 12614, pp. 157–174, 2021.
https://doi.org/10.1007/978-3-030-71058-3_10

PCIe network where one GPU is connected to another through a PCIe switch. In such systems, multi-GPU application performance is constrained by the lower bandwidth of PCIe and the indirect connections between GPUs. With the introduction of GPUDirect Peer-to-Peer that enables direct data access and transfer capability among multiple GPUs and GPU-oriented interconnects such as NVLink, programmers can directly read or write local graphics memory, peer GPU memory or the system memory, all in a common shared address space [13]. The higher bandwidth of such interconnects improve the performance of applications utilizing inter-GPU communication.

To handle the communication between multiple GPUs, CUDA API offers various data transfer options to the programmer under the hood of Unified Virtual Addressing (UVA), Zero-copy Memory and Unified Memory paradigms. Explicit data transfers can be carried out in the traditional way using CUDA's memory copy functions but with Zero-copy Memory or Unified Memory operations, the memory management is handled by the CUDA driver and programmer is free from the burden of tracking data allocations and transfers among host and the GPUs in a node. However, in such a scenario, users are unaware of the underlying communication taking place between the GPUs.

In this pool of varying communication types and methods for single node multi-GPU systems, communication remains as a critical programming component and performance contributor [31]. As a result, identifying communication between GPUs can guide the programmer in many aspects. Firstly there are many cases of communication that result in implicit data transfers, and these unforeseen communications will occur if the programmer is indifferent towards the topology and device capabilities. For example, an application might not have any implicit communication with an all-to-all GPU topology, but might have them with a Hyper-cube Mesh topology such as in DGX-1, where some GPUs do not have direct interconnect to some others, and transfers among them may require explicit routing, as NVLink is not self-routed [16]. Secondly, it is possible for there to be bugs in an application such that the result is not affected, however the bug causes an unexpected communication pattern, which may be hard to infer from debugging alone. Finally, monitoring and identifying communication among multiple GPUs can help reason about scalability issues and performance divergence between different implementations of the same application, and guide the programmer to utilize the GPU interconnects for better performance [8]. For instance, a single GPU application when naively scaled up to multiple GPUs, may follow a master-slave communication pattern, which would mean that it is not effectively using the GPU interconnects. All in all, identifying which groups of GPUs communicate in what volume and their quantitative comparison offer avenues to detect performance bugs and tune software for scalability.

Even though there are communication identification tools for MPI applications on distributed systems (e.g. EZTrace [33]) and for multi-threaded applications on shared memory systems (e.g. ComDetective [29]), to our knowledge, there is no communication monitoring tool designed for single node multi-GPU systems. In this work, we propose COMSCRIBE, a tool that can monitor, identify, and quantify different types of communication among GPU devices. The tool can generate a communication matrix that shows the amount of data movement between two pairs of GPUs or with host. In addition, it can automatically identify the types of communication i.e. explicit transfers using CUDA primitives or implicit transfers using Zero-copy Memory or Unified Memory operations. COMSCRIBE is built on top of NVIDIA's profiling tool *nvprof* [25] that provides a timeline of all activities taking place on a GPU such as kernel execution, memory copy or memory set, data transmitted or received through NVLink. However, *nvprof* does not readily generate communication matrices and the *nvprof* trace consists of extraneous information that is unnecessary for a user who is concerned with communication among GPUs. Our tool overcomes this limitation and works in two steps: First, it collects intra-node multi-GPU and CPU-GPU memory transfer information during execution with *nvprof*. Then, it performs post-processing to quantify communication among GPUs as well as the host, and identify communication types. Our contributions are summarized below:

- We present COMSCRIBE, a tool for generating communication matrices that show both the number of transfers and amount of data transferred between every GPU-GPU and CPU-GPU pair in a node.
- The tool also identifies different types of communication such as explicit data transfers using CUDA primitives or implicit transfers using Zero-copy Memory or Unified Memory.
- We validate our tool against known communication patterns using 11 benchmarks from Comm|Scope [28], MGBench [7] and NVIDIA on a multi-GPU V100-DGX2 system and demonstrate how COMSCRIBE is used for detecting a communication bug in one of these benchmarks.
- We present communication matrices for 2 well-known deep neural network models and demonstrate how COMSCRIBE can be used for explaining different implementations of data parallelism in deep learning.

COMSCRIBE is available at https://github.com/ParCoreLab/ComScribe.

2   Background

In this section we will discuss various data exchange scenarios with CUDA data transfer primitives that are supported by NVIDIA GPUs. Traditionally, for point-to-point CPU-GPU and GPU-GPU communication, programmers initiate explicit data transfers using `cudaMemcpy`. GPU-GPU transfers involve copying through host memory, which not only requires careful tracking of device pointer allocations but may also result in performance degradation [17]. With the introduction of GPUDirect Peer-to-Peer and GPU-oriented interconnects among multiple GPUs, one GPU can directly transfer or access data at another GPU's memory within a shared memory node [13,15,16,18]. For host-initiated explicit peer-to-peer memory copies, `cudaMemcpyPeer` is used, which also requires passing device IDs as arguments, so that CUDA can infer the direction of transfer.

With CUDA 4.0, NVIDIA introduced a new "unified addressing space" mode called Unified Virtual Addressing (UVA), allowing all CUDA execution – CPU and GPU – in a single address space. Applications using UVA with peer-access do not require device IDs to be specified to indicate the direction of transfer for an explicit host-initiated copy. Instead, by using `cudaMemcpy` with transfer kind `cudaMemcpyDefault`, CUDA runtime can infer the location of the data from its pointer and carry out the copy. However, if the peer access is disabled, implicit transfers through the host will occur, resulting in communication overhead.

Similar to CUDA explicit bulk transfers, data accesses between host and device are also possible with Zero-copy Memory, which requires mapped pinned memory. Pinned allocations on the host are mapped into the unified virtual address space and device kernels can directly access them [24]. Similarly, implicit peer-to-peer data accesses between GPUs are possible during kernel execution in Zero-copy Memory paradigm.

In CUDA 6.0, NVIDIA introduced a single address space called Unified Memory. With data allocated using Unified Memory, CUDA becomes responsible for migrating memory pages to the memory of the accessing CPU or GPU on demand. Pascal GPU architecture via its Page Migration Engine is the first that supports virtual memory page faulting and migration [14]. Unified Memory offers ease of programming as managed memory is accessible to CPU and GPUs with a single pointer and does not require explicit memory transfers among them.

Multi-GPU applications are developed using any of the above CUDA data transfer primitives with respect to the GPU hardware, CUDA version and application model. We cover all types of communication options available for intra-node communication using CUDA, and present a tool for generating a communication matrix and identifying the types of communication for single node multi-GPU applications.

3   Types of Communication

As discussed in the previous section, various data transfer primitives are available in the CUDA programming model, each requiring different software or hardware support. Therefore, we have divided these communication types into two categories: Peer-to-Peer and Host-Device shown in Fig. 1. These categories are further divided into sub-categories based on the data transfer options utilized, e.g. explicit transfers using `cudaMemcpy` and `cudaMemcpyPeer`, or implicit transfers using Zero-copy Memory or Unified Memory operations. In order to make reference to the sub-categories easier, we have assigned them a case number. We should also note that synchrony is not a consideration here, because we are interested in the type and amount of the transfer. For example, whether we use `cudaMemcpy` or `cudaMemcpyAsync` does not matter, as both methods will result in the same amount of data transfer, though at different times. In the following subsections, we explain each category and their sub-categories as cases.

3.1   Peer-to-Peer Communication

Peer-to-Peer communication refers to a data transfer between two GPUs that support peer-to-peer memory access. This type of communication depends on

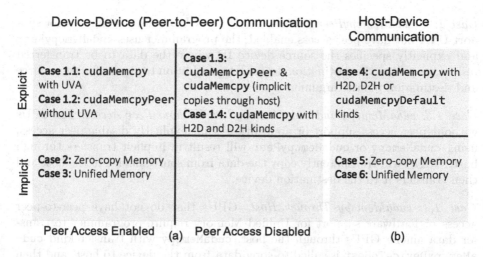

Fig. 1. Types of communication in a multi-GPU system. D2H stands for "Device to Host", H2D stands for "Host to Device".

whether peer access is enabled or disabled and whether the application is using UVA, Zero-copy Memory or Unified Memory.

Peer-to-Peer Explicit Transfers: The host can be explicitly programmed to carry out peer-to-peer transfers using CUDA API. GPU's support for peer access determines the communication pattern in the node, for instance, in a node where GPUs do not have peer access, GPU-GPU communication will happen through the host. Furthermore, the choice of CUDA primitives depend on the utilization of UVA in data transfers. For example, cudaMemcpyDefault transfer kind can not be used without UVA.

Case 1: cudaMemcpy and cudaMemcpyPeer. The host can explicitly initiate a peer-to-peer transfer using either cudaMemcpy or cudaMemcpyPeer. These functions have several cases to consider:

Case 1.1: cudaMemcpy With UVA. UVA enables a single address space for all CPU and GPU memories. It allows determining the physical memory location from the pointer value and simplifies CUDA memory copy functions. For GPUs with peer access and UVA, data transfers between devices are initiated by the host, using cudaMemcpyDefault as the transfer kind with cudaMemcpy, also known as a UVA memory copy. cudaMemcpyDefault is only allowed on systems that support UVA and it infers the direction of transfer from pointer values, e.g. if two pointers point to different devices, then a peer-to-peer memory transfer occurs without specifying in which memory space source and destination pointers are. An alternative to this would be to use cudaMemcpy with the transfer kind cudaMemcpyDeviceToDevice instead.

Case 1.2: cudaMemcpyPeer Without UVA. For CUDA devices that do not support UVA but have peer access enabled, the programmer uses `cudaMemcpyPeer` and explicitly specifies the source device ID where the data to be transferred resides, as well as the destination device ID, in addition to the buffer size, source and destination pointer arguments.

Case 1.3: cudaMemcpy and cudaMemcpyPeer Without Peer Access. For GPUs without peer access support or applications that explicitly disable peer access, using `cudaMemcpy` or `cudaMemcpyPeer` will result in implicit transfers through host. CUDA will transparently copy the data from source device to the host and then transfers it to the destination device.

Case 1.4: cudaMemcpy Through Host. GPUs that do not have peer-to-peer access or hardware support for Unified Memory require programmer to transfer data among GPUs through the host. `cudaMemcpy` with transfer kind `cudaMemcpyDeviceToHost` is called to copy data from the device to host, and then again with transfer kind `cudaMemcpyHostToDevice` to transfer data from host to another device. This movement of data through host introduces additional overhead, similar to *Case 1.3.*

Peer-to-Peer Implicit Transfers: One can use UVA or Unified Memory to transfer data among GPUs with peer access with very little programming effort. For a kernel, its data can reside in device memory, in another GPU or in system memory. During the kernel execution, CUDA can infer the location of kernel's data and implicitly migrate it to the local device memory if required [22].

Case 2: Zero-Copy Memory. Devices that support UVA and have peer access enabled can access each others' data through the same pointer. During execution, device kernels can implicitly read or write data into the memory of their peer GPUs. Zero-copy Memory transfers occur over the device interconnects without any explicit control by the programmer. The interconnect speed, access pattern and degree of parallelism affect the performance of these transfers [28].

Case 3: Unified Memory. With Unified Memory, data is allocated with `cudaMallocManaged`, which returns a pointer that is accessible from CPU and any GPU in the shared memory node. In this case, if a single pointer is allocated on one device using CUDA managed memory and another device accesses it during kernel execution, then the GPU driver will migrate the page from one device memory to another [14]. Page migrations occur between devices in the event of a page fault, which results in an implicit data transfer.

3.2   Host-Device Communication

Similar to peer-to-peer communication between GPUs, CUDA explicit data transfer primitives, Zero-copy Memory and Unified Memory operations exist for communication between host and device. The following cases describe each option in more detail.

Case 4: cudaMemcpy. Traditionally, after initializing data on the host, the data is transferred to the device using `cudaMemcpy` with the transfer kind of `cudaMemcpyHostToDevice`. Data is transferred from device to host using `cudaMemcpy` with the transfer kind of `cudaMemcpyDeviceToHost`. Using transfer kinds such as `cudaMemcpyHostToDevice` and `cudaMemcpyDeviceToHost` mean that the direction of transfer is explicitly specified by the programmer. Or, with the support of UVA, these transfers can happen without explicitly describing the direction by calling `cudaMemcpy` with `cudaMemcpyDefault` as the transfer kind. CUDA will infer the direction of transfer by analyzing the pointer, similar to *Case 1.1*.

Case 5: Zero-Copy Memory. Zero-copy Memory paradigm uses mapped pinned memory that allows a GPU to directly access host memory over PCIe or NVLink interconnect. Page-locked mapped host memory is allocated using `cudaHostAlloc` or `cudaHostRegister` with `cudaHostRegisterMapped`. Next, the device pointer referring to the same memory is acquired with `cudaHostGetDevicePointer` and therefore no explicit data transfers are needed. During kernel execution, the device pointer directly accesses the mapped pinned host memory [24]. However, it must be noted that only unidirectional data transfers that are `read` and `write` operations by the device are possible in this case as the host is unable to perform `write` operations in Zero-copy Memory paradigm [28].

Case 6: Unified Memory. As mentioned in *Case 3*, for Unified Memory, data is allocated via `cudaMallocManaged` which returns a pointer accessible from any processor. If a pointer is allocated on host using `cudaMallocManaged` and the device accesses it during kernel execution, then driver will migrate the page from host to device memory. This holds true for the host as well. In the event of a page fault, page migration occur.

4   Design and Implementation of ComScribe

We have developed COMSCRIBE on top of *nvprof* to identify multi-GPU and CPU-GPU communications. *nvprof* is a light-weight command-line profiler available since CUDA 5.0 [25]. Although NVIDIA's latest profiling tool *Nsight System* is a system-wide performance analysis tool designed to visualize an application's behaviour [27], it does not provide its output in a machine-readable format. On the other hand, *nvprof*'s profiling output can be stored in a text or csv format, which is machine-readable and can be parsed by our tool. Though, *nvprof* profiles data transfers between CPU-GPU and GPU-GPU during the execution of an application, the data required for generating intra-node communication matrices i.e. total amount of data shared between each pair of devices in a node for each type of communication is not readily available, requiring extra effort by the programmer to extract such information. For example, for each kernel or memory copy, detailed information such as kernel parameters, shared memory usage and memory transfer throughput are recorded. As a result, it becomes difficult for the user to observe the total data movement and types of communication between each pair of GPUs in a node. COMSCRIBE represents the

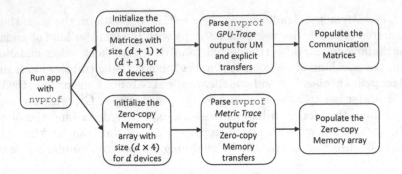

Fig. 2. Workflow diagram of COMSCRIBE

communication pattern in a compact though descriptive manner to the user, in the light of the data obtained and parsed from *nvprof*.

The *nvprof* profiler has 5 modes namely *Summary*, *GPU-Trace*, *API-Trace*, *Event/Metric Summary* and *Event/Metric Trace*. Among these only GPU-Trace and Event/Metric Trace modes are necessary for our tool. The GPU-Trace mode provides information of all activities taking place on a GPU such as kernel execution, memory copy and memory set and is used by COMSCRIBE for generating communication matrices for explicit and Unified Memory data transfers. For Zero-copy Memory transfers, the amount of data transmitted and received through NVLink by a single GPU in a node is drawn from *nvprof*'s Metric Trace mode. Since *nvprof* operates in one mode at a time and the information for all types of communication is not available through a single mode, COMSCRIBE runs the application twice with *nvprof* to collect necessary information.

COMSCRIBE parses *nvprof*'s output for memory copies, accumulates the communication amount for each GPU-GPU and CPU-GPU pair, infers the types of communication and then generates intra-node communication matrices for an application using CUDA's explicit data transfer primitives or Unified Memory. COMSCRIBE can generate these matrices for both the number of bytes transferred, and the number of data transfers. For Zero-copy Memory, *nvprof*'s Metric Trace mode lacks information about the sending or receiving GPU, making it infeasible to generate communication matrix. Instead our tool constructs a bar chart that represents the data transmitted to and received from another GPU or CPU for write and read operations, respectively for each GPU.

4.1   ComScribe Workflow

To generate communication matrices, our tool runs the application code with *nvprof*'s GPU-Trace and Metric Trace modes. The profiling output is parsed only for memory copies by our tool. The type of memory copy helps COMSCRIBE identify the CUDA data transfer primitive. The workflow is shown in Fig. 2 and explained below:

1. **Running application with nvprof.** By running the application with *nvprof*'s GPU-Trace and Metric Trace modes, all activities taking place in

the node such as kernel executions and memory copies are recorded in a chronological order.

2. **Initialization of communication matrices and Zero-copy Memory array.** Depending on the number of devices, d, available in the node, communication matrices represented as two-dimensional arrays of size $(d+1) \times (d+1)$ are initialized to zero where $+1$ accounts for CPU. Communication matrices are generated for both explicit data transfers and Unified Memory transfers. For Zero-Copy Memory transfers, a one-dimensional array of size $(d \times (4)$ is initialized to recorded data transferred and received through NVLink and system memory. A Zero-copy Memory read or write can be identified for a GPU's memory and host memory, so in total this gives 4 types of transfer for every device.

3. **Recording data transfers.** *nvprof's* GPU-Trace mode output is parsed by COMSCRIBE, which reads each recorded event to detect if it is an event of data transfer between GPU-GPU or CPU-GPU. On each memory copy, the source device ID, destination device ID, size of data transferred is extracted. The size is converted into bytes, then by looking at the source and destination device IDs, the communication event is recorded to the communication matrix, where y-axis indicates receivers and x-axis indicates senders. In this matrix, we can also see the host as a sender or receiver, at the 0th index with the letter H. Data movements within a GPU such as local memory copies are also recorded, which appear as non-zero entries in the diagonal of the communication matrix. Moreover, memory copies are characterized to identify the types of communication. For Zero-copy Memory transfers the Metric Trace mode output is parsed to record data movement for each GPU.

4. **Generating Results.** After the memory copy information are recorded in communication matrices, these matrices are plotted for each identified type of communication, in the case of explicit and Unified Memory transfers. Zero-copy Memory transfers are represented in the form of a bar chart.

5   Evaluation

This section evaluates COMSCRIBE on selected micro-benchmarks from the MGBench and Comm|Scope [7,28] benchmark suites. We also present communication matrices for macro-benchmarks including NVIDIA's Ising-GPU and Multi-GPU Jacobi Solver, MGBench's Game of Life (GOL) and study two deep learning applications: E3D-LSTM and Transformer [7,21,23,35,38] as use-cases. The evaluation is conducted on a DGX-2 system consisting of 16 NVIDIA Tesla V100 GPUs, allowing simultaneous communication between 8 GPU pairs at 300 GBps through 12 integrated NVSwitches [20]. We use CUDA v10.0.130.

5.1   Micro-benchmarks from Comm|Scope and MGBench

To validate our tool, we have selected 8 micro-benchmarks with known communication patterns, 6 from Comm|Scope and 2 from MGBench based on their

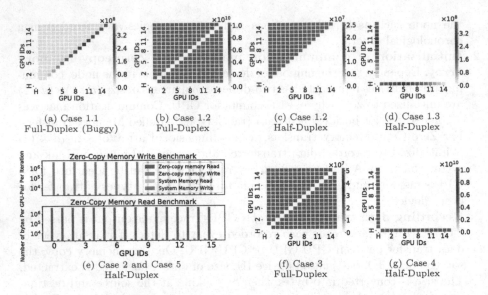

Fig. 3. COMSCRIBE results on several micro-benchmarks from Comm|Scope (Figs. 3a, 3c, 3d, 3e and 3f) and MGBench (Figs. 3b and 3g) benchmark suites.

communication types using explicit data transfers with peer access enabled and disabled, as well as implicit data transfers using Unified Memory and Zero-copy Memory operations. We have observed that the communication matrices for number of bytes transferred and number of transfers are very similar in these benchmarks, therefore we only include the former in this section. Each Comm|Scope micro-benchmark is run with 100 iterations and transfers 256 KB data. Whereas, MGBench by default runs with 100 MB for memory transfers and for a total of 100 iterations.

Figures 3a–3d show the communication matrices generated by COMSCRIBE for the micro-benchmarks that use peer-to-peer explicit transfers. Benchmarks in Figs. 3a and 3b use `cudaMemcpyAsync` and `cudaMemcpyPeerAsync` data transfer primitives, respectively for peer-to-peer full-duplex communication with peer access enabled (*Case 1.1 and 1.2*). However, the pattern in the communication matrix in Fig. 3a is not as expected – should have been similar to the one in Fig. 3b, which shows the data movement as a result of bidirectional transfers between peer GPUs. We observe data transfers in one direction between GPUs along with data movement within the GPU, which translates to local memory copies. With the help of COMSCRIBE, we were able to spot this incorrect communication pattern and identify a communication bug in Comm|Scope's *cudaMemcpyAsync-duplex* micro-benchmark on GitHub[1]. After investigating the benchmark code, we realized that the source and destination pointers of the

---

[1] https://github.com/c3sr/comm_scope/blob/master/src/cudaMemcpyAsync-duplex/gpu_gpu_peer.cpp.

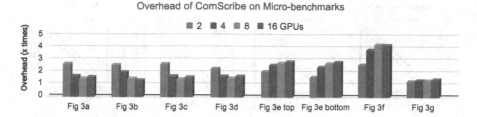

Fig. 4. COMSCRIBE's overhead (mostly stemming from *nvprof*) for Comm|Scope and MGBench micro-benchmarks on 2, 4, 8, and 16 GPUs.

second copy are unintentionally pointing to the same device, resulting in data movement within the device.

Figures 3c and 3d present results for peer-to-peer half-duplex micro-benchmarks where unidirectional communication between each pair of GPUs is expected. However, the key difference between two is that the benchmark in Fig. 3c uses `cudaMemcpyPeerAsync` with peer access (*Case 1.2*) while the benchmark in Fig. 3d uses `cudaMemcpyPeerAsync` without peer access (*Case 1.3*). Figure 3c and 3d demonstrate how peer access being enabled or disabled affects the communication pattern. In Fig. 3c, the transfers are made directly to the peer GPU, whereas, in Fig. 3d, the data is implicitly transferred through host memory as peer access is disabled.

Figures 3e and 3f show results for implicit transfers that occur through Zero-copy Memory and Unified Memory operations (*Case 2, 3 and 5*). Zero-copy Memory bar-chart generated by COMSCRIBE in Fig. 3e shows the number of bytes received and transmitted by a single GPU in Comm|Scope Zero-copy Memory GPU-GPU read and write half-duplex micro-benchmarks, respectively, where a small amount of system memory write is detected as well (*Case 5*). The benchmark in Fig. 3f uses Unified Memory for peer-to-peer full-duplex communication. We can observe communication between all pairs of GPUs in the node as a result of bidirectional Unified Memory data transfers. However, the total number of bytes transferred among each pair of GPUs is twice than expected due to prefetching i.e. after GPU0 transfers data to GPU1, in the next iteration the data is prefetched from GPU1 to GPU0 before it is sent to GPU2.

Figure 3g illustrates the communication type of *Case 4* with the MGBench's Scatter-Gather micro-benchmark that uses `cudaMemcpyAsync` with transfer kind `cudaMemcpyHostToDevice` to scatter data from host to all GPUs and then gathers data back from GPUs to host using `cudaMemcpyAsync` with transfer kind `cudaMemcpyDeviceToHost`.

5.2   Overhead

Figure 4 presents the overhead of running COMSCRIBE with the micro-benchmarks. *nvprof* is the main contributor to the overhead of COMSCRIBE as post-processing of *nvprof* profiling outputs is negligible. On average, an over-

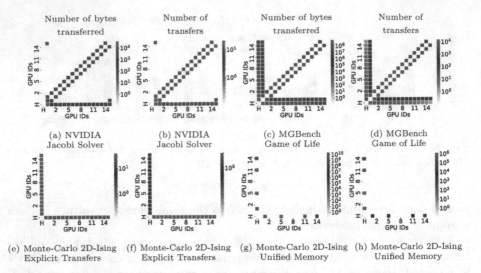

(a) NVIDIA
Jacobi Solver

(b) NVIDIA
Jacobi Solver

(c) MGBench
Game of Life

(d) MGBench
Game of Life

(e) Monte-Carlo 2D-Ising   (f) Monte-Carlo 2D-Ising   (g) Monte-Carlo 2D-Ising   (h) Monte-Carlo 2D-Ising
Explicit Transfers   Explicit Transfers   Unified Memory   Unified Memory

Fig. 5. COMSCRIBE results on macro-benchmarks from NVIDIA (Figs. 5a, 5b, 5e, 5f, 5g and 5h) and MGBench (Figs. 5c and 5d).

head of 2.17x is observed, due to the fact that COMSCRIBE runs the application with *nvprof* twice, once with GPU-Trace mode for explicit and Unified Memory transfers, and then once more with Metric Trace mode for Zero-copy Memory transfers.

5.3   Macro-benchmarks from NVIDIA and MGBench

We present insightful communication matrices for three macro-scale applications using 16 GPUs. These applications are NVIDIA's Multi-GPU Jacobi Solver, NVIDIA's Monte Carlo Simulation 2D Ising-GPU, and MGBench's Game of Life [7,21,23]. Unlike micro-benchmarks, here we include both matrices: number of bytes transferred and number of transfers. We use log scale instead of linear scale in the figures to make the small transfers visually noticeable.

Figures 5a and 5b show a communication pattern that is prevalent among stencil applications such as Jacobi solver: a GPU shares a "halo region" with it's nearest neighbors and it communicates with them in every iteration to exchange and update the halo cells. This access pattern can be thought of as a "window" [6] and shows itself as non-zero entries on the diagonal in the communication matrix. Note that this application uses circular boundary condition where every cell including the ones at the boundary has a neighbor in all directions, which presents itself as communication between GPU0 and GPU15.

Game of Life, shown in Figs. 5c and 5d, is also a type of stencil application. It's domain is distributed among GPUs, and the state of the domain in the next iteration is computed by every GPU using the current state. Similarly, there is a halo region that needs to be updated every iteration, and the nearest-neighbor communication reflects itself as non-zero entries in the diagonal of the

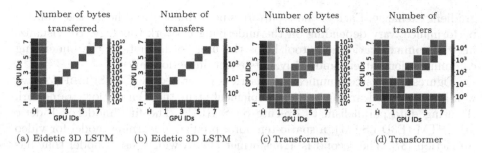

(a) Eidetic 3D LSTM   (b) Eidetic 3D LSTM   (c) Transformer   (d) Transformer

Fig. 6. COMSCRIBE results on two Deep Neural Network models implemented in TensorFlow framework using data parallelism across 8 GPUs

communication matrix. Unlike Jacobi, this application does not employ a circular boundary condition. Note that the communication values are not equal among the GPUs because this benchmark runs the application in increments, starting from 1 GPU, increasing one at a time until the desired amount of GPUs, 16 in our case, is reached. As a result, GPU0 is used in all 16 runs, GPU1 is used in 15 runs, and so on. We can observe this at the diagonals of both figures and from the L shape pattern in Fig. 5c in which the number of bytes transferred and number of transfers decrease as the GPU IDs increase.

Figures 5e–5h shows the results of GPU-accelerated Monte Carlo simulations of 2D Ising Model. The algorithm uses a scatter-gather pattern where independent simulations are run on each GPU and then they are gathered at the host for averaging. Scatter-gather is distinguishable as it forms an L shape pattern on the communication matrix, where the host sends data to all GPUs, and receives data from all. We observe that this application uses both explicit transfers and Unified Memory at the same time, which is identified by COMSCRIBE. By looking at the explicit transfer's communication matrices, we can immediately see the intended communication pattern, which is also complied by the Unified Memory transfers. Moreover, this application (Figs. 5g and 5h) serves as an example for the type of communication presented as *Case 6*.

5.4   Use-Cases: Deep Neural Network (DNN) Models

This section demonstrates the communication matrices for two DNN models. GPUs are commonly used by the deep learning frameworks to accelerate both the training and inference. Due to its simplicity and desired weak scaling, the dominant distributed DNN training strategy is to use data parallelism, where input is split among multiple GPUs each of which holds a replica of the model [30,34]. In stochastic gradient descent (SGD) [2], where the training is done in minibatches, the weights of the DNN need to be updated. In the update phase, the results of the replicas have to be averaged to obtain the gradient of the whole minibatch [5]. The averaged version then needs to be accessed by all the replicas to update their parameters. The pervasiveness of data parallelism has resulted in having multiple underlying implementations (communication patterns) for the gradient exchange. Each of these pattern's performance, and hence the training performance, vary depending on the underlying network topology. By visualizing the communication, our tool helps the user to understand the underlying communication pattern and analyze its effect on performance.

Figures 6 shows communication matrices generated by COMSCRIBE for two well-known deep learning models implemented in the TensorFlow framework [1] using data parallelism to execute on 8 GPUs. The first model is Eidetic 3D LSTM (E3D-LSTM), a spatio-temporal predictive learning model for video prediction [37]. The second is Transformer [36], a widely used model that has considerably influenced the design of SoTA Transformer based models in the NLP domain. From the communication matrices of these two models, two variations of communication used for implementing data parallelism can be observed. In the E3D-LSTM case, the gradients are sent from GPUs to host, they are averaged, then sent from host to GPU0. After this, GPU0 scatters the gradients to all other GPUs. For Transformer, the gradients are exchanged using the nearest neighbor communication, as a result the largest amount of communication occurs between neighboring pairs of GPUs. While in E3D-LSTM, the second largest communication is self communication happening due to the huge memory allocated temporarily for 3D-convolutions. In Transformer, it occurs between GPU0 and host for the purpose of training checkpoint, where a copy of the model state and its parameters are sent to the host. The remaining communication takes place between the host and devices to distribute the training samples in the batch across the GPUs. Note that the models we used in our demonstration are large models having O (1 billion) parameters that is why the last type of communication is relatively small. However, it might have higher relative importance for smaller models.

6   Related Work

EZTrace is a generic trace generation framework for programs that are written using OpenMP, MPI, PThreads and CUDA [33]. It generates trace for such programs in two steps: first, it collects the necessary information by intercepting function calls and recording events during program execution using the FxT library [10], then it performs a post-mortem analysis on the recorded events. The total message size exchanged and number of messages for peer-to-peer and collective communications can be generated for MPI with the help of EZTrace, but for CUDA this feature is limited. For CUDA applications, a log of recorded events is generated that includes the total message size exchanged and number of messages for CPU-GPU communication that uses cudaMalloc-cudaMemcpy pair only. In comparison, our tool detects a much diverse set of communication types and generates communication matrices for GPU-GPU communication including all CUDA explicit data transfer primitives, Zero-copy Memory and Unified Memory operations.

Comm|Scope [28] is a set of micro-benchmarks to measure latency and bandwidth for CUDA data transfer primitives with different data placement scenarios.

This includes NUMA-aware point-to-point CPU-GPU and GPU-GPU explicit data transfer primitives in CUDA as well as Zero-copy Memory and Unified Memory operations. Although our work and Comm|Scope are parallel in motivation to categorize types of communication, Comm|Scope does not focus on identifying and quantifying GPU communications. NUMA-aware communication affects the performance, however it does not change the amount of data shared among GPUs, thus it is not included in our work. Moreover, we consider additional CUDA data transfer primitives like `cudaMemcpyPeer` and transfer kind `cudaMemcpyDefault`.

Li et al. [15,16] developed Tartan, a multi-GPU benchmark suite consisting of micro-benchmarks for characterizing GPU interconnects and 14 application benchmarks for evaluating how multi-GPU execution performance is affected by different GPU interconnects. Tartan includes micro-benchmarks to evaluate interconnects including PCIe, NVLink 1.0, NVLink 2.0, NV-SLI, NVSwitch and Infiniband systems with GPUDirect RDMA for point-to-point and collective intra-node and inter-node GPU-GPU communication. It measures communication efficiency, bandwidth and latency of GPU-GPU explicit memory copies and the NVIDIA Collective Communications Library (NCCL) on the interconnects. However, Tartan is not a tool but rather a benchmark suite, whereas, we offer a tool that captures the total amount of data transferred for intra-node peer-to-peer communication.

A number of tools that generate communication patterns for multi-core applications exist in the literature. ComDetective [29] is a sampling based tool that uses Performance Monitoring Units (PMUs) and debug registers to detect inter-thread data transfers and generates communication matrices for multi-threaded applications for shared memory systems. Likewise, Azimi et al. [3] and Tam et al. [32] leverage kernel support to access PMUs and the kernel generates the communication pattern for the applications. Barrow-Williams et al. [4] and Cruz et al. [9] employ simulator-based approach to collect memory access traces for generating communication patterns. Lastly, Numalize [11,12] uses binary instrumentation to intercept memory accesses and captures communication between threads accessing the same address in memory. However, none of these tools can be used to identify multi-GPU communication.

7   Conclusion

In single node multi-GPU systems, communication is a critical programming component and performance contributor. For such systems, we categorize various data transfer options offered by CUDA API to the programmer, into explicit data transfer primitives and implicit transfers using Unified Memory and Zero-copy Memory operations for Peer-to-Peer and Host-Device communications. We developed COMSCRIBE on top of NVIDIA's profiling tool *nvprof* that identifies, quantifies and generates communication matrices for GPU-GPU and CPU-GPU communications in a node. COMSCRIBE's workflow is presented, followed by it's evaluation on several micro- and macro-benchmarks as well as two deep learning applications. Communication matrices generated by our tool can be used by programmers to differentiate types of communication, study the communication patterns and detect communication bugs in a multi-GPU application.

Acknowledgement. Some of the authors from Koç University are supported by the Turkish Science and Technology Research Centre Grant No: 118E801. The research presented in this paper has benefited from the Experimental Infrastructure for Exploration of Exascale Computing (eX3), which is financially supported by the Research Council of Norway under contract 270053.

References

1. Abadi, M., et al.: TensorFlow: a system for large-scale machine learning. In: Proceedings of the 12th USENIX Conference on Operating Systems Design and Implementation, OSDI 2016, pp. 265–283. USENIX Association, USA (2016)
2. Amari, S.: Backpropagation and stochastic gradient descent method. Neurocomputing **5**(4–5), 185–196 (1993)
3. Azimi, R., Tam, D.K., Soares, L., Stumm, M.: Enhancing operating system support for multicore processors by using hardware performance monitoring. ACM SIGOPS Oper. Syst. Rev. **43**(2), 56–65 (2009)
4. Barrow-Williams, N., Fensch, C., Moore, S.: A communication characterisation of Splash-2 and Parsec. In: 2009 IEEE International Symposium on Workload Characterization (IISWC), pp. 86–97. IEEE (2009)
5. Ben-Nun, T., Hoefler, T.: Demystifying parallel and distributed deep learning: an in-depth concurrency analysis. ACM Comput. Surv. (CSUR) **52**(4), 1–43 (2019)
6. Ben-Nun, T., Levy, E., Barak, A., Rubin, E.: Memory access patterns: the missing piece of the multi-GPU puzzle. In: International Conference for High Performance Computing, Networking, Storage and Analysis (SC), 15–20 November 2015 (2015). https://doi.org/10.1145/2807591.2807611
7. Ben-Nuun, T.: MGBench: multi-GPU computing benchmark suite (CUDA) (2017). https://github.com/tbennun/mgbench. Accessed 29 Jul 2020
8. Buono, D., Artico, F., Checconi, F., Choi, J.W., Que, X., Schneidenbach, L.: Data analytics with NVLink: an SpMV case study. In: ACM International Conference on Computing Frontiers 2017, CF 2017, pp. 89–96 (2017). https://doi.org/10.1145/3075564.3075569
9. da Cruz, E.H.M., Alves, M.A.Z., Carissimi, A., Navaux, P.O.A., Ribeiro, C.P., Méhaut, J.F.: Using memory access traces to map threads and data on hierarchical multi-core platforms. In: 2011 IEEE International Symposium on Parallel and Distributed Processing Workshops and Phd Forum, pp. 551–558. IEEE (2011)
10. Danjean, V., Namyst, R., Wacrenier, P.-A.: An efficient multi-level trace toolkit for multi-threaded applications. In: Cunha, J.C., Medeiros, P.D. (eds.) Euro-Par 2005. LNCS, vol. 3648, pp. 166–175. Springer, Heidelberg (2005). https://doi.org/10.1007/11549468_21
11. Diener, M., Cruz, E.H., Alves, M.A., Navaux, P.O.: Communication in shared memory: concepts, definitions, and efficient detection. In: 2016 24th Euromicro International Conference on Parallel, Distributed, and Network-Based Processing (PDP), pp. 151–158. IEEE (2016)
12. Diener, M., Cruz, E.H., Pilla, L.L., Dupros, F., Navaux, P.O.: Characterizing communication and page usage of parallel applications for thread and data mapping. Perform. Eval. **88**, 18–36 (2015)

13. Foley, D., Danskin, J.: Ultra-performance pascal GPU and NVLink interconnect. IEEE Micro **37**(2), 7–17 (2017)
14. Harris, M.: Unified memory for cuda beginners — nvidia developer blog (June 2017). https://devblogs.nvidia.com/unified-memory-cuda-beginners/
15. Li, A., et al.: Evaluating modern GPU interconnect: PCIe, NVLink, NV-SLI, NVSwitch and GPUDirect. IEEE Trans. Parallel Distrib. Syst. **31**(1), 94–110 (2020)
16. Li, A., Song, S.L., Chen, J., Liu, X., Tallent, N., Barker, K.: Tartan: evaluating modern GPU interconnect via a multi-GPU benchmark suite. In: 2018 IEEE International Symposium on Workload Characterization (IISWC), pp. 191–202 (2018)
17. Micikevicius, P.: Multi-GPU programming (2012). https://on-demand.gputech conf.com/gtc/2012/presentations/S0515-GTC2012-Multi-GPU-Programming.pdf
18. NVIDIA: NVIDIA GPUDirect technology (2012). http://developer.download. nvidia.com/devzone/devcenter/cuda/docs/GPUDirect_Technology_Overview.pdf
19. NVIDIA: NVIDIA DGX-1 with the Tesla V100 system architecture. White Paper (2017). https://images.nvidia.com/content/pdf/dgx1-v100-system-architecture-whitepaper.pdf. Accessed 28 Jul 2020
20. NVIDIA: DGX-2 : AI servers for solving complex AI challenges — NVIDIA (2018). https://www.nvidia.com/en-us/data-center/dgx-2/. Accessed 28 Jul 2020
21. NVIDIA: Multi-gpu-programming-models: examples demonstrating available options to program multiple GPUs in a single node or a cluster (2018). https:// github.com/NVIDIA/multi-gpu-programming-models. Accessed 29 Jul 2020
22. NVIDIA: CUDA runtime API (July 2019). https://docs.nvidia.com/cuda/pdf/ CUDA_Runtime_API.pdf. Accessed 29 Jul 2020
23. NVIDIA: Ising-gpu: GPU-accelerated Monte Carlo simulations of 2d Ising model (2019). https://github.com/NVIDIA/ising-gpu. Accessed 29 Jul 2020
24. NVIDIA: Best practices guide: CUDA toolkit documentation (2020). https://docs. nvidia.com/cuda/cuda-c-best-practices-guide/index.html#zero-copy. Accessed 12 May 2020
25. NVIDIA: CUDA profiler user's guide (July 2020). https://docs.nvidia.com/cuda/ pdf/CUDA_Profiler_Users_Guide.pdf. Accessed 28 Jul 2020
26. NVIDIA DGX A100: universal system for AI infrastructure — NVIDIA (2020). https://www.nvidia.com/en-us/data-center/dgx-a100/. Accessed 28 Jul 2020
27. NVIDIA: NVIDIA Nsigh systems documentation (2020). https://docs.nvidia.com/ nsight-systems/index.html. Accessed 28 Jul 2020
28. Pearson, C., et al.: Evaluating characteristics of CUDA communication primitives on high-bandwidth interconnects. In: Proceedings of the 2019 ACM/SPEC International Conference on Performance Engineering, ICPE 2019, pp. 209–218. Association for Computing Machinery, New York (2019). https://doi.org/10.1145/ 3297663.3310299
29. Sasongko, M.A., Chabbi, M., Akhtar, P., Unat, D.: ComDetective: a lightweight communication detection tool for threads. In: Proceedings of the International Conference for High Performance Computing, Networking, Storage and Analysis, pp. 1–21 (2019)
30. Shazeer, N., et al.: Mesh-TensorFlow: deep learning for supercomputers. In: Advances in Neural Information Processing Systems, pp. 10414–10423 (2018)
31. Sourouri, M., Gillberg, T., Baden, S.B., Cai, X.: Effective multi-GPU communication using multiple CUDA streams and threads. In: Proceedings of the International Conference on Parallel and Distributed Systems, ICPADS 2015, 10 April 2015, pp. 981–986 (2014). https://doi.org/10.1109/PADSW.2014.7097919

32. Tam, D., Azimi, R., Stumm, M.: Thread clustering: sharing-aware scheduling on SMP-CMP-SMT multiprocessors. ACM SIGOPS Oper. Syst. Rev. **41**(3), 47–58 (2007)

33. Trahay, F., Rue, F., Faverge, M., Ishikawa, Y., Namyst, R., Dongarra, J.: EZTrace: a generic framework for performance analysis. In: 2011 11th IEEE/ACM International Symposium on Cluster, Cloud and Grid Computing, pp. 618–619. IEEE (2011)

34. Valiant, L.G.: A bridging model for parallel computation. Commun. ACM **33**(8), 103–111 (1990)

35. Vaswani, A., et al.: Attention is all you need. CoRR abs/1706.03762 (2017). http://arxiv.org/abs/1706.03762

36. Vaswani, A., et al.: Attention is all you need. In: Advances in Neural Information Processing Systems, pp. 5998–6008 (2017)

37. Wang, Y., Jiang, L., Yang, M.H., Li, L.J., Long, M., Fei-Fei, L.: Eidetic 3d LSTM: a model for video prediction and beyond. In: International Conference on Learning Representations (2018)

38. Wang, Y., Jiang, L., Yang, M.H., Li, L.J., Long, M., Fei-Fei, L.: Eidetic 3d LSTM: a model for video prediction and beyond. In: International Conference on Learning Representations (2019). https://openreview.net/forum?id=B1lKS2AqtX

Application and Dataset

A Benchmark of Ocular Disease Intelligent Recognition: One Shot for Multi-disease Detection

Ning Li[1], Tao Li[1,2], Chunyu Hu[1], Kai Wang[1], and Hong Kang[1,3(✉)]

[1] College of Computer Science, Nankai university, Tianjin 300350, China
kanghong@nankai.edu.cn
[2] State Key Laboratory of Computer Architecture, Institute of Computing Technology, Chinese Academy of Science, Beijing 100190, China
[3] Beijing Shanggong Medical Technology Co. Ltd., Beijing 100176, China

Abstract. In ophthalmology, early fundus screening is an economic and effective way to prevent blindness caused by ophthalmic diseases. Clinically, due to the lack of medical resources, manual diagnosis is time-consuming and may delay the condition. With the development of deep learning, some researches on ophthalmic diseases have achieved good results, however, most of them are just based on one disease. During fundus screening, ophthalmologists usually give diagnoses of multi-disease on binocular fundus image, so we release a dataset with 8 diseases to meet the real medical scene, which contains 10,000 fundus images from both eyes of 5,000 patients. We did some benchmark experiments on it through some state-of-the-art deep neural networks. We found simply increasing the scale of network cannot bring good results for multi-disease classification, and a well-structured feature fusion method combines characteristics of multi-disease is needed. Through this work, we hope to advance the research of related fields.

Keywords: Fundus images · Multi-disease · Image classification · Neural network · Computer-aided diagnosis

1 Introduction

Fundus diseases are the leading causes of blindness among human beings worldwide [22]. Among them, diabetic retinopathy (DR), glaucoma, cataract and age-related macular degeneration (AMD) are the most popular ophthalmic diseases. According to related surveys, there will be over 400 million people with DR by 2030, and the glaucoma patients will reach 80 million people worldwide by 2020 [8]. These ophthalmic diseases have become a serious public health problem in the world. Most importantly, the ophthalmic disease has irreversible properties, which could cause unrecoverable blindness. In clinical scenarios, early detection of these diseases can prevent visual impairment. However, the number of ophthalmologists are out of balance compared with that of patients seriously.

F. Wolf and W. Gao (Eds.): Bench 2020, LNCS 12614, pp. 177–193, 2021.
https://doi.org/10.1007/978-3-030-71058-3_11

Moreover, fundus screening manually is time-consuming and relies heavily on ophthalmologists' experience. These reasons make it difficult to perform large-scale fundus screening. Therefore, an automatic computer-aided diagnosis algorithm for ophthalmic diseases screening is important particularly.

However, designing such an effective computer-aided diagnosis algorithm is challenging. For example, microaneurysm is an important reference for DR screening [18]. However, the size of microaneurysm is very small, so that it is hard to be detected and it is easy to be confused with other lesions. Meantime, the low contrast between the lesion pixels and the background pixels, the irregular shape of the lesions and the large differences between the same lesion points caused by different cameras also make it difficult to accurately identify ophthalmic diseases.

Although there have already been some deep learning models for ophthalmic disease screening, and they achieve remarkable performance. We found there are some limitations. 1) *Single disease*. Most of the identification models only concentrate on one ophthalmic disease [26,31], and most of the dataset they use provide annotations for only one kind of ophthalmic disease. However, considering the actual needs of patients with fundus disease in daily life, we believe that establishing a more effective and comprehensive fundus screening system that can detect multiple diseases is necessary. 2) *Single eye*. Existing datasets are based on a fundus image [6,7], but in real clinical scenarios, ophthalmologists usually diagnose patients with information from both eyes.

To solve the problem above-mentioned, in this paper, we release a publicly available dataset for multiple ophthalmic diseases detection. Different from the current published international monocular dataset, our dataset contains 5,000 pairs of binocular images, i.e. 10,000 images in total. Moreover, we provide annotations for 8 diseases on binocular images, which means that there may be multiple diseases for one patient. In addition, multi-disease screening is more complicated than the current single disease screening, and there are few relevant studies to learn from. Hence, we performed experiments on several popular deep learning based classification networks for multi-disease classification. Extensive experiments show simply increasing the scale of network cannot lead to performance improvement, and a well-structured feature fusion method which combines characteristics of multiple diseases is needed.

In summary, the main contributions of our work are as follows. First, we collected, annotated and release a multi-disease fundus image dataset named Ophthalmic Image Analysis-Ocular Disease Intelligent Recognition (OIA-ODIR). Second, we performed experiments on nine popular deep neural network models on this dataset, thereby establishing a benchmark. At last, by presenting this dataset, we hope that it can promote the further development of the clinical multi-disease classification research.

2   Related Work

At present, the works of ocular disease screening are mainly performed on optical coherence tomography (OCT) images and fundus images. With the development of artificial intelligence in the field of medical image processing, some related methods have achieved pleasing results.

2.1 OCT Images Recognition

OCT is one of the commonly used methods for fundus disease examination. After investigation, about 5.35 million OCTs were used in the United States in 2014 [2]. OCT has been widely used in clinical because of the advantages of low-loss, high-resolution, noninvasive medical imaging, compared to other methods. Ophthalmologists can observe the patient's retina layers through OCT images, measure these layers, and find minor early fundus lesions, then provide the corresponding treatment [27].

At present, the focus of some works is done through OCT image recognition, including segmentation [17], detection [24] and classification [23], etc. He et al. [14] proposed a new way for retina OCT layer surface and lesion segmentation without handcrafted graph. A novel method for multiclass drusen segmentation in retinal OCT images was proposed by Asgari et al. [3]. Their method consistently outperforms several benchmarks in some ways by using a decoder for each target category and an additional decoder for the areas among the target layers. Marzieh Mokhtari et al. [20] calculate local cup to disc ratio by fusing fundus images and OCT B-scans to get the symmetry of two eyes, which can detect early ocular diseases better. Mehta et al. [19] proposed a OCT images system for multi-class, multi-label classification, which augments data by using patient information, such as age, gender and visual acuity data.

Although the work of OCT images for ocular diseases screening has been quite mature, the existing public datasets of OCT images are quite few. In addition, comparing with color fundus images, OCT images have higher requirements on acquisition equipment and are more difficult to obtain. In this paper, we provide a new large-scale color fundus image dataset to encourage further research which could be applied in real clinical scenes.

2.2 Fundus Images Recognition

Some related results have been published on fundus image classification. In order not to delay the treatment of patients and to solve the quality classification of fundus images, Zhang et al. proposed an improved residual dense block convolutional neural network to effectively divide fundus images into good quality and poor quality [30]. Zhang et al. described a six-level cataract grading method focusing on multi-feature fusion, which extracted features from residual network (ResNet-18) and gray level co-occurrence matrix (GLCM), the results show advanced performance [31]. Hong et al. developed a 14-layers deep CNN model that can accurately diagnose diseases in the early stages of AMD and help ophthalmologists perform ocular screening [26].

For multiple diseases recognition. Choi et al. used neural networks and random forest to study classification of 10 fundus diseases on STructured Analysis of the REtina (STARE) database [7]. Chelaramani et al. conducted three tasks on a private dataset, including four common diseases classification, 320 fine-grained classification and generated text diagnosis [5]. On a public database named Singapore Malay Eye Study (SiMES) [11], Chen et al. performed multi-label classification of three common fundus diseases on an image, with Entropic Graph regularized Probabilistic Multi-label learning [6].

With the rapid development of artificial intelligence, computer-assisted fundus disease diagnosis have gradually developed. Although the above works have obtained quite good results, they still have limitations to a certain extent. Many of their works are based on a single disease solely, when other fundus diseases need to be detected, the structure need to be redesigned, which undoubtedly makes research cumbersome and inefficient. At the same time, in the process of image processing, some works requires artificial designed features, which makes the operation cumbersome and requires a lot of human prior knowledge.

Currently, many existing datasets for the research on fundus diseases are either too small or the types of diseases are too single, which makes them extremely difficult to apply their work to practical clinical scenarios. Although there are already some fundus datasets for multi-disease research, they are relatively few in number of images and types of diseases. In clinical diagnosis, patients usually have more than one ocular disease, so it is necessary to publish a large-scale fundus image dataset containing multiple diseases.

3 Our Dataset

As the best of our knowledge, there are few publicly available fundus image datasets with multi-disease annotations on one image. However, in clinical application, more than one prediction could be given when observing binocular fundus image. At the same time, ophthalmologists make a diagnosis based on the patient's fundus image, age and other information. This has prompted us to collect and release a multi-modal fundus dataset containing multiple diseases. In this section, we will introduce some details of our dataset.

3.1 Image Collection and Annotation

Collection. The images of OIA-ODIR are derived from our private clinical fundus databases. The database contains more than 1.6 million images totally, and the fundus images are collected from 487 clinical hospitals in 26 provinces across China. Each image contains abnormalities in different areas of the fundus caused by various diseases, these areas include macula, optic cup, optic disc, blood vessels, and the entire fundus background. We conducted statistics and analysis on these fundus disease categories, and unified a more detailed classification of a certain disease category into a category to label each image, i.e., the DR of stage 1, 2, 3, 4 are unified as DR et al.

In order to ensure the high-quality of fundus images, we cleaned the images of our private database by filtering out duplicate images and low-quality images. Then, we selected some samples from the remaining fundus images at a suitable

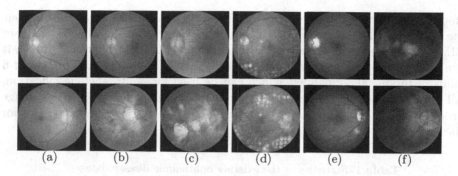

(a)   (b)   (c)   (d)   (e)   (f)

Fig. 1. Examples of images in left (top) and right (bottom) eyes. The diagnostic keywords of each column are provided as [left; right]. (a) normal; normal (b) normal; pathological myopia (c) DR; pathological myopia (d) laser spot, vitreous denaturation, DR; laser spot, DR (e) normal; AMD, DR (f) DR, pathological myopia; pathological myopia

ratio for training and testing. Finally, we obtained 10,000 fundus images with 8 types of annotations from the left and right eyes of 5,000 patients. The labeled categories include normal, diabetic retinopathy (DR), glaucoma, cataract, age-related macular degeneration (AMD), hypertension, myopia, and other diseases.

Annotation. The annotation work of our dataset is done by the professional annotation staff and arbitration team, which took about 10 months to complete. The annotation staff and arbitration team are composed of three ophthalmologists with more than 2 years of clinical experience and three ophthalmologists with more than 10 years of clinical experience in ophthalmology. We strictly follow the corresponding standards and procedures in the process of data annotation. First, three annotators respectively annotate the same batch of fundus images and record the results. If there is any disagreement among the three annotators, the arbitration team will arbitrate the results, the final annotation result shall be based on the consensus of two or more experts. All of these guarantee the persuasiveness of our dataset. At last, some images from our dataset can be seen in Fig. 1.

3.2 Features of Dataset

Currently, there are already some datasets for ophthalmic disease research. For example, in [18], Gao et al. exposed a fundus image dataset called DDR, which can perform three tasks of image classification, semantic segmentation and object detection. Kaggle DR [1] is the largest fundus image dataset currently used for the classification of DR. Kora [4] is widely used in AMD detection, which contains fundus images of 2840 patients. STARE [15] has 397 images and can be used for 14 diseases' classification. The Messidor-2 dataset contains 1,200 fundus images for classification of DR and macular degeneration [10]. A dataset related to glaucoma detection research, named ORIGA, contains 650 fundus images, but the dataset is not available [32]. In addition, there is an unpublished dataset RIM-ONE about optic nerve head segmentation [12]. While e-optha is public, it can only be used for lesion detection [9]. SiMES [11] contains 3150 images of 6 kinds of fundus abnormalities, which can be used for multi-label classification. All these datasets have greatly promoted the development of medical image processing and are of innovative significance. Table 1 shows some statistics for these datasets.

Table 1. Statistics of the existing ophthalmic disease datasets

Dataset	Annotations	Images	Multi-disease	Multi-label	Available
DDR [18]	DR staging	13,673	N	N	Y
Kaggle DR [1]	DR staging	88,702	N	N	Y
KORA [4]	AMD	–	N	N	Y
Messidor-2 [10]	DR staging, AMD	1,200	N	N	Y
ORIGA [32]	Glaucoma detection	650	N	N	N
RIM-ONE [12]	ONH segmentation	783	N	N	N
e-optha [9]	Lesion detection	463	N	N	Y
STARE [15]	14-disease	397	N	N	Y
[28]	36-disease	–	Y	Y	N
SiMES [11]	6-disease	3,150	Y	Y	Y
ODIR	8-disease	10,000	Y	Y	Y

Although many datasets as above have been proposed for ophthalmic disease research, few of them are used for the detection of multiple ophthalmic diseases on one eye, which undoubtedly causes obstacles to the related work for clinical application. As far as we know, our dataset, named OIA-ODIR, is the first internationally launched large-scale multi-type diseases detection dataset based on binocular fundus image. Compared with other fundus image datasets in the same field, our dataset has significant features described as follows.

1. *Multi-disease:* Unlike most existing fundus image datasets, which only focus on one ophthalmic disease, our dataset contains multiple ophthalmic diseases. As shown in Fig. 2, these diseases include abnormalities with lesions in different areas of the fundus. According to the International Classification Standard ICO [29], DR is divided into four stages. The early stage of DR is characterized by various abnormalities on the retina. For example, there are lesions such as hard exudate, soft exudate, bleeding and neovascularization on the fundus image. Compared with advanced DR, the early stage is not serious and the clinical treatment is significant [25]. For glaucoma, the ophthalmologist usually calculates the ratio of the optic cup to the optic disc. When the ratio is greater than 0.5, the patient is judged to have glaucoma. In recent years, ophthalmologists have also diagnosed by the neuroretinal rim loss, the visual field

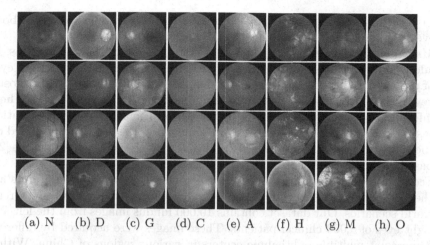

(a) N   (b) D   (c) G   (d) C   (e) A   (f) H   (g) M   (h) O

Fig. 2. Images from each categories. Each column of images comes from the same category, i.e. Normal (N), DR (D), Glaucoma (G), Cataract (C), AMD (A), Hypertension (H), Myopia (M), and Others (O)

and the defect of the retinal nerve fiber layer. Clinically, protocols such as the American Cooperative Cataract Research Group (CCRG) method are generally used to classify cataracts. Experienced ophthalmologists compare the fundus images of patients with standard cataract photos to determine the severity of cataract patients [33]. Nowadays, AMD is also a common cause of blindness in people of an advanced age, and it is closely related to drusen in the macular area [13]. Ophthalmologists diagnose the severity of AMD by the size and number of drusen. In the fundus image of a patient with hypertension, we can see that the arteriovenous diameter has a larger ratio. For pathological myopia, there are clear leopard print shapes in the patient's fundus area.

In the field of ophthalmology research, most of the existing datasets are based on a fundus disease, which makes it difficult to apply related work based on them to the detection of other diseases. Clinically, ophthalmologists may give diagnosis results of various diseases by observing one fundus images. Therefore, as a dataset containing multiple fundus diseases, our dataset is closer to clinical application scenarios.

2. *Binocular-based:* Most of the existing ophthalmic disease detection works are based on a fundus image, but in real clinical scenarios, ophthalmologists usually diagnose patients with information from both eyes. In order that the related work performed on our dataset can be better applied to realistic scenes, our dataset contains fundus images of the left and right eyes of patients. Compared with detection on one eye merely, screening for patients with both eyes is both comprehensive and complicated, because in the process of feature extraction of the image, we have to balance the correlation between the two eyes and their respective characteristics. This makes the classification task on this dataset full of challenges. The ultimate goal of our dataset is

to perform multi-label classification of patients using fundus images of both eyes. Figure 1 shows some images of the patient's left and right eyes.

3. *Multi-modal data:* Our dataset integrates multiple information of patients. In addition to providing researchers with fundus images of the left and right eyes of patients, we also provide age and gender of each patient and the diagnostic keywords of ophthalmologists for each fundus image, as shown in Fig. 1. These information can help researchers better perform multi-disease classification tasks, and can also help them perform some more detailed research based on the dataset, such as generating textual diagnosis [5] and age predicting [21] based on fundus images.

4. *Scale:* In today's data-driven deep learning research, large-scale datasets are the cornerstone of ensuring that a research effort is truly applied to real-world scenarios. Our dataset contains 10,000 fundus images from the left and right eyes of 5,000 clinical patients. These images were acquired by different cameras at multiple ophthalmic centers in various regions of China. With a variety of resolutions and covering large scenes, we hope that it can promote further development in this field.

3.3   Split of Dataset

The OIA-ODIR dataset consists of 10,000 fundus images from 5,000 clinical patients. To evaluate the computer-aided algorithms of ocular diseases recognition, we split the dataset into three parts, i.e. the training set, the off-site test set and the on-site test set, which contains 3,500, 500 and 1,000 patients, respectively. The proportion of the training set and the test set is 7:3. The training set is used for training deep networks, and the off-site test set could be used as the validation set for model selection. The generalization ability of the deep network is evaluated on the on-site test set.

Table 2. Proportion of images per category in training and testing datasets

Labels	N	D	G	C	A	H	M	O
Training case	1138	1130	215	212	164	103	174	982
Off-site testing cases	162	163	32	31	25	16	23	136
On-site testing cases	324	327	58	65	49	30	46	275
All cases	1624	1620	305	308	238	149	243	1393

In detail, the proportion of images per category in the training set and test set is summarized in Table 2. We can observe that there exists serious class imbalance in OIA-ODIR. Specially, the number of fundus images with hypertension (H) is less than one tenth of normal images (N), which is challenging for multi-label diseases recognition.

4 Multi-disease Classification

In order to establish benchmark performance on our proposed OIA-ODIR dataset and evaluate the performance of some popular deep classification networks. In this section, we select nine currently popular deep convolutional neural networks, including Vgg-16, ResNet-18, ResNet-50, ResNeXt-50, SE-ResNet-50, SE-ResNeXt-50, Inception-v4, Densenet and CaffeNet. Their performance will be described below.

4.1 Network Structure

In order to adapt to the characteristics of our OIA-ODIR, we made two modifications on the network structure. Firstly, the input of the network is two images, rather than one. Different from traditional image datasets used for diseases screening, the status of patients take into account both left eyes and right eyes at the same time. Therefore, the inputs of the network are two fundus images and the corresponding ground-truth. Furthermore, in order to better fuse the deep information of two fundus images and find a better baseline feature fusion method, we evaluated three feature fusion methods, including element-wise multiplication, element-wise sum and concat. Secondly, it is multi-label classification task rather than single-label. We added eight classifiers for two-class classification behind the last fully-connected layer of each network to achieve the purpose of multi-label classification. Figure 3 shows some details of our modified network.

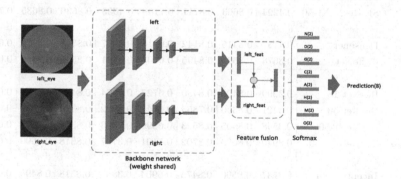

Fig. 3. The structure of multi-label classification network, the input of the network is two fundus images, and the backbone network is used for extracting their features. The feature fusion module fuses two features of left_eye and right_eye into one, and it is further fed into eight classifiers

4.2 Experimental Settings

Running Environment. All the deep networks, pre-trained on ImageNet, were trained and tested based on a publicly available convolutional network framework

Caffe [16]. And, Caffe was compiled with CUDA 8.0 and CUDNN 5.1. The experiments ran on a workstation equipped with three NVIDIA GTX 1080ti GPUs, Intel E5 CPUs and 128 GB memory, and the running operating system is Ubuntu 16.04.

Table 3. The experimental results of nine deep networks on the Off-site and On-site testsets (Final denotes Final-score)

Fusion	Model	Off-site				On-site			
		Kappa	F1	AUC	Final	Kappa	F1	AUC	Final
SUM	Vgg-16	0.4494	0.8730	0.8681	0.7302	0.4397	0.8718	0.8705	0.7273
	ResNet-18	0.4325	0.8635	0.8422	0.7128	0.4137	0.8616	0.8365	0.7039
	ResNet-50	0.3799	0.8452	0.7988	0.6746	0.3827	0.8461	0.7885	0.6724
	ResNeXt-50	0.4588	0.8660	0.8390	0.7213	0.4654	0.8673	0.8386	0.7238
	SE-ResNet-50	0.4140	0.8605	0.8693	0.7146	0.4265	0.8641	0.8689	0.7198
	SE-ResNeXt-50	0.4270	0.8660	0.8785	0.7238	0.4220	0.8666	0.8775	0.7220
	Inception-v4	0.4507	0.8593	0.8800	0.7300	0.4487	0.8583	0.8669	0.7246
	Densenet	0.3914	0.8383	0.8472	0.6923	0.3971	0.8394	0.8460	0.6942
	CaffeNet	0.3885	0.8563	0.8322	0.6923	0.3493	0.8460	0.8293	0.6749
PROD	Vgg-16	0.4359	0.8665	0.8545	0.7190	0.4527	0.8700	0.8628	0.7284
	ResNet-18	0.3593	0.8520	0.8493	0.6869	0.3798	0.8571	0.8583	0.6984
	ResNet-50	0.3545	0.8483	0.8372	0.6800	0.3697	0.8535	0.8408	0.6880
	ResNeXt-50	0.4604	0.8660	0.8578	0.7280	0.4626	0.8674	0.8499	0.7266
	SE-ResNet-50	0.4321	0.8640	0.8613	0.7191	0.4096	0.8601	0.8571	0.7090
	SE-ResNeXt-50	0.4224	0.8663	0.8711	0.7199	0.4033	0.8630	0.8635	0.7099
	Inception-v4	0.5063	0.8793	0.8691	0.7516	0.4505	0.8668	0.8363	0.7178
	Densenet	0.4187	0.8415	0.8142	0.6915	0.3977	0.8338	0.7972	0.6762
	CaffeNet	0.3678	0.8535	0.8495	0.6903	0.3531	0.8525	0.8466	0.6841
Concat	Vgg-16	0.3914	0.8658	0.8806	0.7126	0.3808	0.8641	0.8719	0.7056
	ResNet-18	0.3299	0.8400	0.8480	0.6727	0.3674	0.8485	0.8488	0.6882
	ResNet-50	0.3421	0.8350	0.7853	0.6541	0.3292	0.8320	0.7928	0.6513
	ResNeXt-50	0.3568	0.8605	0.8523	0.6899	0.3383	0.8574	0.8477	0.6811
	SE-ResNet-50	0.3940	0.8660	0.8702	0.7101	0.3707	0.8618	0.8600	0.6975
	SE-ResNeXt-50	0.4179	0.8593	0.8593	0.7121	0.4091	0.8581	0.8606	0.7093
	Inception-v4	0.3737	0.8500	0.8475	0.6904	0.3868	0.8518	0.8499	0.6961
	Densenet	0.3072	0.8495	0.8306	0.6624	0.2772	0.8438	0.8211	0.6473
	CaffeNet	0.3412	0.8485	0.8388	0.6762	0.3467	0.8500	0.8399	0.6789

Evaluation Metrics. We use four evaluation metrics, including Kappa, F1-score (F1), AUC and their mean value, denoted as Final-score, to evaluate the performance of multi-label classification networks. Kappa coefficient is used for consistency check, and it ranges from -1 to 1. F1 is the harmonic mean of precision and recall, which is high only when precision and recall are both high. Since Kappa and F1 only consider a single threshold, while the output of classification networks is probabilistic, so that we use the area under the ROC curve (AUC) to comprehensively consider multiple thresholds. All these four metrics are calculated by sklearn package.

4.3 Experiment Analysis

Nine deep networks were evaluated separately on two test sets, i.e. Off-site and On-site. Meanwhile, we experimentally verified three common feature fusion methods. Table 3 shows the results of our experiments using three different feature fusion methods. In the table we mark the top three results of each feature fusion method with red, green, and blue respectively. We find that compared with the other two feature fusion methods, the experiments using element-wise sum (SUM) feature fusion method gets better comprehensive performance.

Experimental Results. We have performed experiments on our dataset for convolutional neural network structures of different depths and widths. To verify our conjecture, we analyzed the results of each group of experiments on the Off-site and On-site testsets, as shown in Table 3.

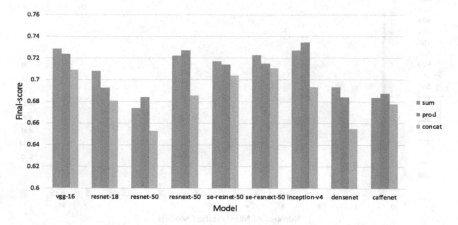

Fig. 4. Comparison of experimental performance among different models (sum denotes element-wise sum, prod denotes element-wise multiplication, Final-score is the mean value on the Off-site and On-site testsets)

In terms of network depth, Vgg-16 shows better performance than other deeper convolutional networks, so we think that simply increasing the depth of the neural network will not bring better results for our task. Correspondingly, in terms of network width, such as ResNeXt-50 and Inception-v4, both have some similar characteristics, they increase the width of the neural network to combine the features of different dimensions to obtain a better result, which is similar with the characteristics of multiple diseases on one eye. At the same time, by introducing the attention mechanism, the SE module can achieve certain effects under certain conditions, such as resnet-50, resnext-50 compared to se-resnet-50, se-resnext-50 in Concat feature fusion mode. In addition, through the distribution of each category on the test set, we found that our samples are imbalance seriously, as shown in Table 2, which also poses a huge challenge to our task. For this issue, we may need more labeled data and sampling methods to support our mission.

On the other hand, through the experimental verification of the three feature fusion methods, as shown in Fig. 4, we find that the results of the two feature fusion methods of element-wise sum and element-wise multiplication are similar on each network model, which further illustrates the correctness of our conclusion above. Meanwhile, for concat feature fusion method, we find that the distribution of evaluation indicators is different from the other two sets of experiments. However, because the evaluation results are not as good as other feature fusion methods, we think that concatenating the features of the left and right eyes simply can't bring a good improvement to our task, and its reference meaning is not significant. In view of the above problems, we believe that a more structured feature fusion method is needed.

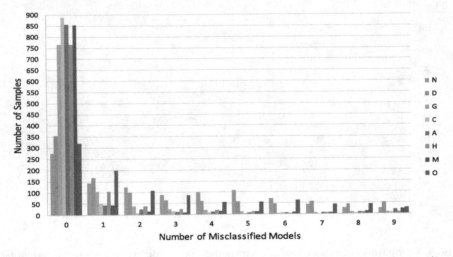

Fig. 5. Statistics on the number of samples with single label misclassified by n (0–9) models

Bad Case Analysis. In order to learn the classification of image samples, on the On-site testset with SUM feature fusion method, we performed statistics on the number of samples that were misclassified by the number of models on each label. Figure 5 shows the details of our statistics. We can find that the analysis of single label is more helpful for our classification task, and most of the samples of each label can be correctly classified by at least 5 models. If the results of multiple models can be effectively integrated in the process of classifier design, we believe that better multi-label classification results will be achieved.

We show some typical samples which are misclassified by most models in Fig. 6. These images reflect some challenges and deficiencies of our dataset. We summarize three key points. 1) *Image quality*. The images in (a) belong to diabetic retinopathy, in which hard exudate can be seen clearly. However, because of some lens stains and lighting problems, these images are misclassified. 2) *Intra-class confusion*. The classification of images in (b) are affected and confused by various fundus abnormalities. For example, cataract prevents the model from identifying hard exudate, hard exudation and drusen are difficult to be distinguish from each other. Which makes most of our misclassified samples are difficult to be extracted valid regional features by models. 3) *Local features are not obvious*. As shown in the images of the first line in (c), the determination of glaucoma requires accurate ratio of optic cup and disc. In the second line of (c), AMD requires more detailed features of the macular area. For these, we need to extract relevant local features to improve the performance of classification.

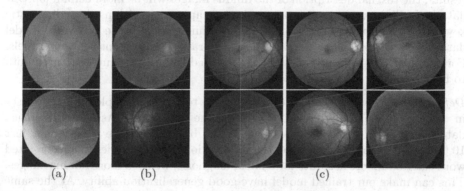

(a)   (b)   (c)

Fig. 6. Examples of misclassified images owing to different reasons. (a) camera lighting and lens stains, (b) multiple diseases interfere with each other, (c) local features are not obvious

5 Discussion

As one publicly available multi-disease recognition dataset, we have discussed the characteristics of our dataset. In this section, we will discuss its challenges, deficiencies and potential applications.

Challenge: First of all, unlike previous studies of medical image processing based on a single fundus image, feature learning using left and right eye fundus images as input requires more considerations, such as the spatial and structural correlation of the two eyes. Second, for the classification of multiple disease labels, different fundus diseases have different local or global characteristics. For example, glaucoma is characterized by the relative size of the optic cup and optic disc, and cataracts are reflected in the clarity of various structures of the fundus. How to make suitable feature extraction schemes for different diseases in model design is a challenging task. And when multiple diseases interact in one fundus image, as shown in Fig. 6(b), it is very difficult to identify them all correctly. Third, for the image itself, as shown in Fig. 2, due to the wide source of our images, there is a wealth of intra-class diversity. In Fig. 2(a), although they are all labeled as normal fundus, there are large differences in color, lighting, and lens shooting conditions, and the same situation also exists in other categories. At the same time, because the images in Other category are composed of a variety of uncommon fundus diseases, the differences within the class are more serious.

Potential Application: On one hand, our dataset can be used as a multi-disease screening dataset. On the other hand, there are several potential applications of our dataset. 1) We can explore the correlation between fundus images and patient's age or gender [21]. Specifically, we can train a deep neural network for age predicting, and use a heat map to visualize the decision basis of the network. 2) In clinical scenarios, it is not enough to provide only classification results, the textual description of the fundus images will be more helpful [5]. Our dataset facilitates the development of image caption algorithms since diagnostic keywords of ophthalmologists for each fundus image are provided. 3) Multi-model data makes it possible to develop more accurate disease identification models. For example, graph neural network can be used to integrate un-structured data to further improve diagnostic accuracy.

Deficiency: As a work to make a bold attempt to detect multiple fundus diseases in a single fundus, our dataset also has some limitations. As a fundus image dataset with real clinical applications as the background, we believe that just 10,000 images can not really meet our application needs. In order to make related work safer and more accurate for clinical diagnosis, we need more fundus images. This can make our trained model have good generalization ability. At the same time, it can be found from Table 2 that there are serious data imbalances in different categories of our dataset. This is because some fundus diseases rarely occur clinically, and because multiple labels need to be labeled on a single image, it is difficult to ensure a balanced ratio between each category. In addition, although our dataset already provided detailed diagnostic keywords for each fundus image, they were finally divided into 8 categories. In future work, we need to perform some more fine-grained classification of fundus diseases. Finally, as an international fundus dataset, the source of images is only limited to some regions in China. In order to have a better geographical diversity of the dataset, we need fundus data from different races around the world.

6   Conclusions

Due to the lack of benchmark dataset hindering further development in automatic classification of clinical fundus images, in this paper, we release a fundus image dataset with multi-disease annotations. The dataset contains 10,000 images from the left and right eyes of 5,000 clinical patients, with rich diversity. At the same time, we evaluate the performance of some existing deep learning models on our dataset, in order to provide a valuable reference for future related work. Experimental results show that simply increasing the depth of the neural network alone cannot improve performance, however increasing the width of the network can bring certain improvement. Moreover, integrating multiple deep networks will be helpful to improve classification performance. At last, the dataset is available at https://github.com/nkicsl/OIA-ODIR.

Acknowledgements. This work is partially supported by the National Natural Science Foundation (61872200), the Open Project Fund of State Key Laboratory of Computer Architecture, Institute of Computing Technology, Chinese Academy of Sciences No. CARCH201905, the Natural Science Foundation of Tianjin (19JCZDJC31600, 18YFYZCG00060).

References

1. Kaggle diabetic retinopathy detection competition. https://www.kaggle.com/c/diabetic-retinopathy-detection. Accessed 18 Feb 2020
2. Alqudah, A.M.: AOCT-NET: a convolutional network automated classification of multiclass retinal diseases using spectral-domain optical coherence tomography images. Med. Biol. Eng. Comput. **58**(1), 41–53 (2020)
3. Asgari, R., et al.: Multiclass segmentation as multitask learning for drusen segmentation in retinal optical coherence tomography. In: Shen, D., et al. (eds.) MICCAI 2019. LNCS, vol. 11764, pp. 192–200. Springer, Cham (2019). https://doi.org/10.1007/978-3-030-32239-7_22
4. Brandl, C., et al.: Features of age-related macular degeneration in the general adults and their dependency on age, sex, and smoking: results from the German KORA study. PLOS ONE **11**(11), e0167181 (2016)
5. Chelaramani, S., Gupta, M., Agarwal, V., Gupta, P., Habash, R.: Multi-task learning for fine-grained eye disease prediction. In: Palaiahnakote, S., Sanniti di Baja, G., Wang, L., Yan, W.Q. (eds.) ACPR 2019. LNCS, vol. 12047, pp. 734–749. Springer, Cham (2020). https://doi.org/10.1007/978-3-030-41299-9_57
6. Chen, X., et al.: Multiple ocular diseases classification with graph regularized probabilistic multi-label learning. In: Cremers, D., Reid, I., Saito, H., Yang, M.-H. (eds.) ACCV 2014. LNCS, vol. 9006, pp. 127–142. Springer, Cham (2015). https://doi.org/10.1007/978-3-319-16817-3_9
7. Choi, J.Y., Yoo, T.K., Seo, J.G., Kwak, J., Um, T.T., Rim, T.H.: Multi-categorical deep learning neural network to classify retinal images: a pilot study employing small database. PLOS ONE **12**(11), e0187336 (2017)
8. Costagliola, C., Dell'Omo, R., Romano, M.R., Rinaldi, M., Zeppa, L., Parmeggiani, F.: Pharmacotherapy of intraocular pressure: part I. Parasympathomimetic, sympathomimetic and sympatholytics. Exp. Opin. Pharmacother. **10**(16), 2663–2677 (2009)
9. Decencière, E., et al.: TeleOphta: machine learning and image processing methods for teleophthalmology. IRBM **34**(2), 196–203 (2013)
10. Decencière, E., et al.: Feedback on a publicly distributed image database: the Messidor database. Image Anal. Stereol. **33**(3), 231–234 (2014)

11. Foong, A.W., et al.: Rationale and methodology for a population-based study of eye diseases in Malay people: The Singapore Malay eye study (SiMES). Ophthalmic Epidemiol. **14**(1), 25–35 (2007)
12. Fumero, F., Alayón, S., Sanchez, J.L., Sigut, J., Gonzalez-Hernandez, M.: RIM-ONE: an open retinal image database for optic nerve evaluation. In: 2011 24th International Symposium on Computer-Based Medical Systems (CBMS), pp. 1–6. IEEE (2011)
13. García-Floriano, A., Ferreira-Santiago, Á., Camacho-Nieto, O., Yáñez-Márquez, C.: A machine learning approach to medical image classification: detecting age-related macular degeneration in fundus images. Comput. Electr. Eng. **75**, 218–229 (2019)
14. He, Y., et al.: Fully convolutional boundary regression for retina OCT segmentation. In: Shen, D., et al. (eds.) MICCAI 2019. LNCS, vol. 11764, pp. 120–128. Springer, Cham (2019). https://doi.org/10.1007/978-3-030-32239-7_14
15. Hoover, A., Kouznetsova, V., Goldbaum, M.: Locating blood vessels in retinal images by piecewise threshold probing of a matched filter response. IEEE Trans. Med. Imaging **19**(3), 203–210 (2000)
16. Jia, Y., et al.: Caffe: convolutional architecture for fast feature embedding. In: Proceedings of the 22nd ACM International Conference on Multimedia, pp. 675–678 (2014)
17. Lee, K., Niemeijer, M., Garvin, M.K., Kwon, Y.H., Sonka, M., Abramoff, M.D.: Segmentation of the optic disc in 3-D OCT scans of the optic nerve head. IEEE Trans. Med. Imaging **29**(1), 159–168 (2009)
18. Li, T., Gao, Y., Wang, K., Guo, S., Liu, H., Kang, H.: Diagnostic assessment of deep learning algorithms for diabetic retinopathy screening. Inf. Sci. **501**, 511–522 (2019)
19. Mehta, P., Lee, A.Y., Lee, C., Balazinska, M., Rokem, A.: Multilabel multiclass classification of OCT images augmented with age, gender and visual acuity data. bioRxiv, 316349 (2018)
20. Mokhtari, M., et al.: Local comparison of cup to disc ratio in right and left eyes based on fusion of color fundus images and OCT B-scans. Inf. Fusion **51**, 30–41 (2019)
21. Poplin, R., et al.: Prediction of cardiovascular risk factors from retinal fundus photographs via deep learning. Nat. Biomed. Eng. **2**(3), 158 (2018)
22. Quigley, H.A., Broman, A.T.: The number of people with glaucoma worldwide in 2010 and 2020. Br. J. Ophthalmol. **90**(3), 262–267 (2006)
23. Rasti, R., Rabbani, H., Mehridehnavi, A., Hajizadeh, F.: Macular oct classification using a multi-scale convolutional neural network ensemble. IEEE Trans. Med. Imaging **37**(4), 1024–1034 (2017)
24. Schlegl, T., et al.: Fully automated detection and quantification of macular fluid in OCT using deep learning. Ophthalmology **125**(4), 549–558 (2018)
25. Sengupta, S., Singh, A., Leopold, H.A., Gulati, T., Lakshminarayanan, V.: Ophthalmic diagnosis using deep learning with fundus images - a critical review. Artif. Intell. Med. **102**, 101758 (2019)
26. Tan, J.H., et al.: Age-related macular degeneration detection using deep convolutional neural network. Fut. Gener. Comput. Syst. **87**, 127–135 (2018)
27. Ting, D.S.W., Wu, W.C., Toth, C.: Deep learning for retinopathy of prematurity screening. Br. J. Ophthalmol. **103**(5), 577–579 (2019)
28. Wang, X., Ju, L., Zhao, X., Ge, Z.: Retinal abnormalities recognition using regional multitask learning. In: Shen, D., et al. (eds.) MICCAI 2019. LNCS, vol. 11764, pp. 30–38. Springer, Cham (2019). https://doi.org/10.1007/978-3-030-32239-7_4

29. Wong, T., Aiello, L., Ferris, F., Gupta, N., Kawasaki, R., Lansingh, V., et al.: Updated 2017 ICO guidelines for diabetic eye care. Int. J. Ophthalmol, 1–33 (2017)
30. Zhang, F., et al.: Automated quality classification of colour fundus images based on a modified residual dense block network. SIViP **14**(1), 215–223 (2019). https://doi.org/10.1007/s11760-019-01544-y
31. Zhang, H., et al.: Automatic cataract grading methods based on deep learning. Comput. Meth. Program. Biomed. **182**, 104978 (2019)
32. Zhang, Z., et al.: ORIGA-light: an online retinal fundus image database for glaucoma analysis and research. In: 2010 Annual International Conference of the IEEE Engineering in Medicine and Biology, pp. 3065–3068. IEEE (2010)
33. Zhou, Y., Li, G., Li, H.: Automatic cataract classification using deep neural network with discrete state transition. IEEE Trans. Med. Imaging **39**(2), 436–446 (2020)

MAS3K: An Open Dataset for Marine Animal Segmentation

Lin Li[1] (ID), Eric Rigall[1] (ID), Junyu Dong[1(✉)] (ID), and Geng Chen[2(✉)] (ID)

[1] Ocean University of China, Qingdao, China
dongjunyu@ouc.edu.cn
[2] Inception Institute of Artificial Intelligence, Abu Dhabi, UAE
geng.chen.cs@gmail.com

Abstract. Recent advances in marine animal research have raised significant demands for fine-grained marine animal segmentation techniques. Deep learning has shown remarkable success in a variety of object segmentation tasks. However, deep based marine animal segmentation is lack of investigation due to the short of a marine animal dataset. To this end, we elaborately construct the first open Marine Animal Segmentation dataset, called *MAS3K*, which consists of more than three thousand images of diverse marine animals, with common and camouflaged appearances, in different underwater conditions, such as low illumination, turbid water quality, photographic distortion, etc. Each image from the *MAS3K* dataset has rich annotations, including an object-level annotation, a category name, an animal camouflage method (if applicable), and attribute annotations. In addition, based on *MAS3K*, we systematically evaluate 6 cutting-edge object segmentation models using five widely-used metrics. We perform comprehensive analysis and report detailed qualitative and quantitative benchmark results in the paper. Our work provides valuable insights into the marine animal segmentation, which will boost the development in this direction effectively.

Keywords: Marine animal segmentation · Underwater images · Camouflaged marine animals

1 Introduction

The ocean covers more than 70% of the earth's surface [42], making it one of the most important ecosystems in the world. Moreover, it contains abundant fishery and energy resources, providing a huge impetus for the development of modern society. Therefore, marine study is of great importance and has been a long-standing research topic. In particular, the marine animal study has gained increasing research efforts in recent years. With the development of artificial intelligence techniques, deep learning has been applied to a number of marine animal related studies, e.g., fish identification [24], underwater image enhancement [30], marine animal identification [42], marine biology and archaeology [37],

© Springer Nature Switzerland AG 2021
F. Wolf and W. Gao (Eds.): Bench 2020, LNCS 12614, pp. 194–212, 2021.
https://doi.org/10.1007/978-3-030-71058-3_12

Fig. 1. Typical examples for the underwater environments. Due to the complex nature of underwater environments, accurately segmenting marine animals from the underwater images is challenging. Images are selected from *MAS3K*.

etc. Among various methods, marine animal segmentation (MAS) is particularly important since it can provide vital information for the identification of diverse marine animals from complex underwater environments, which has great potentials for the fishery industry to carry out better monitoring and supervision.

However, accurate MAS is a challenging task due to the complex nature of underwater environments and the camouflaged properties of marine animals. As shown in Fig. 1, it can be observed that the underwater environment is particularly complex, e.g., brightness issues due to insufficient underwater luminosity, coloration issues caused by underwater turbidity, and similarity of color and texture between foreground and background, which induce significant difficulties for segmenting marine animals from underwater images. In addition, marine animals have rich camouflaged properties. As shown in Fig. 2, various marine animals (e.g., seahorse, fish, and octopus) conceal themselves in their underwater habitats (e.g., corals reef, seabed, and beach). Due to the survival purpose, these animals have developed realistic camouflaged abilities, which makes it an even challenging task to accurately segment marine animals from underwater images.

To address these challenges, a number of methods have been proposed. For instance, image enhancement techniques have been developed to resolve the quality issue of underwater images [22,30]. However, these methods mainly focus on image quality enhancement and are unable to improve the MAS directly. On the other hand, efforts have been made to detect/segment camouflaged objects [14,29]. As clarified in [63], object detection/segmentation methods mainly includes traditional generic object detection (GOD), salient object detection (SOD) and camouflaged object detection (COD). Figure 3 shows the images that are collected from MS-COCO dataset [34] used for GOD, DUT-OMRON [57] dataset used for SOD, and COD10K dataset [14] used for COD. It can be observed that accurate COD is with considerable difficulties due to the low

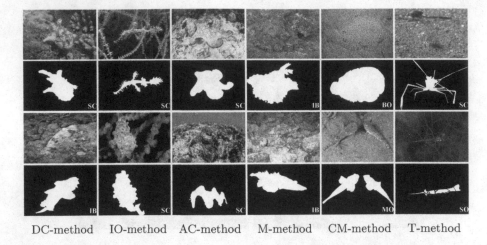

DC-method   IO-method   AC-method   M-method   CM-method   T-method

Fig. 2. Typical examples of marine animal camouflage methods. Please refer to Table 1 for the marine animal attributes and Table 2 for the definitions of different camouflage methods. Images are selected from our *MAS3K* dataset.

boundary contrast between camouflaged object and its surroundings. Thanks to the powerful deep learning techniques, deep based models have shown remarkable success in object detection/segmentation tasks, even the most challenging COD. The progress made in COD offers valuable insights to improve MAS, but is lack of investigation at the current stage. In addition, the most serious problem restricting the development of deep based MAS models is the short of an open marine animal dataset. To the best of our knowledge, currently, there is no object-level labeled dataset that can be used for MAS.

To this end, we elaborately construct the first open marine animal segmentation dataset, called **MAS3K**. Its key features lie in three folds.

1. *MAS3K* contains a total of 3,103 images, where 1,588 are for camouflaged cases, 1,322 are for common cases, and 193 are underwater images in absence of marine animals.
2. The marine animal categories in *MAS3K* cover both vertebrate and invertebrate, including seven super-classes, e.g., *mammals*, *reptile*, *arthropod*, and *marine fish*, etc. Under the super-classes, *MAS3K* dataset has 37 sub-classes, e.g., *crab*, *starfish*, *shark*, and *turtle*, etc.
3. We provide rich annotations for each marine animal image. As shown in Fig. 2, the images are annotated with high quality object-level annotations. In addition, they also have category, attribution, and camouflage method annotations for more fine-grained data analysis and diverse applications. Finally, we employ cross-validation to ensure annotation quality.

Our paper is organized as follows: Section 2 presents a review of related works, including underwater image enhancement, marine animal detection, marine animal camouflage, and camouflaged object detection. Section 3 introduces the

(a) GOD Dataset   (b) SOD Dataset   (c) COD Dataset

Fig. 3. Comparison of GOD, SOD, and COD datasets. The images are shown in the top line, and the corresponding ground truth labels are shown in the bottom line.

proposed *MAS3K* dataset in terms of image collection, data annotation, and dataset features. Section 4 benchmarks 6 deep-based object segmentation models and provides in-depth result analyses. Finally, Sect. 5 concludes the work.

2 Related Work

In this section, we discuss a number of works that are closely related to ours. These works can be classified into four categories, including underwater image enhancement, marine animal detection, marine animal camouflage, and camouflaged object detection.

2.1 Underwater Image Enhancement

Due to the lighting condition and complexity in underwater environment, underwater images usually suffer from low-quality issues, such as color distortion, low-contrast between marine animal and the seabed or seawater, and severe water turbidity. To tackle the aforementioned problems, underwater image enhancement has become an essential step and is widely used as a powerful preprocessing tool before various vision tasks, such as marine animal identification, detection, or segmentation.

In classic methods, hand-crafted filters are used to enforce color constancy and improve color constancy [19,26]. Based on the multi-scale Retinex theory, the human visual simulation systems were utilized to restore the lightness and illumination of the image background [26,61]. The method based on the physical model is also a main class of underwater image enhancement approaches. In [7], the dehazing algorithm was used to enhance the underwater image to compensate for the difference in attenuation along the propagation path, while taking into account the influence of artificial light sources.

In recent years, learning-based perceptual enhancement methods have made significant advances to address the challenges in underwater image enhancement. For instance, GAN-based methods have shown promising performance, and many excellent models have emerged, e.g., WaterGAN [33], Water CycleGAN [31], Dense GAN [20], etc.

2.2 Marine Animal Detection

Marine animal detection has gained increasing research effort in recently years. Based on the detection object, we divided existing methods into three categories, including fish, scallop, and coral reef detection models.

Methods in the first category aim to detect fishes from underwater images. For instance, Villon et al. [51] compared the traditional machine learning approach and deep learning approach for the task of automatic detection and identification of fishes. Specifically, the traditional approach first extracts HOG features from underwater images, and then utilizes an SVM classifier for fish identification. In contrast, deep learning approach identify fishes in an end-to-end manner, without using hand crafted features. The experimental results in [51] indicate that a well-trained convolutional neural network (CNN) outperforms the traditional machine learning approach relying on HOG features and SVM classifier. In addition, Siddiqui et al. [49] employed a very deep CNN along with cross-layer pooling to enhance the discriminative ability of fish detection.

The second category includes the methods for scallop detection. Dawkins et al. [10] effectively identified scallops from very challenging underwater images by a multi-step procedure, including initial image analysis, candidate extraction, feature computation, and a two-level final classification. Rasmussen et al. [47] presented a deep-based scallop detection model, which is based on the variant of YOLOv2 [48]. This detection model achieves high accuracy scallop detection in real-time and is applied in an autonomous underwater vehicle.

In the last category, Mahmood et al. [38] proposed to use fine-tuned VGGNet for the identification of coral reefs. In [1], the standard reflectance image and the coral fluorescence image are fused in a 5-channel CNN for coral reef detection tasks. Despite their advantages, existing methods suffer from two major limitations. First, they all aim to predict the coarse annotations of marine animals, i.e., bounding boxes. Finer annotations, e.g., segmentation masks, can provide richer information and are greatly desired. Second, they usually focus on the detection of one specific kind of marine animals, which restricts the universality and application scenarios of the trained model.

2.3 Marine Animal Camouflage

As aforementioned, marine animals have rich camouflaged properties. The marine animal camouflage has been well studied in the ecology community. For instance, McFall-Ngai et al. [40] and Johnsen [27] have studied the relationship between the camouflage methods of marine animals and the depth of the ocean where they live in. Their studies show that the most deep sea animals usually use one or several camouflage methods, e.g., transparency [27], reflection, and counter illumination [40]. The first two camouflage methods usually exist within the top 100 m of the ocean, while the last one exists from 100 m to 1000 m. In addition, marine animals also conceal themselves using several common camouflage methods.

In general, there are six kinds of widely existed camouflage methods [8,52]. For instance, mimesis is a camouflage mechanism, where animals conceal themselves to avoid the interest of observers. For predators, mimesis is used to avoid scaring off the prey, while for preys, it is used to avoid being discovered by the predator. The color matching technique is widely used by the salmonid fish (e.g., the brown trout), who finds habitats that have similar color with its body so that the chance to be recognized is decreased [8]. Distraction camouflage method, such as disruptive coloration, is used by the animals that dazzle or confuse their predators by using their complex body colors. This technique is used by the four-eye butterfly fish, which has two black round marks on its back, similar to the real eyes. Animals with irregular outlines take advantage of their complex outline to mislead an observer's sight so that it takes longer to identify. Along with another approach, octopuses can change their coloration in real-time to maintain resemblance to their surroundings when they move [36]. This phenomenon is named active camouflage.

2.4 Camouflaged Object Detection

A number of approaches have been developed to detect camouflaged objects from natural images. These methods, named camouflaged object detection (COD), belong to the object detection, which aims to detect/segment objects from images and can be classified into three categories, including generic object detection (GOD) [5,63], salient object detection (SOD) [4,11,16–18,21,59,64], and COD [14,29]. In computer vision, GOD is one of the most fundamental research topics. As clarified in [63], deep based GOD models usually predict the coordinates of bounding boxes to detect the target object. SOD aims to identify the objects that attract the human attention [23,35,60,62]. Differing from GOD, the prediction target of SOD is a pixel-level segmentation mask. As suggested in [14], the high intrinsic similarities, i.e., color, texture, brightness, between the target object and the background make COD far more challenging than GOD and SOD. Camouflaged object detection has promoted the development of object detection that exhibits camouflaged characteristics under complex environmental conditions (e.g., medical image segmentation [15,54]), and provides valuable insights to solve the task of MAS.

A number of COD datasets have been constructed for the development of deep-based COD models. For instance, CHAMELEON [50] dataset contains 76 images, 10 of which contain marine animals, and is crafted manually for presenting various camouflage efficiency. These images were taken from the Internet using Google search with the keyword "camouflaged animal". CAMO [29] dataset

Fig. 4. Matting label examples. The images are shown in the top line, and the corresponding ground truth labels are shown in the bottom line.

is constructed for promoting camouflaged object segmentation. The dataset contains 1,250 camouflaged images with pixel-by-pixel annotations, 14% of which are underwater animal images, while the 1,250 images from MS-COCO are non-camouflaged. Compared with existing datasets, COD10K [14] dataset is the largest COD dataset with a total of 10,000 images, over 78 object categories. All the images have rich annotations, especially the alpha-matting, which makes the dataset suitable to various visual tasks. At present, COD10K dataset is the most competitive for COD tasks.

3   Proposed Dataset

In this section, we describe our *MAS3K* dataset in detail from three aspects, including image collection, data annotation, and dataset features. Figures 1 and 2 show some example images from *MAS3K* dataset.

3.1   Image Collection

Our dataset contains a total of 3,103 images, including 1,588 camouflaged images, 1,322 common images, and 193 background images, covering a total of 37 categories of marine animals. These images are from three sources, which are detailed as follows.

Existing Object Detection Datasets. One of the main sources of the camouflaged images in our dataset is from the COD10K dataset [14], which is by far the largest and most comprehensive COD dataset. Some marine animal images from the existing SOD datasets have also been collected once they meet the requirements of our dataset. These images are from SED2 [2], DUTS [53], DUT-OMRON [57], MSRA-10K [6], ECSSD [56], HKU-IS [32], SOD [41], SOC [11].

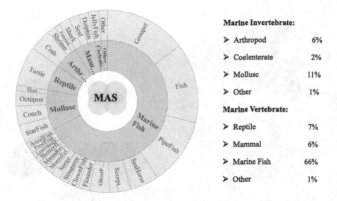

Marine Invertebrate:

➤ Arthropod   6%

➤ Coelenterate   2%

➤ Mollusc   11%

➤ Other   1%

Marine Vertebrate:

➤ Reptile   7%

➤ Mammal   6%

➤ Marine Fish   66%

➤ Other   1%

Fig. 5. Marine animal categories. Marine animal super-class and sub-class for *MAS3K*.

Existing Underwater Image Datasets. We consider three underwater datasets, including the *"labeled fishes in the wild"* dataset [9], UIEB dataset [30], and MUED dataset [25]. Underwater images of *labeled fishes in the wild* dataset are collected from a remotely operated vehicle. This dataset contains 2,061 images for fishes in various species and sizes. However, the annotation of the dataset is bounding-box, not an object-level segmentation mask. The UIEB dataset contains 950 images and is used for the underwater image enhancement task. The MUED dataset contains 4,400 underwater images for 220 marine animals under the different underwater environments. We have selected images that meet the characteristics of our *MAS3K* dataset and annotated these images at the matting-level, which is described in Sect. 3.2.

Internet. Nearly one-third of marine animal images of *MAS3K* dataset are from the Internet. We search Unsplash[1] and Google Images[2] with the keywords: *marine animal, ocean animal, fish, underwater, camouflaged animal, unnoticeable animal, camouflaged fish, seahorse, octopus*, etc. Note that the relevant websites release public-domain stock photos, which are free from copyright. Consistent with the object-level annotation of the COD10K dataset, the images in *MAS3K* dataset are labeled according to the annotation method described in Sect. 3.2.

Furthermore, we collect 195 underwater images without marine animals as part of the *MAS3K* dataset. These images are mainly from SOC dataset [11], Unsplash, and Google Images.

---

[1] https://unsplash.com/.

[2] https://www.google.com/imghp.

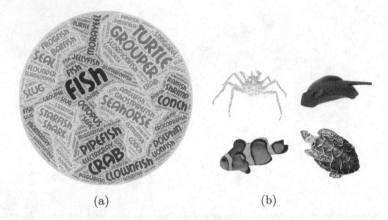

(a)   (b)

Fig. 6. Marine animal categories. (a) Word cloud of sub-class. (b) Some examples of categories, i.e., crab, clownfish, stingaree, and turtle.

3.2   Data Annotation

Our *MAS3K* dataset provides the following four kinds of annotations.

Objects Level Annotation. Inspired by the COD10K dataset [14], we use object-level annotation for our dataset. To be consistent with the COD10K, the images of our *MAS3K* dataset are labeled with the high-quality alpha-matting level annotation, as shown in Fig. 4.

Categories. As shown in Fig. 5, the marine animal categories in *MAS3K* include vertebrates and invertebrates. We divide these marine animals into 7 super-class, including *mammals, reptile, marine fish, arthropod , coelenterate, mollusc,* and *other*. Under the super-class, the *MAS3K* dataset includes 37 sub-categories, e.g., *conch, octopus, flounder,* and *seal,* etc. If the number of images in one sub-class is less than 15, we categorize the images in the super-class *"other"*. The word cloud of sub-class and some examples of marine animals are shown in Fig. 6(a) and (b), respectively.

Attributes. Consistent with [11,44], the *MAS3K* dataset has informative attribute labels for each image. Specifically, we annotate each image with seven attributes, including big object, small object, multiple objects, occlusion, shape complexity, indefinable boundaries, and out-of-view, which are detailed in Table 1. Figure 7(a) and (b) provide the details regarding the co-attribute distribution and multi-dependencies among the attributes of our *MAS3K* dataset.

Camouflage Methods. In our dataset, we introduce six methods of camouflaged images, defined as follows: mimesis (M-method), color matching (CM-method), disruptive coloration (DC-method), irregular outline (IO-method),

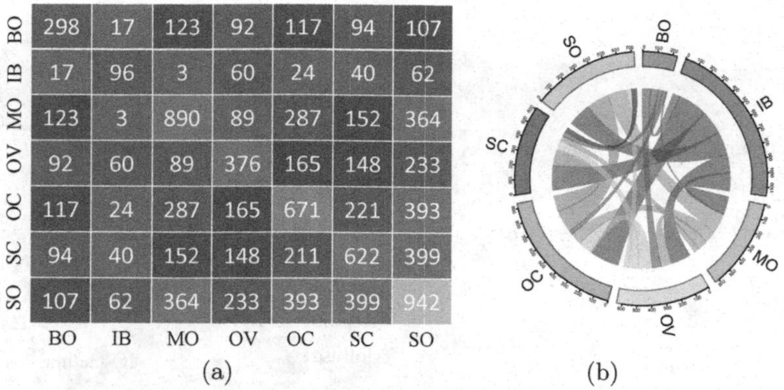

	BO	IB	MO	OV	OC	SC	SO
BO	298	17	123	92	117	94	107
IB	17	96	3	60	24	40	62
MO	123	3	890	89	287	152	364
OV	92	60	89	376	165	148	233
OC	117	24	287	165	671	221	393
SC	94	40	152	148	211	622	399
SO	107	62	364	233	393	399	942

(a)　　　　　　　　　　　　　　　　(b)

Fig. 7. Dataset attributes. (a) Co-attribute distributions of *MAS3K* dataset. (b) Multi-dependencies among the attributes in *MAS3K* dataset.

Table 1. Attribute descriptions [14].

Attribute	Description
Big Object (BO)	Object area/Image area ≥ 0.5
Indefinable Boundaries (IB)	Similar colors between object and background
Multiple Objects (MO)	Number of objects in each image ≥ 2
Out-of-View (OV)	Object is incomplete
Occlusions (OC)	Object is obscured by others
Shape Complexity (SC)	Object has small and thin parts (e.g. animal foot Or whiskers)
Small Object (SO)	Object area/Image area ≤ 0.1

Table 2. Camouflage methods.

Camo. Method	Description [3, 8]
M-Method	*Mimesis.* Having the appearance of a common object, outwitting the observer's attention
CM-Method	*Color Matching.* Having similar colors with the environment it is in
DC-Method	*Disruptive Coloration.* Having complex coloration pattern or disruptive marks that breaks up its boundaries, so that predators fail to detect it
IO-Method	*Irregular Outline.* Having complex outline that misleads an observer in determining its shape
AC-Method	*Active Camouflage.* Being able to naturally and dynamically change its coloration according to its background environment
T-Method	*Transparency.* Having some parts of their bodies transparent, decreasing their visibility from an observer's eye

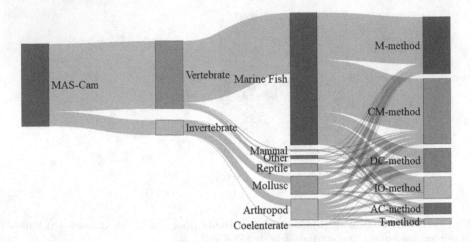

Fig. 8. Camouflage methods distribution in *MAS3K* dataset.

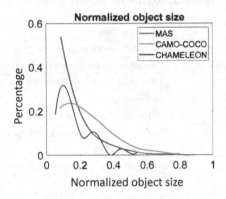

Fig. 9. Comparison between *MAS3K* and existing datasets in terms of normalized object size.

activate camouflage (AC-method), and transparency (T-method). Their detailed descriptions are listed in Table 2. Figure 8 shows the distribution of camouflage methods in each super-class, where CM-method is the most used camouflage method. In addition, it can be observed that a camouflaged image can have multiple camouflage methods.

To ensure the quality of image annotation, one researcher annotates the image, while another researcher is responsible for validating the mask labels.

3.3   Dataset Features and Statistics

Object Size. According to [28], there is a large gap between the object detection performance between small and large objects. As shown in Fig. 9, we plot the standardized object size. It can be clearly seen that the proportion

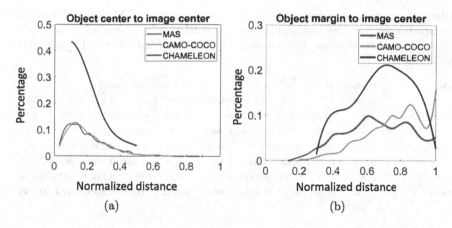

Fig. 10. Comparison between *MAS3K* and existing datasets in terms of center bias.

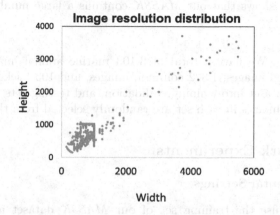

Fig. 11. Image resolution distribution of our *MAS3K* dataset.

of small objects in *MAS3K* dataset is significantly higher than that in the other two datasets. Hence, compared to the CAMO and CHAMELEON, our *MAS3K* dataset is more challenging.

Center Bias. This regularly happens when taking photos since humans naturally tend to focus on the center of the scene. We utilize the strategy described in [11] to analyze this bias. Figure 10(a) and (b) indicate whether it is the normalized ratio from the center of the object to the center of the image or the normalized ratio from the margin of the object to the center of the image, our *MAS3K* dataset has a broader range distribution than the other two datasets. Hence, our *MAS3K* dataset outperforms other datasets in terms of center bias.

Resolution Distribution. As described in [58], a high-resolution image provides more boundary detail information for model training and better

Table 3. Quantitative benchmark results on different datasets. "↑" indicates the higher the score the better. The best results are in boldface. Five widely-used metrics are considered in our evaluation. Evaluation toolbox: https://github.com/DengPingFan/CODToolbox

Models	CAMO-CHAM-test [29,50]					MAS3K-test (ours)				
	$mIoU$ ↑	F_β^w ↑	S_α ↑	mE_ϕ ↑	MAE ↓	$mIoU$ ↑	F_β^w ↑	S_α ↑	mE_ϕ ↑	MAE ↓
2019 BASNet [46]	0.467	0.548	0.679	0.748	0.127	0.511	0.572	0.732	0.791	0.076
2019 PoolNet [35]	0.608	0.695	0.774	**0.834**	**0.080**	0.604	0.685	0.799	0.867	0.045
2019 EGNet [62]	0.602	687	0.784	0.819	0.082	0.596	0.677	0.806	0.853	0.047
2019 SCRN [55]	**0.643**	**0.705**	**0.816**	**0.834**	0.081	0.649	**0.686**	**0.830**	0.863	0.047
2020 U2Net [45]	0.463	0.537	0.704	0.724	0.133	0.541	0.615	0.776	0.802	0.058
2020 SINet [14]	0.632	0.698	0.799	0.832	0.082	**0.652**	0.678	**0.830**	**0.874**	**0.044**

performance during testing. Figure 11 is the image resolution distribution of our dataset, and shows that our *MAS3K* contains a large number of Full HD 1080p images.

Dataset Splits. We have a total of 3,103 marine animal images, including 1,588 camouflaged images, 1,322 common images, and 193 background images. We divide the dataset into training, validation, and testing sets with a ratio of 6:2:2. Note that images in each set are randomly selected from the sub-class.

4   Benchmark Experiments

4.1   Experimental Settings

Datasets. We use the training set of our *MAS3K* dataset as the training dataset for the experiment, and it contains 1,769 images. The two benchmark datasets used for inference are CAMO-CHAM-test, and *MAS3K*-test. The CAMO-CHAM-test dataset consisting of 191 marine animal camouflaged images, which are from the CHAMELEON [50] and CAMO [29] datasets. The *MAS3K*-test dataset consists of 1,141 images from our *MAS3K* dataset.

Competitors. In this study, we evaluate/compare existing state-of-the-art (SOTA) object segmentation methods, including one COD model, SINet [14], and five SOD models, including SCRN [55], EGNet [62], PoolNet [35], BASNet [46], and U2Net [45].

Evaluation Criteria. We use five metrics to evaluate the results with the toolbox provided by [15]. These metrics include mean Intersection over Union ($mIoU$), weighted F-measure (F_β^w) [39], structural similarity measure (S_α, with $\alpha = 0.5$) [12], mean E-measure (mE_ϕ) [13], and mean absolute error (MAE) [43].

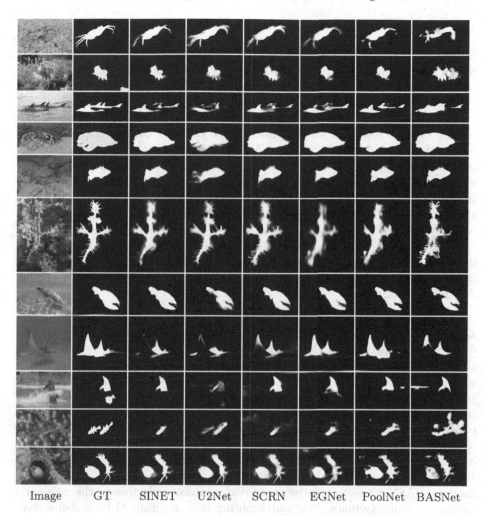

Image   GT   SINET   U2Net   SCRN   EGNet   PoolNet   BASNet

Fig. 12. Visual comparison of different methods.

mIoU is the average of the intersection of the predicted result and the ground truth divided by their union, i.e., the mean detection accuracy. F_β^w is based on weighted precision and recall values. S_α calculates both the object-aware and region-aware structure similarities. mE_ψ combines local pixel values and image-level average values in one formula for capturing both image-level statistics and local pixel matching information. *MAE* calculates the mean absolute difference value between the normalized prediction and the ground truth for evaluating the overall pixel-level relative error.

4.2   Results

Quantitative Evaluation. We summarize the quantitative results in Table 3, where 6 SOTA object segmentation models are considered. In addition, comprehensive analyses are performed on two datasets based on five widely-used evaluation metrics.

We first present the results regarding the CAMO-CHAM-test, which is a testing dataset based on the CHAMELEON [50] and CAMO [29]. As can be observed in Table 3, SCRN provides the best performance in terms of most evaluation metrics, including $mIoU$, F_β^w, S_α, and mE_ϕ. PoolNet outperforms SCRN in terms of MAE and provides the same mE_ϕ result, but shows unsatisfactory performance in other evaluation metrics. SINet is a competitive method, which shows the second best performance in terms of $mIoU$, F_β^w, and S_α.

We then present the results for our $MAS3K$-test dataset. In general, SINet is the best model in comparison with others. Specifically, it provides the best results in terms of $mIoU$, S_α, mE_ϕ, and MAE, and shows the third best performance in terms of F_β^w. SCRN is the second best model, which provide particularly good F_β^w and S_α results.

Qualitative Evaluation. To further compare the benchmark models, we perform visual inspection on the predicted probability maps. As shown in Fig. 12, the benchmark models are all able to segment the marine animals from the underwater images, but have their own emphasises. Specifically, SINet shows particularly good performance in restoring the edge details of the probability maps. U2Net is able to segment the most complete foreground from the images, e.g., it is the only method capable of segmenting two fishes from the image shown in the second last row. However, U2Net is unable to recover sharp edges and usually provides blurry boundaries in the probability maps. SCRN shows balanced performance in different sets of visual results. Compared with other models, BASNet shows unsatisfactory performance, reflecting in the noisy and unclear probability maps. It is worth noting that accurate MAS is still a challenging task. As can be observed in the third last row, none of the benchmark models is unable to segment the complete dolphin due to the disturbances of splash in the image.

5   Conclusion

In this paper, we have proposed the first MAS dataset, $MAS3K$. We consider the images of marine animals with camouflaged and common appearances and provide rich annotations for each image. Our dataset is derived from diverse resources, including existing object detection datasets, underwater image datasets, and the Internet. In addition, we perform in-depth analyses regarding the dataset features, such as the center bias and resolution distribution. Finally, based on $MAS3K$, we compare 6 cutting-edge object segmentation models and perform comprehensive analyses using five widely-used evaluation metrics. Our work offers valuable insights into the development of MAS techniques, which will eventually boosts various real applications in marine study. The *MAS3K* benchmark dataset will be made publicly available at https://github.com/LinLi-DL/MAS.

References

1. Beijbom, O., et al.: Improving automated annotation of benthic survey images using wide-band fluorescence. Sci. Rep. **6**, 23166 (2016)
2. Borji, A., Cheng, M.M., Jiang, H., Li, J.: Salient object detection: a benchmark. IEEE Trans. Image Process. **24**(12), 5706–5722 (2015)
3. Carraway, L.N., Verts, B., et al.: A bibliography of Oregon mammalogy (1982)
4. Chen, Q., et al.: EF-Net: a novel enhancement and fusion network for RGB-D saliency detection. Pattern Recogn. **112**, 107740 (2020)
5. Cheng, M.M., Liu, Y., Lin, W.Y., Zhang, Z., Rosin, P.L., Torr, P.H.: BING: binarized normed gradients for objectness estimation at 300fps. Comput. Vis. Media **5**(1), 3–20 (2019)
6. Cheng, M.M., Mitra, N.J., Huang, X., Torr, P.H., Hu, S.M.: Global contrast based salient region detection. IEEE Trans. Pattern Anal. Mach. Intell. **37**(3), 569–582 (2014)
7. Chiang, J.Y., Chen, Y.C.: Underwater image enhancement by wavelength compensation and dehazing. IEEE Trans. Image Process. **21**(4), 1756–1769 (2011)
8. Cott, H.B.: Adaptive Coloration in Animals. Oxford University Press, Methuen (1940)
9. Cutter, G., Stierhoff, K., Zeng, J.: Automated detection of rockfish in unconstrained underwater videos using Haar cascades and a new image dataset: labeled fishes in the wild. In: 2015 IEEE Winter Applications and Computer Vision Workshops, pp. 57–62. IEEE (2015)
10. Dawkins, M., Stewart, C., Gallager, S., York, A.: Automatic scallop detection in benthic environments. In: 2013 IEEE Workshop on Applications of Computer Vision, pp. 160–167. IEEE (2013)
11. Fan, D.-P., Cheng, M.-M., Liu, J.-J., Gao, S.-H., Hou, Q., Borji, A.: Salient objects in clutter: bringing salient object detection to the foreground. In: Ferrari, V., Hebert, M., Sminchisescu, C., Weiss, Y. (eds.) ECCV 2018. LNCS, vol. 11219, pp. 196–212. Springer, Cham (2018). https://doi.org/10.1007/978-3-030-01267-0_12
12. Fan, D.P., Cheng, M.M., Liu, Y., Li, T., Borji, A.: Structure-measure: a new way to evaluate foreground maps. In: Proceedings of the IEEE International Conference on Computer Vision, pp. 4548–4557 (2017)
13. Fan, D.P., Gong, C., Cao, Y., Ren, B., Cheng, M.M., Borji, A.: Enhanced-alignment measure for binary foreground map evaluation. arXiv preprint arXiv:1805.10421 (2018)
14. Fan, D.P., Ji, G.P., Sun, G., Cheng, M.M., Shen, J., Shao, L.: Camouflaged object detection. In: Proceedings of the IEEE/CVF Conference on Computer Vision and Pattern Recognition, pp. 2777–2787 (2020)
15. Fan, D.P., et al.: PraNet: parallel reverse attention network for polyp segmentation. arXiv preprint arXiv:2006.11392 (2020)
16. Fan, D.P., Lin, Z., Zhang, Z., Zhu, M., Cheng, M.M.: Rethinking RGB-D salient object detection: models, data sets, and large-scale benchmarks. In: IEEE Transactions on Neural Networks and Learning Systems (2020)

17. Fan, D.-P., Zhai, Y., Borji, A., Yang, J., Shao, L.: BBS-Net: RGB-D salient object detection with a bifurcated backbone strategy network. In: Vedaldi, A., Bischof, H., Brox, T., Frahm, J.-M. (eds.) ECCV 2020. LNCS, vol. 12357, pp. 275–292. Springer, Cham (2020). https://doi.org/10.1007/978-3-030-58610-2_17

18. Fu, K., Fan, D.P., Ji, G.P., Zhao, Q.: JL-DCF: joint learning and densely-cooperative fusion framework for RGB-D salient object detection. In: Proceedings of the IEEE/CVF Conference on Computer Vision and Pattern Recognition, pp. 3052–3062 (2020)

19. Fu, X., Zhuang, P., Huang, Y., Liao, Y., Zhang, X.P., Ding, X.: A retinex-based enhancing approach for single underwater image. In: 2014 IEEE International Conference on Image Processing, pp. 4572–4576. IEEE (2014)

20. Guo, Y., Li, H., Zhuang, P.: Underwater image enhancement using a multiscale dense generative adversarial network. IEEE J. Oceanic Eng. **45**, 862–870 (2019)

21. Huang, Z., Chen, H.X., Zhou, T., Yang, Y.Z., Wang, C.Y.: Multi-level cross-modal interaction network for RGB-D salient object detection. arXiv preprint arXiv:2007.14352 (2020)

22. Islam, M.J., Luo, P., Sattar, J.: Simultaneous enhancement and super-resolution of underwater imagery for improved visual perception. arXiv preprint arXiv:2002.01155 (2020)

23. Itti, L., Koch, C., Niebur, E.: A model of saliency-based visual attention for rapid scene analysis. IEEE Trans. Pattern Anal. Mach. Intell. **20**(11), 1254–1259 (1998)

24. Jäger, J., Simon, M., Denzler, J., Wolff, V., Fricke-Neuderth, K., Kruschel, C.: Croatian fish dataset: fine-grained classification of fish species in their natural habitat. In: British Machine Vision Conference, Swansea (2015)

25. Jian, M., Qi, Q., Dong, J., Yin, Y., Zhang, W., Lam, K.M.: The OUC-vision large-scale underwater image database. In: 2017 IEEE International Conference on Multimedia and Expo, pp. 1297–1302. IEEE (2017)

26. Jobson, D.J., Rahman, Z., Woodell, G.A.: A multiscale retinex for bridging the gap between color images and the human observation of scenes. IEEE Trans. Image Process. **6**(7), 965–976 (1997)

27. Johnsen, S.: Hidden in plain sight: the ecology and physiology of organismal transparency. Biol. Bull. **201**(3), 301–318 (2001)

28. Kisantal, M., Wojna, Z., Murawski, J., Naruniec, J., Cho, K.: Augmentation for small object detection. arXiv preprint arXiv:1902.07296 (2019)

29. Le, T.N., Nguyen, T.V., Nie, Z., Tran, M.T., Sugimoto, A.: Anabranch network for camouflaged object segmentation. Comput. Vis. Image Underst. **184**, 45–56 (2019)

30. Li, C., Guo, C., Ren, W., Cong, R., Hou, J., Kwong, S., Tao, D.: An underwater image enhancement benchmark dataset and beyond. IEEE Trans. Image Process. **29**, 4376–4389 (2019)

31. Li, C., Guo, J., Guo, C.: Emerging from water: underwater image color correction based on weakly supervised color transfer. IEEE Signal Process. Lett. **25**(3), 323–327 (2018)

32. Li, G., Yu, Y.: Visual saliency based on multiscale deep features. In: Proceedings of the IEEE Conference on Computer Vision and Pattern Recognition, pp. 5455–5463 (2015)

33. Li, J., Skinner, K.A., Eustice, R.M., Johnson-Roberson, M.: WaterGAN: unsupervised generative network to enable real-time color correction of monocular underwater images. IEEE Robot. Autom. Lett. **3**(1), 387–394 (2017)

34. Lin, T.-Y., et al.: Microsoft COCO: common objects in context. In: Fleet, D., Pajdla, T., Schiele, B., Tuytelaars, T. (eds.) ECCV 2014. LNCS, vol. 8693, pp. 740–755. Springer, Cham (2014). https://doi.org/10.1007/978-3-319-10602-1_48
35. Liu, J.J., Hou, Q., Cheng, M.M., Feng, J., Jiang, J.: A simple pooling-based design for real-time salient object detection. In: Proceedings of the IEEE Conference on Computer Vision and Pattern Recognition, pp. 3917–3926 (2019)
36. Lu, M., Wagner, A., Van Male, L., Whitehead, A., Boehnlein, J.: Imagery rehearsal therapy for posttraumatic nightmares in U.S. veterans. J. Trauma. Stress **22**(3), 236–239 (2009)
37. Ludvigsen, M., Sortland, B., Johnsen, G., Singh, H.: Applications of geo-referenced underwater photo mosaics in marine biology and archaeology. Oceanography **20**(4), 140–149 (2007)
38. Mahmood, A., et al.: Automatic annotation of coral reefs using deep learning. In: MTS/IEEE Conference OCEANS16, Monterey, pp. 1–5. IEEE (2016)
39. Margolin, R., Zelnik-Manor, L., Tal, A.: How to evaluate foreground maps? In: Proceedings of the IEEE Conference on Computer Vision and Pattern Recognition, pp. 248–255 (2014)
40. McFall-Ngai, M.J.: Crypsis in the pelagic environment. Am. Zool. **30**(1), 175–188 (1990)
41. Movahedi, V., Elder, J.H.: Design and perceptual validation of performance measures for salient object segmentation. In: 2010 IEEE Computer Society Conference on Computer Vision and Pattern Recognition-Workshops, pp. 49–56. IEEE (2010)
42. Pedersen, M., Bruslund Haurum, J., Gade, R., Moeslund, T.B.: Detection of marine animals in a new underwater dataset with varying visibility. In: Proceedings of the IEEE Conference on Computer Vision and Pattern Recognition Workshops, pp. 18–26 (2019)
43. Perazzi, F., Krähenbühl, P., Pritch, Y., Hornung, A.: Saliency filters: contrast based filtering for salient region detection. In: 2012 IEEE Conference on Computer Vision and Pattern Recognition, pp. 733–740. IEEE (2012)
44. Perazzi, F., Pont-Tuset, J., McWilliams, B., Van Gool, L., Gross, M., Sorkine-Hornung, A.: A benchmark dataset and evaluation methodology for video object segmentation. In: Proceedings of the IEEE Conference on Computer Vision and Pattern Recognition, pp. 724–732 (2016)
45. Qin, X., Zhang, Z., Huang, C., Dehghan, M., Zaiane, O.R., Jagersand, M.: U2-Net: going deeper with nested U-structure for salient object detection. Pattern Recogn. **106**, 107404 (2020)
46. Qin, X., Zhang, Z., Huang, C., Gao, C., Dehghan, M., Jagersand, M.: BASNet: boundary-aware salient object detection. In: Proceedings of the IEEE Conference on Computer Vision and Pattern Recognition, pp. 7479–7489 (2019)
47. Rasmussen, C., Zhao, J., Ferraro, D., Trembanis, A.: Deep census: AUV-based scallop population monitoring. In: Proceedings of the IEEE International Conference on Computer Vision Workshops, pp. 2865–2873 (2017)
48. Redmon, J., Farhadi, A.: YOLO9000: better, faster, stronger. In: Proceedings of the IEEE Conference on Computer Vision and Pattern Recognition, pp. 7263–7271 (2017)
49. Siddiqui, S.A., et al.: Automatic fish species classification in underwater videos: exploiting pre-trained deep neural network models to compensate for limited labelled data. ICES J. Mar. Sci. **75**, 374–389 (2017). Handling editor: Howard Browman
50. Skurowski, P., Abdulameer, H., Błaszczyk, J., Depta, T., Kornacki, A., Kozieł, P.: Animal camouflage analysis: Chameleon database (2018, unpublished manuscript)

51. Villon, S., Chaumont, M., Subsol, G., Villéger, S., Claverie, T., Mouillot, D.: Coral reef fish detection and recognition in underwater videos by supervised machine learning: comparison between deep learning and HOG+SVM methods. In: Blanc-Talon, J., Distante, C., Philips, W., Popescu, D., Scheunders, P. (eds.) ACIVS 2016. LNCS, vol. 10016, pp. 160–171. Springer, Cham (2016). https://doi.org/10.1007/978-3-319-48680-2_15

52. Wallace, A.R.: The colours of animals. Nature **42**(1082), 289–291 (1890)

53. Wang, L., et al.: Learning to detect salient objects with image-level supervision. In: Proceedings of the IEEE Conference on Computer Vision and Pattern Recognition, pp. 136–145 (2017)

54. Wu, Y.H., et al.: JCS: an explainable COVID-19 diagnosis system by joint classification and segmentation. arXiv preprint arXiv:2004.07054 (2020)

55. Wu, Z., Su, L., Huang, Q.: Stacked cross refinement network for edge-aware salient object detection. In: Proceedings of the IEEE International Conference on Computer Vision, pp. 7264–7273 (2019)

56. Yan, Q., Xu, L., Shi, J., Jia, J.: Hierarchical saliency detection. In: Proceedings of the IEEE Conference on Computer Vision and Pattern Recognition, pp. 1155–1162 (2013)

57. Yang, C., Zhang, L., Lu, H., Ruan, X., Yang, M.H.: Saliency detection via graph-based manifold ranking. In: Proceedings of the IEEE Conference on Computer Vision and Pattern Recognition, pp. 3166–3173 (2013)

58. Zeng, Y., Zhang, P., Zhang, J., Lin, Z., Lu, H.: Towards high-resolution salient object detection. In: Proceedings of the IEEE International Conference on Computer Vision, pp. 7234–7243 (2019)

59. Zhang, J., et al.: UC-Net: uncertainty inspired RGB-D saliency detection via conditional variational autoencoders. In: Proceedings of the IEEE/CVF Conference on Computer Vision and Pattern Recognition, pp. 8582–8591 (2020)

60. Zhang, P., Wang, D., Lu, H., Wang, H., Ruan, X.: Amulet: aggregating multi-level convolutional features for salient object detection. In: Proceedings of the IEEE International Conference on Computer Vision, pp. 202–211 (2017)

61. Zhang, S., Wang, T., Dong, J., Yu, H.: Underwater image enhancement via extended multi-scale retinex. Neurocomputing **245**, 1–9 (2017)

62. Zhao, J.X., Liu, J.J., Fan, D.P., Cao, Y., Yang, J., Cheng, M.M.: EGNet: edge guidance network for salient object detection. In: Proceedings of the IEEE International Conference on Computer Vision, pp. 8779–8788 (2019)

63. Zhao, Z.Q., Zheng, P., Xu, S.t., Wu, X.: Object detection with deep learning: a review. IEEE Transactions on Neural Networks and Learning Systems **30**(11), 3212–3232 (2019)

64. Zhou, T., Fan, D.P., Cheng, M.M., Shen, J., Shao, L.: RGB-D salient object detection: a survey. arXiv preprint arXiv:2008.00230 (2020)

Benchmarking Blockchain Interactions in Mobile Edge Cloud Software Systems

Hong-Linh Truong[1][(✉)] ⓘ and Filip Rydzi[2]

[1] Department of Computer Science, Aalto University, Espoo, Finland
linh.truong@aalto.fi
[2] Bratislava, Slovakia

Abstract. As blockchain becomes an essential part of many software systems in the edge and cloud, the developer starts to treat blockchain features like commodity software components that can be integrated into edge and cloud software systems. For the developer it is quite challenging to determine, customize, and evaluate suitable blockchain features for software systems in the edge and cloud environments. In this paper, we conceptualize important blockchain interactions in mobile edge computing software systems (MECSS) and present generic techniques for evaluating these interactions. We determine different interaction patterns for different deployments of compute resources and networks. We abstract and represent application-level mobile edge computing (MEC) features and blockchain features to create MECSS deployment models to be coupled with testbed deployments for benchmarking application-level interactions within application contexts. Based on that, we develop a generic framework for building and executing benchmarks of application-level blockchain interactions within MECSS. We will demonstrate our framework for vehicle-to-everything communication scenarios with two main blockchain technologies, Hyperledger Fabric and Ethereum, using various types of compute resources in edge and cloud infrastructures.

Keywords: Benchmark · Testing · Blockchain · Edge computing · Microservices

1 Introduction

To date, blockchain technologies have been widely exploited in different types of software systems [8,38]. Applications and systems utilize blockchain as commodity features to support verifiable and open transactions. One of the challenges for the application developer is the question of which blockchain features should be integrated in which part of the developer's complex software systems. Especially, in our focus, mobile edge computing software systems (MECSS) [21,31] have increasingly leveraged blockchain potentials due to application requirements [12,15,18,39]. For the developer, combining blockchain features with MEC

F. Rydzi—Independent.

F. Wolf and W. Gao (Eds.): Bench 2020, LNCS 12614, pp. 213–231, 2021.
https://doi.org/10.1007/978-3-030-71058-3_13

features is extremely challenging because the complexity and diversity of software services, system configurations and interactions.

The need for development tools for blockchain-based software is high [27] and we lack tools to support the design and evaluation of combined features from MEC and blockchain for different realistic deployments. Especially, our work is concerned with the application-level interactions in MEC that need blockchain features. Determining such interactions is time-consuming. Furthermore, software development knowledge for integrating edge computing with blockchain is hard to acquire, due to several challenges [6,14,35]. Therefore, generic methods and tools to enable testing of such interactions play an important role. Such tools and methods are different from current benchmarking and testing for particular blockchain systems, individual blockchain features, or for individual MEC resources, as we need to develop generic ways to evaluate *integration interaction patterns* in which blockchain-based data exchanges are carried within suitable MEC design models, reflecting application developer needs. Furthermore, key quality metrics and appropriate deployments, including underlying computing resources and application topologies, must be considered at the application level. As we also discuss in the related work (see Sect. 5), many works provide high-level recommendations of using blockchain features and blockchain systems, but they do not treat combined blockchain features with other features within contexts of interactions in MECSS.

This paper identifies such interactions and supports methods to evaluate the interactions in the development of MECSS with blockchain features. A MECSS includes various components deployed in MEC infrastructures that interact with each other. Without loss of generality and based on the development trend, we concentrate on MECSS components developed as microservices [24,28]: we focus on interactions in such microservices, not low-level networks or infrastructures in MEC. We (i) treat blockchain features like software components that can be taken from existing blockchain libraries/frameworks, (ii) consider common integration of such features based on different needs, and then (iii) test such features for MECSS, especially for application-level interactions within MECSS. To help the developer to perform a systematic way of benchmarking interactions, we choose a known MECSS application domain – the vehicle-to-everything (V2X) – to explain our work. We will use scenarios in V2X to present our methods and software prototype. We first present an abstract view on MECSS and their blockchain features, key interactions in the interest of testing, and their software coupling from an application viewpoint (see Sect. 2). We then contribute a benchmark framework with features of automatic deployment and execution of benchmarks (see Sect. 3).

Our framework is designed for evaluating blockchain features based on a complex dependency of blockchain features, application-related operations, system topology and resources running blockchain features. Utilizing our framework, we carry out several experiments to present how our framework could provide insights into realistic deployments of MECSS for the developer (see Sect. 4). We illustrate our work with well-known blockchain systems, like Hyperledger Fabric and Ethereum, using edge and cloud infrastructures.

2   Aspects in Benchmarking Blockchain Features for MECSS

2.1   Mobile Edge Computing Software Systems

Several papers have conceptualized mobile edge computing and fog computing [7] with multiple layers. Practically, we focus on applications atop a common 3-level of MEC infrastructures, shown in Fig. 1. In this 3-level abstract infrastructure model, a mobile component mc is movable and interacts with other mobile components, edge units, edge data centers and clouds. The level 1 edge $edge_{l1}$ indicates typical edge units/devices/systems which are very close to the mobile component, serving for a limited number of mobile components. The level 2 edge $edge_{l2}$ is deployed in edge data centers with reasonable capabilities, e.g. connected telco base stations. Finally, cloud-based data centers offer $cloud$ services for mc, $edge_{l1}$ and $edge_{l2}$ components. Such infrastructures are common in many real deployments and scenarios in smart building, vehicle communication and smart factory. Mapping to the 5 layers of edge/fog/cloud in [21], our mc is at layer 5, $edge_{l1}$ is at layer 2, $edge_{l2}$ at layer 3 and $cloud$ is at layers 2 and 1. In this paper, we will use the V2X communication scenarios [2,12,13,16,17,23,25] to demonstrate our work.

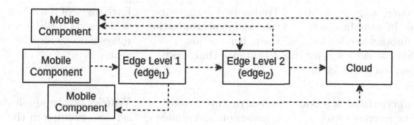

Fig. 1. Simplified view of three-level MEC with two layers of edges

Given the above-mentioned view on MEC infrastructures, we consider distributed, application-required components as microservices residing in different levels in the above-mentioned view. With the assumption that underlying networks and operating systems of MEC have different mechanisms to enable us to compose and deploy these microservices to build MECSS (e.g., via containerization), we will address the service developer concerns in application-level interactions utilizing blockchain features. MECSS have different application-level software features, covering typical MEC software features at the application level, such as sending and receiving messages from message brokers, blockchain features, like read/writing blockchain transactions and consensus/mining execution, and application-specific features, such as reporting events or performing data analytics. Such features will be implemented within microservices deployed in resources in the 3-level MEC infrastructural model. There are many types of interactions, shown in Table 1, in existing MEC use cases that one can find in the literature and real-world applications (e.g., [2,12,13,16,17,23,25]).

For such application-level features working properly, many system services have to be deployed or available to offer infrastructure- and platform-level features, such as message brokers, blockchain nodes, message flow engines, etc.

Table 1. Example of key interactions that should be benchmarked

Interactions: description	Example of metrics	V2X data exchange scenarios
mc–mc: a service in a mc interacts directly with a service in another mc	Transaction acceptance rate, transaction acceptance time	Vehicles directly exchange driving data [36]
mc–$edge_{l1}$–mc: a service in a mc interacts with a service in another mc via a service in $edge_{l1}$	Transaction acceptance rate, transaction acceptance time, cost	Vehicles send road warnings via a road side unit (RSU) [17,25]
mc–$edge_{l2}$–mc: a service in a mc interacts with another service in another mc via a service in a $edge_{l2}$	Transaction acceptance rate and synchronization state, transaction acceptance time, cost	Exchanges of data between vehicles over a data broker deployed in an edge node in mobile base stations
mc–$edge_{l1}$–$edge_{l2}$–mc: a service in a mc interacts with another service in another mc via a service in a $edge_{l1}$ via a service in $edge_{l2}$	Transaction acceptance rate and synchronization state, transaction acceptance time, cost	Exchanges of data between vehicles via a RSU, which relays data to an edge data center
mc–$edge_{l2}$–$cloud$: a service in a mc interacts with a service in a $cloud$ via a service in a $edge_{l2}$	Infrastructure costs, transaction acceptance rate and synchronization state	Vehicles invoke application services running in the edge and the cloud to sell traffic/environmental data
mc–$edge_{l1}$–$edge_{l2}$–$cloud$: a service in a mc utilizes various services in $cloud$ via services in $edge_{l1}$ and in $edge_{l2}$	Infrastructure costs, transaction acceptance rate and synchronization state	Vehicles invoke application services running in the edge and the cloud, e.g. payment for using fast lanes [2]

2.2 Application-Required Features for Blockchain-Based MECSS

To develop a blockchain-based MECSS, many common IoT, edge and cloud infrastructure- and platform-level features are needed. Let $MEC_F = \{mec_f\}$ represent such features. A feature $mec_f \in MEC_F$ is provided by a component. Thus, we can have $MEC_F = \{mosquitto\_mqtt\_broker, v2xpaas, kafka\}$ as an example where features are provided by the Eclipse Mosquitto MQTT broker[1], Apache Kafka[2] or a V2X Platform-as-a-Service [25]. These components are deployed and run as microservices, leading to the set of service instances $MEC_S = \{s(mec_f)_i\}$. With blockchain-based MECSS, such services will be integrated with blockchain features. From the application viewpoint, blockchain can be used as composite or individual features based on primitive operations, like *creating, signing, validating, mining,* and *verifying* [10]. We work at the blockchain features level for different interactions of MECSS. Generally, we consider $BC_F = \{bcf_i\}$ as a set of application-specific blockchain features that should be benchmarked. For example, in the experiments of this paper we focus on $BC_F = \{creator, consensus, all\}$ where *creator* is a composite feature including operations *creating, signing* and *submitting* a transaction, *consensus* is atomic feature reflecting the *mining* process, and *all* means all needed blockchain operators. To use blockchain we will need several blockchain nodes, $BC_N = \{bc_n\}$, offering bcf_i. For testing purposes, BC_F and concrete BC_N will be mapped into concrete blockchain implementations. For example, let $BC_N = \{standard_n, miner_n\}$, we can have $standard_n \in \{Client_{hyperledger}, PeerNodes_{hyperledger}, ETHNode_{eth}\}$ whereas $miner_n \in \{OrdererNode_{hyperledger}, MinerNode_{eth}\}$; these roles/nodes specified in Ethereum[3] and Hyperledger Fabric [5].

We define $MECSS = \{MEC_S, BC_N\}$. For a benchmark, we have a $MECSS$ deployment including MEC_S and BC_N executed in a testbed deployment of a set of containers or VMs across edge and cloud infrastructures. Given blockchain features and interactions, we need to consider main couplings between blockchain features and interactions. Such couplings are based on the design of blockchain-based software systems. For example, let $C_{MEC} = \{mc, edge_{l1}, edge_{l2}, cloud\}$ be the nodes in the previous discussed MEC model and let a set $BC_F = \{creator, consensus\}$ be the blockchain features. In order to perform benchmark, we will need to have a specification of couplings (c, f), whereas $c \in C_{MEC}$ and $f \in BC_F$.

2.3 Benchmarked Metrics

When developing blockchain features for MECSS, there are many metrics that the developer wants to consider [1,11,32,37,40]; such metrics are important and they have been well-documented in the literature. Table 2 shows examples of important metrics, which should be assessed. Besides these common metrics, the developer usually needs different types of metrics for different requirements. Thus, the developer should be able to customize possible metrics to be tested/measured. In our framework, we do not define such metrics but assume that benchmark functions (see Sect. 3) will implement suitable metrics defined in the literature. This way allows us to extend benchmark functions even for evaluating application-specific metrics, instead of evaluating features of specific blockchain frameworks without application interaction patterns.

---

[1] https://mosquitto.org/.

[2] https://kafka.apache.org/.

[3] https://docs.ethhub.io/using-ethereum/running-an-ethereum-node.

Table 2. Examples of importance metrics for interactions

Metrics	Description
Transaction (Tx) Acceptance Time	The ratio of accepted transactions to the total transactions submitted
Synchronization State	The number of nodes, which lost their synchronization
Transaction (Tx) Acceptance Rate	The number of the submitted transactions accepted by blockchain
Infrastructure resource utilization	Typical CPU, memory, bandwidth of infrastructures
Cost	Cost for blockchain operations and for other related operations and infrastructures

2.4 MECSS Under Test and Infrastructures

A benchmark for interactions in MECSS needs a suitable MEC infrastructure. Resources for a MECSS and their dependencies are also considered based on application requirements. Realistically, all components should be deployed in the real systems suitable for different scenarios. However, practically, currently it is impossible to have the realistic infrastructure for MEC, especially for large-scale and complex topologies of MEC resources. Therefore, we apply symbiotic engineering principles for IoT Cloud systems by having real resources combined with emulation components:

- mc: emulated with multiple configurations using container with resource constraints or powerful machines.
- $edge_{l1}$: emulated by VMs/containers with reasonable capabilities, as it is resource-constrained in real deployments.
- $edge_{l2}$ and *cloud*: based on real systems using micro data centers or cloud resources.

The developer can use existing cloud and edge providers, e.g., Google Compute Engine[4], for running benchmarks.

2.5 Coupling Software and Infrastructure Artefacts

Figure 2 presents a deployment topology model of artefacts and their configurations for benchmarks. The deployment model is used to define suitable deployments for specific application needs w.r.t. MECSS and blockchain-based interaction evaluation. Resources are defined by `ContainerConfiguration` and `NetworkConfiguration`. `BlockchainArtefact` and `ApplicationArtefact` are used to describe blockchain and application-specific features, respectively. The

---

[4] https://cloud.google.com/compute/docs/instances/.

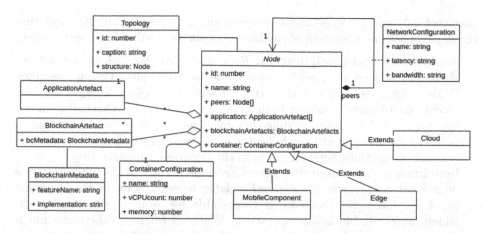

Fig. 2. Relationships between software and infrastructural artefacts

deployment topology model is crucial for understanding required software artefacts and corresponding configurations that will be deployed into a suitable testbed
for evaluating interactions. For example, a Node will specify software artefacts to be
deployed in a specific mc, $edge_{l1}$, $edge_{l2}$ or $cloud$, including blockchain software and
other services, whereas ContainerConfiguration specifies information about the
container environment hosting such software artefacts. Nodes are connected to create a topology of machines (a test infrastructure) through suitable network configuration (specified by NetworkConfiguration). Based on this deployment model,
we will define deployment configurations, explained in Sect. 3.3.

3   Framework for Benchmarks

3.1   Overview

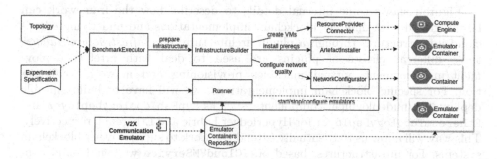

Fig. 3. Main components of the benchmark framework

Figure 3 outlines the architecture of our framework for developing and executing
benchmarks for MECSS. Inputs for benchmarks are specified via (i) topology

(see Sect. 2.5) and (ii) experiment specification. *BenchmarksExecutor* performs the deployment and execution of emulator containers in suitable infrastructures.

- **deployment and configuration:** *BenchmarkExecutor* uses *Infrastructure-Builder* to invoke *ResourceProviderConnector* to acquire virtual machines (VMs). After acquiring VMs, *ArtefactDeployer* deploys application and blockchain artefacts according to the topology specification. Depending on the topology, a VM can host multiple container-based services running artefacts. *InfrastructureBuilder* utilizes *NetworkConfigurator* to set the configuration of network connections between nodes in the deployed infrastructure.
- **benchmark execution:** *BenchmarkExecutor* invokes *Runner* to start the dockerized component *InteractionEmulator* in each node in the deployed topology. *InteractionEmulator* is responsible for running the benchmark, which carries out blockchain operations. When all *InteractionEmulator* finish their running experiments, the framework will download the logs and results of the experiment from all nodes across the deployed topology. Finally, *Runner* will stop docker containers hosting *InteractionEmulator* and stop blockchain nodes and virtual machines.

InteractionEmulator includes all necessary features for emulating application-level blockchain interactions. This component basically emulates or implements interactions of exchanging data over blockchain. Thus, it emulates both data source and receiver in MECSS by connecting blockchain nodes and performing blockchain operations. The developer can select, customize and utilize suitable *InteractionEmulator* for application designs. During the benchmarks operations are monitored to collect data for analyzing metrics. *InteractionEmulator* is a customized component, in which the developer would emulate/test blockchain-based operations for suitable interactions using benchmark functions (see Sect. 3.2). Several *InteractionEmulator* can be managed in *EmulatorContainersRepository*. For example, in our experiment, a `V2XCommunicatorEmulator` is used (see Sect. 4) for benchmarking interactions in V2X. The use of *InteractionEmulator* allows us to add new functions for testing a different, new type of interactions.

Figure 4 shows some internal details to describe how the framework can be integrated with different blockchain implementations and underlying edge-/cloud infrastructures through a plugin architecture. For *InfrastructuralBuilder*, three different classes of plugins are used to deal with artefact deployment/undeployment, virtual machines provisioning and network configuration. For specific blockchain implementations, we will have to build suitable deployment/undeployment components, such as `HypFabTopologyDeployer` and `EthereumTopologyDeployer` for Hyperledger Fabric and Ethereum, respectively. This way will allow us to eventually extend the work to support other blockchain systems. For infrastructures, based on `ICloudVMService` we could build connectors to suitable infrastructure providers, enabling benchmarking and testing using different edge and cloud resources. Similar to artefacts and infrastructures deployment/undeployment, different plugins for running emulators performing benchmarks have to be developed for suitable blockchain features. For example, `RunnerHypFab` and `RunnerEthereum` are used for suitable emulators running in

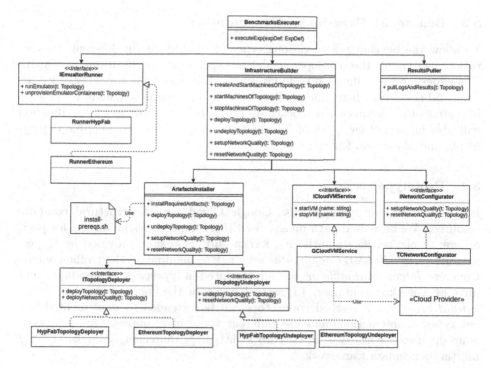

Fig. 4. Main classes for plugins in the framework

Hyperledger Fabric and in Ethereum, respectively. Using common interfaces and plugins design, we could extend and include new benchmark functions for other blockchain technologies.

3.2 Benchmark Functions

One of the key features is to support the development of benchmark functions based on end-to-end interactions in the design of the developer. As discussed in the previous subsection, such benchmark functions are encapsulated into emulators which are executed as container-based microservices. In our approach we enable the developer to develop them via *InteractionEmulator* containers.

In our framework, the developer writes required functions based on *InteractionEmulator* templates, then the framework will take *InteractionEmulator* to run it. Key functions that the developer has to develop:

- emulated data and parameters for using data: data can be loaded, e.g., from files. Examples of parameters are sending/reading frequencies and number of records to be used.
- key benchmark functions: perform end-to-end test operations and report metrics

These functions are configured with existing features of the framework to build container-based emulators.

3.3 Benchmark Experiment Configuration

To allow the benchmarks of various types of interactions in different configurations, we enable the developer to define experiment specifications in YAML. The experiment specification includes information about the topology of infrastructural resources where blockchain artefacts will be deployed. Node to indicate infrastructural resources and blockchain artefacts. The experiment specification will also include other types of information, such as different possible deployments and blockchain features.

3.4 Prototype

In our current prototype, we use Google Cloud for infrastructural compute resources. We have used geth image[5] for Ethereum, and official images for peer, orderer, tools, certificate authority, Kafka and Zookeeper provided by Hyperledger Fabric[6]. *NetworkConfigurator* uses tc[7] to manipulate the traffic control. Concrete *InteractionEmulator* are implemented in typescript and nodejs, running in a docker container. In general, most of the components, like *InteractionEmulator* and testbed connectors can be extended to implement different types of interactions and use different types of resources. Our prototype is an open source available in GitHub at https://github.com/rdsea/kalbi/tree/master/benchmark_framework.

4 Experiments

4.1 Flexibility in Benchmark Configurations

One of the key requirements is the flexibility in configuring benchmarks that we illustrate in this section through examples of creating experiments through the parameterization of experiment configurations. For experiments, we use the V2X Communication scenarios whereas mc is a vehicle, $edge_{l1}$ is a RSU, $edge_{l2}$ is a resource in an edge data center, and *cloud* is a public cloud resource. We implement V2XCommunicatorEmulator for experiments. There are many combinations of MEC and blockchain features and deployment topologies, thus we have many MECSS deployments that we cannot present here all[8]. Table 3 shows examples of deployments; note that each types of interaction has different deployments of features. Table 4 gives dynamic configuration for testbed deployment. All machines are with Intel Xeon E5, Sandy Bridge 2.6 GHz and Ubuntu 18.04. Network configurations for the experiments are varied, shown in Table 5. For each of deployments, we can select suitable configurations for emulating mc, $edge_{l1}$, $edge_{l2}$ or

---

[5] https://github.com/ethereum/go-ethereum.
[6] https://github.com/hyperledger/fabric.
[7] http://manpages.ubuntu.com/manpages/bionic/man8/tc.8.html.
[8] Detailed deployment configurations and logs as well as benchmark results can be found at: https://github.com/rdsea/kalbi/tree/master/experiments.

cloud. Furthermore, experiments are also configured with different blockchain implementations. Due to the flexibility of our framework, it is easy to create several experiments. For example, when focusing on a topology called *large scale* where we have max 48 *mc* and (i) for interaction $mc\text{--}edge_{l1}\text{--}mc$: one $edge_{l1}$, (ii) for interaction $mc\text{--}edge_{l2}\text{--}mc$: one $edge_{l2}$, and (iii) for interaction $mc\text{--}edge_{l1}\text{--}edge_{l2}\text{--}mc$: one $edge_{l2}$, two $edge_{l1}$, we carried out 180 experiments for Ethereum and 144 experiments for Hyperledger Fabric.

Table 3. Example of the deployment of blockchain features for interaction 4 – *mc–edge$_{l1}$–edge$_{l2}$–mc*

Blockchain features deployment				
Deployment ID	*mc*	*edge$_{l1}$*	*edge$_{l2}$*	*cloud*
0	*creator*	*consensus*	*creator*	–
1	*creator*	*all*	*creator*	–
2	*creator*	*creator*	*all*	–
3	*creator*	*creator*	*consensus*	-
4	*creator*	*consensus*	*consensus*	–
5	*creator*	*all*	*consensus*	–
6	*creator*	*consensus*	*all*	–
7	*creator*	*all*	*all*	–
8	*all*	*all*	*all*	–
9	*all*	*consensus*	*all*	–
10	*all*	*creator*	*all*	–
11	*all*	*creator*	*creator*	–
12	*all*	*consensus*	*creator*	–
13	*all*	*all*	*creator*	–
14	*all*	*creator*	*consensus*	–
15	*all*	*consensus*	*consensus*	–
16	*all*	*all*	*consensus*	–

Table 4. Example of VM configurations for running containers

Component	CPU	RAM	Storage (GB)
cloud	4vCPU	16 GB	60 SSD
edge$_{l2}$	4vCPU	16 GB	60 SSD
edge$_{l1}$	1vCPU	2 GB	16 SSD
mc (light)	1vCPU	2 GB	20 SSD
mc (medium)	2vCPU	4 GB	20 SSD
mc (big)	4vCPU	8 GB	20 SSD

Table 5. Example of used network configurations

Type	Latency	Bandwidth
3G	200 ms	1000 kbps
4G	100 ms	10000 kbps
5G	5 ms	54 mbps

Table 6. Examples of best benchmarks results

Input				Result	Performance						Reliability			
					Transaction acceptance time						Transaction acceptance rate			Not-sync nodes count
Interaction Id	Blockchain framework	Scale		Experiment ID	Minimum time	Maximum time	Median time	Average time			Accepted count	Failed count		
2	Ethereum	Small	24		240	6510	2316.5	2507.7			200	0		0
2	Ethereum	Large	94		979	23013	5691.5	6617.78			4800	0		0
2	Hyperledger Fabric	Small	188		2044	2072	2054	2054.45			200	0		0
2	Hyperledger Fabric	Large	272		50	6956	124	487.18			4800	0		0
3	Ethereum	Small	53		474	5120	1862	2153.24			200	0		0
3	Ethereum	Large	125		429	16774	3698.5	4444.62			4800	0		0
3	Hyperledger Fabric	Small	233		2038	2064	2049	2049.55			200	0		0
3	Hyperledger Fabric	Large	302		49	5708	154	494.91			4800	0		0
4	Ethereum	Small	61		199	4914	2151.5	2188.34			200	0		0
4	Ethereum	Large	149		306	47711	5218.5	6529.1			4618	182		0
4	Hyperledger Fabric	Small	260		2041	2063	2048.5	2050.21			200	0		0

4.2   Insights from Benchmarks for Developers

Table 6 presented a small set of results to illustrate the richness of our framework. Several results can be obtained through the framework by parameterizing experiment specifications. Our goal is to illustrate the framework. In the following we will only focus on few aspects of how the developer could benefit from our methods and framework.

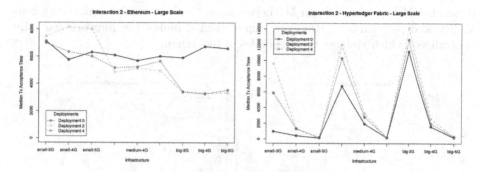

Fig. 5. Medians of transaction acceptance times for interaction 2 ($mc\text{–}edge_{l1}\text{–}mc$)

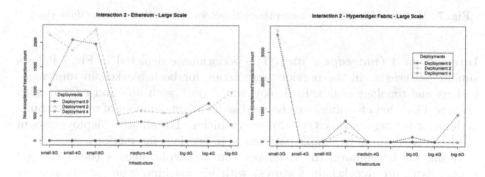

Fig. 6. Number of rejected transactions for interaction 2 ($mc\text{–}edge_{l1}\text{–}mc$)

Interaction 2 ($mc\text{–}edge_{l1}\text{–}mc$). Figures 5 and 6 depict a dependency between the infrastructure and performance and reliability respectively, among all blockchain deployments for this interaction. For a large scale topology, the experiments didn't achieve 100% reliability, except deployment 0 (where mc is configured with *creator* and $edge_{l1}$ with *all* blockchain features). However, the deployment 0 is centralized (consensus algorithm is running only in $edge_{l1}$ (RSU)). For deployment 2 (mc with *all* and $edge_{l1}$ with *creator* blockchain features) and deployment 4 (mc and $edge_{l1}$ with *all* blockchain features) results is strongly dependent on the used infrastructure. However, for a better resource configuration for *mc*, we obtained a worse performance. It is possible that *mc* created more transactions when utilizing more powerful configuration, leading to longer synchronization time. Hyperledger Fabric has shown better results for the large scale (the best deployment is for experiment 272, not shown in the paper).

Considering that the goal of a developer is to find a single deployment and infrastructure configuration. Deriving from several benchmark results and the above observations, the developer might choose Hyperledger Fabric, deployment 0, small VM type for *mc* and 5G network, as the best results concerning reliability and performance. However, deployment 0 makes the network partially centralized, which violates the principles of blockchain.

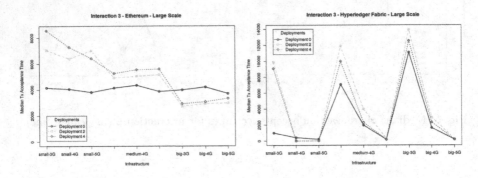

Fig. 7. Medians of transaction acceptance times for interaction 3 (mc–$edge_{l2}$–mc)

Interaction 3 (mc–$edge_{l2}$–mc). The performance depicted in Fig. 7 follows similar patterns as in the previous interaction for both blockchain implementations and topology scales. In deployment 2 (*mc* with *all* and $edge_{l2}$ with *creator* blockchain features) we observed an increasing number of rejected transactions for the big machine types for *mc* (vehicles). For all other deployments in the large scale, we have similar patterns as in previous interactions.

From the benchmark, the developer can use deployment 4 (both *mc* and $edge_{l2}$ with *all* blockchain features) with big machine type for *mc* and 5G network. With deployment 0 (*mc* with *creator* and $edge_{l2}$ with *all* blockchain features), medium machine types for *mc* and 5G network we got the best results. From all benchmarks for this interaction, our framework could provide a hint to the developer that Hyperledger Fabric, deployment 0, medium machine type and 5G network is considered as the best deployment and configuration.

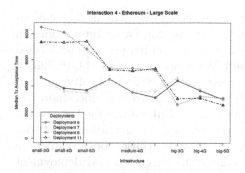

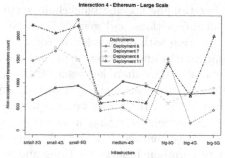

Fig. 8. Median of transaction acceptance times for interaction 4 (mc–$edge_{l1}$–$edge_{l2}$–mc)

Fig. 9. Number of rejected transactions for interaction 4 (mc–$edge_{l1}$–$edge_{l2}$–mc)

Interaction 4 (mc–$edge_{l1}$–$edge_{l2}$–mc). Figure 8 and Fig. 9 showed performance and reliability results, respectively, for this interaction with Ethereum (no Hyperledger Fabric experiments for this scale). Concerning the reliability, the results showed a dependency between infrastructure and number of rejected transactions. In this interaction we achieved the best results for experiment 149 (deployment 8, medium machine types for mc and 5G network).

Additional Discussion. We notice that experiments with different underlying blockchain systems show different performance. In our work, we did not investigate the underlying reasons for the difference. The reason is that it is not our goal to compare different blockchain internal structures and this comparison in MEC will also require intensive work on analyzing blockchain internals and their relationships with MEC middleware and applications. Some related works have studied intensively internal properties of Ethereum and Hyperledger Fabric [9,11,20]. Nevertheless, from the list of experiments, the best configuration from our experiments is based on parameters set in the experiment configuration and might not be the best for the requirements of MECSS designed by the developer (e.g., in V2X, requirements from safety regulation). This raises the importance of having benchmarks with different customization capabilities for the developer.

5 Related Work

There is no lack of survey papers about blockchain, edge computing and IoT, such as [3,4,14,26,33]. In MEC various papers have addressed different issues of blockchain and presented various scenarios [29,35]. Unlike these works, we focus on benchmarking blockchain features with MECSS from software development viewpoint, especially we focus on application-level interactions in an end-to-end view. There are general blockchain benchmark tools[9] but they are focused on

---

[9] e.g., https://github.com/dsx-tech/blockchain-benchmarking and https://github.com/hyperledger/caliper.

understanding specific blockchain systems in general view - not in application-level interactions and generic frameworks for blockchain-based interactions in connection with other relevant software services. Several papers have performed benchmarks and testing of blockchain and blockchain networks [11,19,32,34]. Generally, they share key issues with our paper w.r.t. metrics and software components. However, our paper focuses on generic benchmarks of blockchain features within MECSS so we can provide a distinguished feature for the need of the developer. Note that in our work, we do not focus on definition of metrics to be benchmarked, like [1,11,32]. Instead, we provide utilities for developers to write core benchmark functions and we enable the execution and deployment of benchmarks. Another difference of our framework is the design of *InteractionEmulator* and connectors to allow the developer to create new configurations and benchmark functions to support new types of application-level interactions, which might exist in specific application designs.

The work [22] specifically develops blockchain for V2X and has also performed simulation and benchmark. However, it is a typical benchmark for systems developed for V2X. In our work, we abstract the MECSS to focus on application-level interactions carried out through different services, creating a generic framework for benchmarking blockchain interactions in MEC; we leverage V2X scenarios only for testing our framework.

6   Conclusions and Future Work

In this paper we present a framework for developing and executing benchmarks for blockchain-based mobile edge computing software systems. We have focused on important application-level interactions and metrics for realistic deployment of MECSS. Our framework is generic enough to cover various aspects of deployments and software features. Benchmarking functions for interactions can be defined in *InteractionEmulator* that can be extended, whereas the design of connectors for blockchain, common and infrastructural services allows us to deploy and integrate with different software systems and resources. The contribution is not about specific benchmark values for blockchain but the capabilities to perform benchmarks in a generic way for application specific interactions.

In our current work, we focus on improving the prototype and extending metrics as plugins as well as to support fine-grained couplings of MEC features and blockchain features for MECSS. We are also integrating the benchmark framework and benchmark data with a service for managing knowledge from benchmarks [30] to enable the reuse of knowledge from benchmarks for MECSS design and implementation.

Acknowledgment. Filip Rydzi work was performed as a part of his study at TU Wien. Partial results of this paper were also reported in his master thesis. We thank Google Cloud Platform Research Credits Program for supporting computing resources.

References

1. Hyperledger blockchain performance metrics. https://www.hyperledger.org/wp-content/uploads/2018/10/HL_Whitepaper_Metrics_PDF_V1.01.pdf. Accessed 26 May 2019
2. Vehicle-to-vehicle cooperation to marshal traffic. https://patents.google.com/patent/US9928746B1/en
3. Zheng, Z., Xie, S., Dai, H.N., Chen, X., Wang, H.: Blockchain challenges and opportunities: a survey. Int. J. Web Grid Serv. **14**(4), 352–375 (2018). http://dl.acm.org/citation.cfm?id=3292946.3292948
4. Ali, M.S., Vecchio, M., Pincheira, M., Dolui, K., Antonelli, F., Rehmani, M.H.: Applications of blockchains in the Internet of Things: a comprehensive survey. IEEE Commun. Surv. Tutor. **21**, 1676–1717 (2018). https://doi.org/10.1109/COMST.2018.2886932
5. Androulaki, E., et al.: Hyperledger fabric: a distributed operating system for permissioned blockchains. In: Proceedings of the 13th EuroSys Conference, EuroSys 2018, pp. 30:1–30:15. ACM, New York (2018)
6. Bagchi, S., Siddiqui, M.B., Wood, P., Zhang, H.: Dependability in edge computing. Commun. ACM **63**(1), 58–66 (2019).https://doi.org/10.1145/3362068
7. Bittencourt, L., et al.: The internet of things, fog and cloud continuum: integration and challenges. IoT **3–4**, 134–155 (2018)
8. Chakraborty, P., Shahriyar, R., Iqbal, A., Bosu, A.: Understanding the software development practices of blockchain projects: a survey. In: Proceedings of the 12th ACM/IEEE International Symposium on Empirical Software Engineering and Measurement, ESEM 2018, pp. 28:1–28:10. ACM, New York (2018)
9. Chen, T., et al.: Understanding Ethereum via graph analysis. ACM Trans. Internet Technol. **20**(2), 32 (2020). https://doi.org/10.1145/3381036
10. Christidis, K., Devetsikiotis, M.: Blockchains and smart contracts for the Internet of Things. IEEE Access **4**, 2292–2303 (2016). https://doi.org/10.1109/ACCESS.2016.2566339
11. Dinh, T.T.A., Wang, J., Chen, G., Liu, R., Ooi, B.C., Tan, K.L.: BLOCKBENCH: a framework for analyzing private blockchains. In: Proceedings of the 2017 ACM International Conference on Management of Data, SIGMOD 2017, pp. 1085–1100. ACM, New York (2017)
12. Dorri, A., Steger, M., Kanhere, S.S., Jurdak, R.: BlockChain: a distributed solution to automotive security and privacy. IEEE Commun. Mag. **55**(12), 119–125 (2017). https://doi.org/10.1109/MCOM.2017.1700879
13. Faezipour, M., Nourani, M., Saeed, A., Addepalli, S.: Progress and challenges in intelligent vehicle area networks. Commun. ACM **55**(2), 90–100 (2012)
14. Ferrag, M.A., Derdour, M., Mukherjee, M., Derhab, A., Maglaras, L.A., Janicke, H.: Blockchain technologies for the Internet of Things: research issues and challenges. IEEE IoT J. **6**(2), 2188–2204 (2019). https://doi.org/10.1109/JIOT.2018.2882794
15. Grewe, D., Wagner, M., Arumaithurai, M., Psaras, I., Kutscher, D.: Information-centric mobile edge computing for connected vehicle environments: challenges and research directions. In: Proceedings of the Workshop on Mobile Edge Communications, MECOMM 2017, pp. 7–12. ACM, New York (2017)
16. Guo, H., Meamari, E., Shen, C.: Blockchain-inspired event recording system for autonomous vehicles. CoRR abs/1809.04732 (2018)

17. Harding, J., et al.: Vehicle-to-vehicle communications: readiness of v2v technology for application. Technical report. National Highway Traffic Safety Administration, United States (2014)
18. Kim, N.H., Kang, S.M., Hong, C.S.: Mobile charger billing system using lightweight blockchain. In: 2017 19th Asia-Pacific Network Operations and Management Symposium (APNOMS), pp. 374–377 (September 2017). https://doi.org/10.1109/APNOMS.2017.8094151
19. Kim, S.K., Ma, Z., Murali, S., Mason, J., Miller, A., Bailey, M.: Measuring Ethereum network peers. In: Proceedings of the Internet Measurement Conference 2018, IMC 2018, pp. 91–104. ACM, New York (2018)
20. Lee, X.T., Khan, A., Sen Gupta, S., Ong, Y.H., Liu, X.: Measurements, analyses, and insights on the entire Ethereum blockchain network. In: Proceedings of the Web Conference 2020, WWW 2020, pp. 155–166. Association for Computing Machinery, New York (2020). https://doi.org/10.1145/3366423.3380103
21. Li, C., Xue, Y., Wang, J., Zhang, W., Li, T.: Edge-oriented computing paradigms: a survey on architecture design and system management. ACM Comput. Surv. 51(2), 39:1–39:34 (2018)
22. Li, L., et al.: CreditCoin: a privacy-preserving blockchain-based incentive announcement network for communications of smart vehicles. IEEE Trans. Intell. Transp. Syst. 19(7), 2204–2220 (2018). https://doi.org/10.1109/TITS.2017.2777990
23. Lu, N., Cheng, N., Zhang, N., Shen, X., Mark, J.W.: Connected vehicles: solutions and challenges. IEEE IoT J. 1(4), 289–299 (2014). https://doi.org/10.1109/JIOT.2014.2327587
24. Newman, S.: Building Microservices, 1st edn. O'Reilly Media Inc., Newton (2015)
25. Nokia: Vehicle-to-everything communication will transform the driving experience. https://networks.nokia.com/products/vehicle-to-everything. Accessed 27 May 2019
26. Panarello, A., Tapas, N., Merlino, G., Longo, F., Puliafito, A.: Blockchain and IoT integration: a systematic survey. Sensors 18(8), 2575 (2018). https://doi.org/10.3390/s18082575
27. Porru, S., Pinna, A., Marchesi, M., Tonelli, R.: Blockchain-oriented software engineering: challenges and new directions. In: 2017 IEEE/ACM 39th International Conference on Software Engineering Companion (ICSE-C), pp. 169–171 (2017)
28. Qu, Q., Xu, R., Nikouei, S.Y., Chen, Y.: An experimental study on microservices based edge computing platforms (2020)
29. Rahman, M.A., et al.: Blockchain-based mobile edge computing framework for secure therapy applications. IEEE Access 6, 72469–72478 (2018). https://doi.org/10.1109/ACCESS.2018.2881246
30. Rydzi, F., Truong, H.: Sharing blockchain performance knowledge for edge service development. In: 5th IEEE International Conference on Collaboration and Internet Computing, CIC 2019, Los Angeles, CA, USA, 12–14, December 2019, pp. 20–29. IEEE (2019). https://doi.org/10.1109/CIC48465.2019.00012
31. Taleb, T., Dutta, S., Ksentini, A., Iqbal, M., Flinck, H.: Mobile edge computing potential in making cities smarter. IEEE Commun. Mag. 55(3), 38–43 (2017). https://doi.org/10.1109/MCOM.2017.1600249CM
32. Thakkar, P., Nathan, S., Vishwanathan, B.: Performance benchmarking and optimizing hyperledger fabric blockchain platform. CoRR abs/1805.11390 (2018)
33. Viriyasitavat, W., Anuphaptrirong, T., Hoonsopon, D.: When blockchain meets Internet of Things: characteristics, challenges, and business opportunities. J. Ind. Inf. Integr. 15, 21–28 (2019)

34. Walker, M.A., Dubey, A., Laszka, A., Schmidt, D.C.: PlaTIBART: a platform for transactive IoT blockchain applications with repeatable testing. In: Proceedings of the 4th Workshop on Middleware and Applications for the Internet of Things, M4IoT 2017, pp. 17–22. ACM, New York (2017)

35. Xiong, Z., Zhang, Y., Niyato, D., Wang, P., Han, Z.: When mobile blockchain meets edge computing. IEEE Commun. Mag. **56**(8), 33–39 (2018). https://doi.org/10.1109/MCOM.2018.1701095

36. Xu, Q., Mak, T., Ko, J., Sengupta, R.: Vehicle-to-vehicle safety messaging in DSRC. In: Proceedings of the 1st ACM International Workshop on Vehicular Ad Hoc Networks, VANET 2004, pp. 19–28. ACM, New York (2004)

37. Xu, X., et al.: A taxonomy of blockchain-based systems for architecture design. In: 2017 IEEE International Conference on Software Architecture (ICSA), pp. 243–252 (April 2017). https://doi.org/10.1109/ICSA.2017.33

38. Xu, X., Weber, I., Staples, M.: Architecture for Blockchain Applications. Springer, Switzerland (2019). https://doi.org/10.1007/978-3-030-03035-3

39. Zhang, L., et al.: Blockchain based secure data sharing system for internet of vehicles: a position paper. Veh. Commun. **16**, 85–93 (2019)

40. Zheng, P., Zheng, Z., Luo, X., Chen, X., Liu, X.: A detailed and real-time performance monitoring framework for blockchain systems. In: 2018 IEEE/ACM 40th International Conference on Software Engineering: Software Engineering in Practice Track (ICSE-SEIP), pp. 134–143 (2018)

Author Index

Printed in the United States
By Bookmasters